Dining Out

**First Dates, Defiant Nights,
and Last Call Disco Fries at
America's Gay Restaurants**

Dining Out

Erik
Piepenburg

GRAND
CENTRAL

New York   Boston

Grand Central Publishing
Hachette Book Group
1290 Avenue of the Americas, New York, NY 10104
grandcentralpublishing.com
@grandcentralpub

First Edition: June 2025

Grand Central Publishing is a division of Hachette Book Group, Inc. The Grand Central Publishing name and logo is a registered trademark of Hachette Book Group, Inc.

The publisher is not responsible for websites (or their content) that are not owned by the publisher.

The Hachette Speakers Bureau provides a wide range of authors for speaking events. To find out more, go to hachettespeakersbureau.com or email HachetteSpeakers@hbgusa.com.

Grand Central Publishing books may be purchased in bulk for business, educational, or promotional use. For information, please contact your local bookseller or the Hachette Book Group Special Markets Department at special.markets@hbgusa.com.

Print book interior design by Amy Quinn.

Library of Congress Cataloging-in-Publication Data has been applied for.

ISBNs: 9780306832161 (hardcover); 9780306832192 (ebook)

Printed in Canada

MRQ

Printing 1, 2025

To Sonia and Paul, my mom and dad,
for encouraging me always.

To Blanca and Agnes, my grandmothers, for reading with me.

And to David and Brian, for getting me.

"It's no secret. Not here."

Interior. A gay restaurant.
L.A. Law. Aired Oct. 31, 1991.

Contents

Introduction:
What's Good Tonight?

I had a terrible first date at a gay restaurant in 1997. I was twenty-six, and I'd met him the night before at a popular gay bar in Chicago named Sidetrack that we all called Sidetracks. On big overhead monitors, the bar played bloopers from *The Price Is Right*, clips of peak Joan Crawford in *Mildred Pierce*, and Ultra Naté music videos—crutches for our eyes, before iPhones. It was a musicals-themed night, so we all shushed one another when Jennifer Holliday appeared on every screen to belt "And I Am Telling You I'm Not Going"—the clip from her Tony Awards performance, of course.

I don't remember my date's name but he was around my age and blessed with a dreamy triple-combo that knocked me out: a skater-skinny frame, mussed black hair over a pale complexion, and blue bedroom eyes. He looked like a punk version of my boyhood crush—teen idol and *Tiger Beat* magazine cover dreamboat Robby Benson—but fresh out of a mosh pit, nothing like the frosted blowback theater queens in blousy button-down paisley shirts who were usually there on Mondays. He wore size thirteen sneakers—his answer to my opening question. It worked.

He was at Sidetracks by himself that night, and I was too. At first we flirted from afar, then closer, chatting mouth to ear. I asked whether he'd have dinner with me the following evening at my favorite local restaurant: the Melrose, a twenty-four-hour diner in the Lakeview neighborhood—or Boystown, as we called Chicago's North Side gay enclave in the late '90s. He'd never been to the Melrose Restaurant, as it was officially called, even though he said he lived in the neighborhood—the first red flag. He didn't seem excited about going to a diner for a first date—the second red flag—even though I promised him the food was terrific. He said yes. I melted.

But, the next night, once we settled into our window-seat booth and started talking, he didn't seem into the Melrose, or me. "Why do you like it here?" he asked, looking concerned, as if I had lured him to a 7-Eleven parking lot for Funyuns and Jolt. "I'm a diner gay, I guess," I said, with a giggle. "Got it," he replied unsmiling, scanning the oversize menu.

He got a cheeseburger and fries, a meal as boring as he turned out to be, although I appreciated how he understood that the best way to eat well at a diner is to eat a meal that must be made fresh to order, not food that's been sitting around waiting to be reheated. (*Do* order grilled cheese. Do *not* order meatloaf.) As our conversation lurched along, I caught him eyeing another guy at a table across the full and fully gay dining room, and that's when I knew it was time to finish my blueberry silver dollar pancakes and split the check, and the Melrose.

We both knew it wasn't a match as we silently stood in line to pay our bills. I took a spoonful of the free jelly beans that the Melrose kept in a jar at the cashier stand, so that my lips would taste like grape and cherry in case I could squeeze a kiss out of this clunker of a date with the kind of hottie who usually never paid attention to a gay-with-a-belly like me.

After I gave him a hug good-bye and lied that it was great to meet him, he took off. I waited until he turned the corner, then went back into the Melrose and restfully, blissfully ate rice pudding by myself.

A bad date, a satisfying meal, the promise of sex: That's what happens, or used to happen, at gay restaurants like the Melrose.

Located at the corner of Melrose and Broadway, the Melrose was a gay restaurant that didn't look gay, not right away. The booths and chairs were upholstered in shades of avocado and russet. I knew at least one of the servers was gay, but he was in his forties and partial to bushy mustaches and sensible knit pullovers, not busy midriffs and leggy rainbow-colored short shorts like servers at the glittery drag brunches that had gotten popular around town. There were no puns on the menu about buns or kielbasa, though if there had been, nobody would have been offended.

The Melrose was a gay restaurant because gay people made it one. It was where older gay couples sampled each other's roast beef and mashed potato specials without asking first, as across the dining room, a four-top of butches feasted on chunky patty melts and audibly crisp chicken fingers. I once watched a table of loud-mouthed drag queens scarf down platters of grease-soaked bacon-and-cheese potato skins at two a.m. after they'd taken their bows at Foxy's or Berlin, two of my favorite gay clubs that are now just memories. During weekend brunch hours, the Melrose transformed into the dining equivalent of a hopping gay bar, but with egg-white skillets and the roar of gossip instead of overpriced Cosmos and the thump of Chicago house music.

I was a Melrose regular. I ate there several times a week after midnight on my way home from my first journalism job, as the night-shift web producer at the NBC station downtown. If I couldn't sleep, I'd go to the Melrose and read a book over a gooey grilled Cheddar on rye with fries, followed by a slice of warmed blueberry pie bearing a scoop of vanilla ice cream the size of my fist. Sometimes, I ate at the small counter to watch the cooks hustle, untempted by gay apps like Grindr or Scruff because they didn't exist. I lived a few blocks from the Melrose, which is how, on one chilly winter morning circa 1999, next to me in bed was the same otter—the scrawny and extra-hairy type, my favorite—from the night before, who'd looked at me with a coy smile when we got up to pay our bills at the same time.

Melrose meals were within my modest budget and, most important, delicious, far better than typical greasy-spoon fare, thanks to cooks who knew their way around a hot grill and didn't skimp on size. The menu rarely changed. Like most diners, it emphasized breakfast, which is why the dining room always smelled of syrup and sizzle, like maple butter melting on hot links. My go-to meal, no matter the time of day, was the chubby broccoli-and-Cheddar omelet, made with eggs so expertly fluffed, each forkful went down like chiffon. Without fail, it arrived at my table oozing pylon-orange cheese and snuggled against a heaping hill of humble buttery home fries. No Melrose meal was complete for me without a cup of its signature homemade sweet-and-sour cabbage soup—a tangy fusion of chunky tomatoes, vinegary broth, and thick-cut pieces of cabbage hugged by dill sprigs. A tall glass case near the front door was illuminated from within to show off fancy layer cakes and homey fruit pies. My favorite dessert was a squat sundae cup filled with creamy rice pudding, with a tall wig of whipped cream that the server dusted with cinnamon à la minute.

Location helped make the Melrose gay. It was an avenue over from Halsted Street, the blocks-long Boystown strip that bustled nightly with party people promenading between bars, nightclubs, and Steamworks, the neighborhood's big and busy bathhouse. Many of the diners who frequented the Melrose were white gay men who could afford to live in gentrifying Boystown—Gen Xers like me who spent their twenties in Chicago working, sleeping around, and otherwise coming of age. Before gay life went digital, we learned where to party and eat from newspapers and bar guides that the Melrose and other local businesses stacked high near their entrances. During the summer, the Melrose was a popular spot for

Cubs fans headed to and from nearby Wrigley Field—my way of saying that straight people ate there too. Not once did I see gays and straights clash at the Melrose, even during brunch when gay men cranked up the dining room to inferno levels of flaming. The only time I saw someone kicked out was for being drunk and belligerent, not for being gay, or homophobic.

In 2017, after fifty-six years in business, my beloved Melrose closed, for reasons that remain unclear. A year later, it was replaced by Eggsperience, a family-owned restaurant chain. Better that, I suppose, than some soul-sucking Chick-fil-A or a bank branch. But it's not the same. While "I'll see you at the Melrose" sounds gay, even a little chic, "Let's go to Eggsperience" sounds phony, like ad copy rushed into print. It breaks my heart to think that, in being replaced, the Melrose might inevitably be forgotten. I left Chicago in 2001 and always go back to Lakeview when I visit, but not to Eggsperience. Pushing open those familiar glass doors would offer me nothing but a double whammy of crushing nostalgia: for a restaurant that's no longer there and for an age—my twenties, that gay golden decade—that isn't either. When I'm with my partner, David, and I see or hear the word "Melrose"—walking down Melrose Avenue in West Hollywood, for example—I'll look at him with a sad face. He ate with me at the Melrose, too, and appreciates how much its absence breaks my heart.

When gay restaurants close, gay reliquaries empty of memories and meaning. Gone are favorite waitresses and go-to meals, safe spaces and party places in the night's last hours. For me and other gay people who love to eat out, losing a gay restaurant is a kind of dispossession.

It's painful, too, when gay bars close. Just ask lesbians, whose bars have dwindled and disappeared in recent years. But overall, queer people have been good about remembering, valuing, and documenting queer bars and their histories and significance, their evolution and design, regardless of whether the bars are still open or not. You can fill a library with books, plays, films, and songs about the Stonewall Inn and other gay bars and how they "helped shape a sense of gay identity that went beyond the individual to the group," as historian Allan Bérubé once wrote.[1] No surprise there: Bars are widely accepted as *the* LGBTQ+ social institution because they provide or offer the promise of community, sex, mobilization, entertainment, and friendship.

Allan H. Spear, a Minnesota state senator who in 1974 became one of the first openly gay lawmakers in the United States, put it this way: "Much maligned by gay liberationists as an exploitative institution, the gay bar needs to be seen historically—much like the Irish saloon or the Jewish coffeehouse or the African American barber shop—as a building block of community, a free space where the sense of camaraderie that later led to liberation was first formed."[2]

Restaurants have served the same purposes and more, and still do. Yet we don't know *nearly* as much about gay restaurants as we do about gay bars. This is strange, since knowing why and where gay people eat helps us understand who gay people are, in ways that gay bars don't, because they can't.

What can you do at a gay restaurant that you can't at a gay bar? Share hot-to-the-touch falafel on an anxiously awaited first date. Argue over and organize a protest with plates of flapjacks and unlimited coffee refills from sundown to sunrise. Learn and hone a culinary craft that can become a Michelin-quality career. Gather over disco fries with your queer high school drama club when you still look too young to use a fake ID. Share sobriety stories over mozzarella sticks with strangers after a 12-Step meeting. Pick at nachos during a support group with scared, lonely, and closeted people from around your state whose drive to the restaurant took longer than the meal. Pay honest-to-god attention to what's on television while you eat, as gay fans of the soap opera

All My Children did at the *All My Children* Lunch Bunch, a week-day watch party that took place in the early '80s at Hobo's restaurant in Portland, Oregon.[3] Eat out as an elder on a budget and be served by people who remember your name and that you like your coffee decaf and your wheat toast buttered, not dry.

Or, as I did, read *Dancer from the Dance* alone in a booth with cherry pie at an almost empty Melrose diner on a weekday midnight hour.

In 2008, David and I had our first official date at a diner. We'd met earlier that day when our mutual friend Mekado invited us both to screenings at New York's gay and lesbian film festival. Afterward, I could tell that David and I were both eager to keep hanging out. He and I, plus Mekado and my friend Clark, went to the nearby Skylight Diner, a blue-and-white, glass-and-chrome spot that opened in 1996 at 34th Street, just off Ninth Avenue in Midtown Manhattan. I don't remember what movie we saw or what I wore or what I ate, but I remember flirting with David across the table, giving him coy but lingering looks as I took bites of my grilled cheese. Like some randy fifteen-year-old, I stared at him as I slowly slid thick steak fries in and out of my mouth. David cruised me back just as intently, moving his knees closer to mine under the table. I was drawn to how his green-and-white striped polo shirt accentuated his beautiful blue eyes. I felt heat. That same night, David, Mekado, and I went to another movie—*Choke*, a dark comedy about a con man who fakes choking in restaurants—the better for David and I to extend our day into the night. David and I went on a picnic the next week, and have been together ever since. We rarely go back to the Skylight, but with Clark we eat all the time at diners in Hell's Kitchen, where we have lived for almost twenty years.

I'm still a diner gay.

Just as it's impossible to understand America without talking about its LGBTQ+ people, no portrait of America's culinary history or queer past is complete without memories of LGBTQ+ restaurants where moments big and small shaped individuals and communities. That's why, as the Melroses of the country become footnotes in gay history, I wrote this book to illustrate how gay restaurants nourished, changed, and continue to inspire LGBTQ+ people and food cultures in the United States, and how the mainstreaming of gay dining is, in turn, impacting how Americans eat out regardless of sexual orientation or gender identity.

In 2021, I reported a story about gay restaurants that ran on the front page of the *New York Times* Food section at the start of Pride Month.[4] When I originally pitched the piece, it was about the gay restaurant's impending death, which is what I thought was happening because that's what I saw happening in New York City. At the time, there were still a few honest-to-goodness gay restaurants left in Manhattan, including the Chelsea mainstays Elmo and Cafeteria, although every time I walked by Cafeteria, the tables outside looked more homogenized—straighter, less eccentric, more monied—than I remembered from when I first started eating there in the '90s. Most of the New York gay restaurants where I came of age as a young gay man are long gone. Among them was East of Eighth, the place to be on Saturday nights if you were gay and wanted a decently priced, aspirationally upscale meal of, say, matzo ball soup and sirloin tip meatloaf, and didn't mind or notice the tacky attempts at white-tablecloth respectability. Another was the Manatus, a West Village diner popular with Stonewall-generation seniors. In 2014, the Manatus closed when the owners lost their lease, victims of a rent hike that reached $50,000 per month.[5] As of this writing, it's an upscale Italian restaurant called Saint Theo's that offers a $22 watermelon and feta salad and $26 pesto fusilli.

My article was published during some of the darkest days of the coronavirus pandemic, when many restaurants were closing or hanging on by repurposing their business models for delivery and takeout. One of the casualties was MeMe's Diner, a popular queer restaurant in Brooklyn that closed in November 2020, citing the hardships of the city's shutdown measures and a lack of government support.[6] The National LGBT Chamber of Commerce, an advocacy organization, told me at the time that COVID-19 hit their restaurant members especially hard, particularly those dependent on daily foot traffic in big cities. I figured gay restaurants were disappearing because of COVID-19 but also because those of us who valued gay restaurants were getting older, and dining-out tastes and queer culture had changed to the point where the gay restaurant model was passé. I assumed gay restaurants were in hospice with little chance of being revived.

I was thrilled to be wrong. LGBTQ+ restaurants are thriving across the country, in big metropolitan areas but also in smaller cities, such as Salt Lake City, Utah, and Green Bay, Wisconsin. I wasn't ready for all the stories people told me about gay restaurants where they fell in love, had a quickie, mourned a lover, or came out. And I wasn't alone in my love of the Melrose. I was overjoyed to see this reader's memory in the comments section of my article:

> I remember one Sunday . . . It was the usual bustling scene: The sassy waitresses with beehive hairdos who called everyone "hon" while topping up coffee, tables full of families, older couples, first-daters and, in one corner, four cheerful BDSM gentlemen in full leather, chains, and boa constrictor–sized whips, enjoying pancakes while passing around the Sunday paper and talking about the Cubs.

So many folks I interviewed had gay restaurant stories like that one, but they had never shared those stories with anyone other than the people who were at the table when the memories were made. My article easily could have been ten times as long as it ended up being. After the story came out, I heard from friends and strangers about their own gay restaurant memories. That got me digging even more, and I realized there was a book to be written after talking with people who were both interested and invested in gay restaurants: chefs, owners, wait staff, historians, academics, cultural geographers, entrepreneurs and, most important, patrons.

So: What *is* a gay restaurant? It's the question I received more than any other as I spent over three years traveling the country, researching and eating.

Many people I spoke with assumed that what I meant by a gay restaurant was one that was gay-owned or had a gay chef and gay servers. While those elements were germane, for my purposes they were secondary considerations. I agree with historian Hugh Ryan, who told me a gay restaurant was a place where queer folks can "assume an overlap of experience with most of the people there and get a sense of what it is to be queer." In other words, it's a restaurant where queer people open the doors and think: *These are my people.* That was my primary interest in identifying gay restaurants: Who's eating there, not just who's cooking or running the place.

The most common type of gay dining space is the bar-restaurant, although, weirdly, that's not the case in New York City, where most of the gay bars (at least the ones I've been to) don't serve food. David Gersten, a longtime entertainment publicist and co-owner of the 9th Avenue Saloon, a gay bar in Hell's Kitchen, told me there are a host of reasons why. Space is the primary issue; as he explained, "We don't have room for a kitchen." Staffing would also increase, as would overhead and spoilage costs. Health codes would have to be updated or revised for older buildings. Plus, he's not convinced that gay men in New York want to eat at a bar.

"You can't meet somebody with a hamburger in your mouth," he told me. "You don't want ketchup on your face when you make out with somebody."

Tell that to Wisconsin. In Madison, my friend Todd, a fellow journalist whom I met in the '90s when we both lived in Chicago, took me to the Shamrock, a bar not far from Wisconsin's stately Capitol building. Gay since the late '80s, the Shamrock is an elevated dive. A sturdy wooden bar snakes along the left wall, and in the back, there's a pool table, television screens, and Pride flags aflutter. The real wonders are the grill and fryers that run the length of one wall, exposing the kitchen so customers can watch fish fried to order. The grill includes all the accoutrements of a working kitchen: spatulas, plates, silverware, A1 sauce, potato rolls, basket liners.

Todd took me there on a quiet Sunday night. Wes, our hot-stuff bartender, was in a black muscle tee that showed off his yoga-toned arms. Todd and I watched nearly drooling as Wes did double duty as a short-order cook, plopping frozen cheese curds into the fryer, and minutes later serving those puppies to us in a big plastic basket with a side of the house buttermilk ranch. They were gone in five minutes. Wes said we should come back for the long-running Friday Fish Fry, an event that packs the place with folks hungry for baskets of seafood dinners of cod and jumbo shrimp that come with coleslaw, a dinner roll, and choice of potato, all for around $20. Visit almost any American town with a gay bar and there's a good chance there will be a Wes flipping burgers and piling plates high with curly fries to go with the Cosmos and Dua Lipa remixes. New York gays don't know what they're missing.

Across the country, gay people eat at all kinds of restaurants, from cozy family-run taquerias and working-class pubs to tiny dive bars and James Beard Award–winning bistros. (After eating at Slammers, a bar-restaurant in Columbus, Ohio, I say this with utter certainty: Lesbians love pizza.) Some gay restaurants are well known; one example are the Hamburger Mary's restaurants. Sometimes, a corporate chain develops a gay customer base, such as an International House of Pancakes in Atlanta that in 1981 ran an ad that said: "IHOP Supports LGT Pride."[7] (Back then, the "B" in LGBT wasn't as prevalent as it is today, an unfortunate sign of bisexual invisibility.) How I wish I could have had dinner at Tallywackers, a restaurant that opened in 2015 in Oak Lawn, Dallas's gayborhood, where beefcake servers in tank tops and distended-bulge boxer briefs took their shirts off as the night wore on. The "Hooters for men," as it was called, lasted a year.[8]

Sometimes, you won't know you're in a gay restaurant until you walk inside and look at the menu. For dinner at Cabana Cafe and Cabaret, a Miami restaurant that operated in the '80s, the signature Steak Cabana was an 8-ounce sirloin "char-broiled per your instructions—dragged through sequins to make your taste buds sparkle—then padded like Dana's thighs."[9] (I don't know who Dana was, but Cabana assumed its customers did. My guess is she was a *thicc-ass* drag queen.) The Wizlitt Omelette was a "fashionable three egg omelette" covered with cheese, a mushroom sauce, and "bacon accessories." You know you're in a gay restaurant when your dish comes with "bacon accessories."

Often, a restaurant will become gay by location or convenience. Mom-and-pop diners that in the latter half of the twentieth century found themselves in newly created gay neighborhoods, such as the Castro in San Francisco and Boystown in Chicago, turned gay organically, embracing their gay neighbors and the gentrification they brought with them. (The other option—to fight being known as a gay-welcoming restaurant—usually did not end well, once the queer community started spending their money elsewhere.) Looks can be deceiving, though: Just because there's a Pride flag in the window, it doesn't necessarily make a restaurant gay or the neighborhood safe.

If there's a hot spot for gay restaurants today, it's San Diego. Almost every place to eat along University Avenue in Hillcrest, the city's gay neighborhood, is a gay one. During my visit there in October 2023, even the McDonald's hung a banner that said "living my truth," next to a heart in the colors of the Progress Pride flag. At Urban MO's, I got the special (and cheap) peach margarita and a heaping plate of heart-exploding macaroni and cheese, served by a blond twink wearing high-waisted denim shorts and a shirt that said "I [heart] Dominant Women." At Inside-OUT, located in the commons of an apartment building, I ate syrup-soaked French toast with a sexually and racially diverse crowd under a fantastic mélange of life-size, kaleidoscopically colored mushrooms and Alice in Wonderland–style flowers, all part of the restaurant's regular Instagram-thirsty redesigns. Nathan, my ridiculously handsome server who looked like George Clooney's otter brother, wore a black collared shirt, a strappy brown leather harness, knee-length shorts, and brown boots—Alpine go-go boy realness. During my weekend in San Diego, it was evident that restaurant owners in Hillcrest are skilled at providing a culinary and visual experience that locals and tourists (gay men and straight women, mostly) want from a gay restaurant: familiar American food, specialty cocktails, hot waiters in leg-baring shorts, and jealousy-inducing decor.

All that gayness has a national history and I will take you there, restaurant by restaurant. In the 1920s and '30s, in cities big and small, gay people ate out despite threats of arrest. During World War II, restaurants attracted gay servicemen and -women who didn't know other gay people existed before the conflict brought them together. In postwar America, gay restaurants began to thrive in earnest, especially in big cities. That was especially the case in Washington, D.C., despite the Lavender Scare that gripped the federal government and put gay people in the crosshairs. In the '70s, neighborhoods like the Castro and the West Village became ground zero for what today we would consider the modern gay restaurant.

In the '80s—the decade I started to realize that I was gay—restaurants served as refuges during the AIDS epidemic. In the '90s, they became more mainstream, as the internet and social media changed how LGBTQ+ people came out, found one another, and socialized. In our new century, gay restaurants may be fewer, but they are more queer than ever by embracing trans, nonbinary, and diverse sexual and gender identities in ways that, a hundred years ago, would have been unthinkable or undefinable.

Before we go any further, a note about diversity and language: If I took a time machine to most of the restaurants in this book and asked diners what it was like to be a queer person eating at an LGBTQIA+ restaurant, they'd be as confused as if I had asked them whether they would like a venti oat milk Frappuccino to go with their Impossible Smash Burger. My twenty-first-century vocabulary about food and sexuality wouldn't make sense or be useful in helping me characterize these people's lives and identities.

I'm not a historian or an academic, but I am a journalist, and here's how I talk about gay restaurants and LGBTQ+ people. In the 1920s, calling a restaurant "gay" would have meant it was vibrant, and "queer" would have meant it was unusual. As the LGBTQ+ community embraced the words "homosexual" and "gay" starting in the '40s, the words changed how the community collectively identified and gathered. When "LGBT" was normalized and "queer" was reclaimed starting in the '80s, it opened new ways of thinking about identity. In twenty years, perhaps someone will pick up this book and find today's terms quaint or offensive.

Calling a restaurant "queer" today is a privilege. Ask someone on Grindr where the good queer restaurants are in Bushwick or West Hollywood, and they'll have several recommendations. Maybe not so much in Oklahoma or Alaska. "Queer" rolls off the tongue for many young people, but for other LGBTQ+ people, especially older folks, "queer" can be fraught, not liberating. Contemporary conceptions of queerness, queer language, and intersectionality may be absent from some of my accounts because it's ahistorical to call a gay man in the '40s queer, or to use "transgender" to describe a person who in the '50s was heterosexual and a self-described transvestite. "Queer" may be a common synonym for LGBT today, but it was not as widely so when I was growing up in the '80s. If a person is dead or declined an interview request, I do my best to ensure that my words match what I know about them, noting when and why I made assumptions. I describe gay people and communities with the evidence I have about who they were at the time, not how I wish today they had been.

I also take the liberty of using the words "gay restaurant" to mean LGBTQIA+ restaurants generally since, to my Gen X ears, "gay" is a more efficient and shorter modifier. I'm specific about the clientele at a restaurant when it's accurate to do so; I write about lesbian restaurants and trans buffets if that's what they are. I asked people to describe their sexual and gender identities and their personal pronouns, so I didn't make assumptions about their orientation or gender identity. If a restaurant is still open, I say that. If I know when a restaurant closed, I let you know, even if the date is approximate. If I don't give an answer, assume it's because the restaurant is no longer in business.

When I write about myself, I write as a gay man, not a queer one, because "queer" carries with it maverick connotations that don't align with my identity. Even though I'm half-Latino, look at me and you'll think, "That's a white gay guy." My experience as a gay man in America—and that includes eating at restaurants—is miles away from the experiences of people of color who are visibly nonwhite, people with disabilities, and people whose gender identity isn't cis like mine. Make no mistake: How I look affected how I researched this book, from how I was treated when a restaurant owner knew I was eating at their establishment to who responded to my cold outreach on social media for interviews. A white-looking cis guy like me is and always has been served differently at restaurants, gay and not. I tried to bring with me an understanding and humbleness about that privilege every time I walked into a dining room, did a phone interview, and wrote a paragraph.

Okay, back to the question: *What is a gay restaurant?* The best answer, of course, comes from *Dynasty.*

In 1983, ABC's hit primetime soap opera was in its fourth season. Among the many plotlines was a convoluted custody case involving Steven Carrington, the gay son of the wealthy tycoon Blake Carrington. Steven was semi-out from the first episode—a groundbreaking and scandalous assertion of male homosexuality on American television during the homophobic and Christian Nationalist Reagan administration. Blake was so upset over his son's sexual identity and his desire to be more open about it that in one early episode, he acerbically said that if only homosexuality were still considered a disease, he would endow a foundation called "The Steven Carrington Institute for the Treatment and Study of Faggotry." Blake spoke for many Americans at the time who considered homosexuality an illness and something best left to sad, dark bars in sketchy, remote neighborhoods.

In a *Dynasty* episode that aired on November 2, 1983, Sammy Jo, Steven's ex-wife, testifies against him in a bitter custody hearing, claiming he would be a poor father for their son, Danny. Sammy Jo—played to perfection by '80s ingenue Heather Locklear—says this while looking stunning in a luscious raspberry wool mock turtleneck mini-dress accented with a dramatic black obi belt, and a wide-brimmed black hat that frames her feathered blond hair with an evil patina.

To convince the court that Steven is an unfit dad, Sammy Jo testifies that she saw Steven flirt with a man as they ate at a gay restaurant in New York.

"A gay restaurant?" the lawyer for her side replies, as if he had never heard of so ridiculous a place. "Now, why do you say that?"

"It's very obvious," she responds, her voice like ice. "All you had to do was look around."

I'm getting hungry. Let's eat.

The Elder Stateswoman

Annie's Paramount Steak House, Washington, D.C.

Before diving into the many histories and permutations of America's gay restaurants, we need to talk about *the* American gay restaurant. For that, I turned to a gregarious, no-nonsense, smile-producing, and hug-hungry heterosexual great-grandmother who loved to pour strong drinks and had a message for all her guests but especially her beloved gay ones: In my house, you come as you are.

Georgia Katinas dropped a teeny pin into my hand.

"For you," she said.

It was near the end of our conversation, late one morning over coffee (mine) and paperwork (hers) at Annie's Paramount Steak House, the Washington, D.C., restaurant her family owns and operates. To mark the seventy-fifth anniversary of Annie's in 2023, Georgia commissioned tiny oblong enameled pins as gifts to her loyal customers. Each one said "Annie's" in minuscule script, and they came in five-year increments in ten colors to commemorate how long the wearer had been eating there. At some point, I must have told Georgia that I first ate at Annie's in 1993, which was why she gave me the lime-colored thirty-year pin.

Georgia, who has managed Annie's since 2019, originally ordered twenty-five of the forty years–plus pins, figuring she wouldn't need more. But she ran out and had to order fifty more—that's how many customers, most of them gay men, had been dining at Annie's since at least the late 1960s. "That just shows an incredible level of community," she said, as employees in black dress shirts and black pants washed glasses, wiped down tables, and made fresh pots of coffee ahead of the lunchtime rush.

Annie's is one of the oldest gay restuarants, if not the oldest surviving gay restaurant, in the country. ("Gay, but straight-friendly," as Georgia reminds me.) It's located on 17th Street in D.C.'s once very gay but now straighter and still gentrified Dupont Circle neighborhood, where I lived in the mid-'90s. Annie's looks gay all over. Outside, rainbow flags share space with Italianate architectural touches, including window hoods and cornice details. Inside, Pride flags offset the pecan-brown wood paneling and sleet-gray decor in the dining room, and large street-facing windows make it easy for passersby to see how gay their dining experience will be. Annie's checks every box of what you want your gay restaurant to be: It's known for a good time with good food for lots of tastes, it welcomes anyone under the queer umbrella, and it's deeply invested in its community and the people who live there. It's tenderly masculine and unpretentiously congenial—my kind of gay restaurant.

It helps that the food is all about comfort, mostly in the American diner tradition but elevated a notch, with touches of Greece, where the Katinas family is from. Popular items include steak, of course, but also the Athenian chicken and Annie's signature Bull in the Pan, a platter of sirloin tips served sizzling. To accommodate more than just meat eaters, there's now a vegetarian Beyond Burger on the menu. On the day I tried it, the waiter who took care of me was Mano Vodjani, an efficient and no-nonsense man Annie hired in 1974 and who still makes customers feel as special as if they were dining at Daniel, the renowned French restaurant on New York's Upper East Side.

Annie's isn't a foodie destination. In 2010, *The Washington Post*'s restaurant critic Tom Sietsema criticized the "gloppy Caesar salad" and the "juiceless and vapid" pork chops.[1] But it wasn't a total pan; he praised the strong drinks and the "homey" mashed potatoes, the "crisp" coleslaw, and the "decent" Cajun-spiced rib eye. He also pointed out that a visitor would encounter "more air-kissing than you see at fashion week in New York, London, Milan and Paris combined." Say gay without saying gay.

Annie's remains a gay draw for reasons beyond comfort food. In fact, Annie's is such a gay legacy restaurant that in 2019, the James Beard Foundation named it an American Classic, an award that honors restaurants with "timeless appeal" that "serve quality food that reflects the character of their communities." In its announcement, the foundation praised Annie's for its "hefty" steaks and strong cocktails, but also lauded the restaurant's "inclusiveness and respect."[2] Unlike some of the other distinctions, the American Classic Award acknowledges not only the food but also the ethos of a long-standing restaurant, making this particular honor even more special.

David Hagedorn, a food critic, writer, and chef based in Washington, D.C., gushed about Annie's in an essay that accompanied the announcement. "The steaks are good, the burgers fat and juicy, and the clam strips are ever at-the-ready to act as conveyances for tartar and cocktail sauces," he wrote.[3] Annie's used to make so many martinis and Manhattans, he noted, that bartenders made batches in Sysco mayonnaise jugs. According to David, Annie's is in a gay restaurant league of its own.

"It's just always had that reputation of being a place that everyone would feel comfortable in," he told me. "That's part of its staying power. They're not doing it just to take our money. They've demonstrated a real commitment to the community." That includes being an early sponsor of the Gay Men's Chorus of Washington, D.C., and of other LGBTQ+ causes.

In 1985, Annie's moved a block north from its original location to 1609 17th Street NW. (The popular gay bar JR's took over its old space.) It became so popular in the '90s that men who had been eating there for thirty years would walk in on a busy Friday night and "be pissed that they didn't have a table right away," Georgia said.

Since taking over as manager, Georgia has ushered Annie's into the twenty-first century by starting an Instagram account, a small step for most restaurants but a big one for Annie's, which didn't have much of a website until 2019. Annie's is no longer open twenty-four hours on the weekend, a casualty of COVID-19-related supply chain issues, staffing challenges, and changes in dining habits.

———————

I first got to know Annie's in 1993, when I was in my early twenties and had just started graduate school at American University in Washington, D.C. I lived in Dupont Circle, which at the time was *the* neighborhood for white gay men who could afford it, which I did by working through grad school and living with three room-mates of various iterations in an apartment at 2222 Q Street. Every Friday like clockwork, I went to the now-closed Lambda Rising bookstore to pick up the *Washington Blade*, the city's gay weekly newspaper. As with most extant gay newspapers, the print edition of the *Blade* has slimmed down since the 1990s, as advertising, including for gay restaurants, has shifted away from print or dis-appeared. But in the '90s, I could count on there always being a full-page ad reminding gays that Annie's was open twenty-four hours on weekends.

Not that Annie's customers needed reminding: Each time I ate at Annie's in the early-morning hours, two a.m. and on, the mood in the packed dining room was festive and flirty. The minute I walked in the door I was hit with the aroma of seared meat and syrup, mixed with sweat wafting off the bodies of horny gay men still hopeful for a last-call hookup. Annie's was my after-hours spot on the way home from the gay mega-club Tracks, where I first met Tommy, who reeled me in with his sly smile, wet brown eyes, and wicked sense of humor. We became boyfriends that night. (We're still friends to this day.) There was usually a wait.

Annie's wasn't alone in the making of D.C.'s long-running gay restaurant scene. In the '70s, the Eagle leather bar had a full-service dining room that was open daily. It served BLTs and ham sandwiches but also upscale dinners, including lobster tail and London broil, with wine pairings listed alongside each entrée. A 1975 menu issued this dare: "Slip into your Levis . . . and eat with the men! If you're man enough"—right above a listing for a Weight Watchers Special Chef Salad for $2.40. David Hagedorn remembered sitting at the Eagle for a community event next to former mayor Marion Barry and being served by a man in leather chaps.

When I think of Annie's, I think of Brian Eft, a former boy-friend. Brian hated to cook and loved to eat out, including at

Annie's. He preferred restaurants that reminded him of eating like a college student: Pizzeria Paradiso for a pepperoni slice, or Burrito Brothers for an arm-size steak burrito. We once had a fight about I don't remember what over tacos and frozen margaritas at El Tamarindo. We made up days later with *gomen wat* at our favorite Ethiopian restaurant, Meskerem. I will never forget how brightly his eyes sparkled during dinner one night under the lights at the Southern-inspired fine dining restaurant Vidalia—in him, I experienced "the warmth of being beheld," to borrow a phrase from the novelist Ling Ma.[4] Brian's eyes always shined after a few glasses of wine, but on this particular night, they were luminescent.

My other favorite memory of Brian involved an annual, uniquely D.C. tradition: the High Heel Race. It started in the '80s as a competitive run that took place between Annie's in its previous location and the gay bar JR's. The goal was simple: contestants put on high heels and raced from one bar to the other, taking a shot before running back. (The race remains a highlight of the district's annual gay calendar.) People traveled to Dupont Circle from across metro D.C. to watch folks run in heels, some of them successfully to the finish line, and others, not more than a few steps. Brian lived on T Street near 17th, a few minutes from Annie's, and on the night I remember most, we made sure to get to 17th early for a good viewing advantage. When the race kicked off, he let loose with high-pitched giggles that didn't stop for the duration of the race. I recall standing behind Brian, holding my hands around his waist with my chin on his shoulder, his beard nestled against my face. Annie's was across the street, and when I think of Brian, Annie's is in the picture too.

When Brian died in 2022, I went to a locker he kept in Maryland and spent an afternoon sorting through his sweaters, scrapbooks, and files of printed-out emails he thought he'd need one day. I didn't find anything related to Annie's, but in one of his many manila folders, I came across a newspaper clipping with an ad for DuPont Italian Kitchen, a restaurant where we liked to split mozzarella sticks. (I and other juvenile D.C. gays referred to the restaurant by its acronym: DIK, as in "Let's eat DIK tonight.") I kept that ad as a reminder of meals with Brian, when food and drinks were our shared language, as if we were in a gay restaurant of our own making. How I wish Brian were still here so we could eat at Annie's and, for dessert, split a slice of pumpkin pie, his favorite. I'd leave him the last bite.

Annie Katinas was born on August 20, 1927, in Washington, D.C. Her brother, George Katinas, the only son of a Greek immigrant family from the island of Naxos, was serving overseas during World War II when his father, John George, who ran a fruit stand in Georgetown, passed away. George was then brought home from the war to be the head of household for his mother, Dialecti, and sisters—Annie, Sue, Kitty, Mary, and Sophie—and he took over the stand, his first step in a life that would be spent in food service and hospitality.

Within a couple of years, George had earned enough money to buy a restaurant. He opened Paramount Steakhouse at 1519 17th Street in 1948, the same year that the sex researcher Alfred Kinsey published *Sexual Behavior in the Human Male*, the ground-breaking study that explained to much of America for the first time what gay sex was and who was having it. (Way more people than Americans thought at the time, including straight men, sometimes.) In the early 1950s, George brought his sisters into the business. Annie and Sue tended bar and helped manage the restaurant. Sophie handled the finances. Kitty, along with Annie's daughters, Kathy and Detra, waitressed. George's son, Paul, was a day manager who worked with Annie's husband, Sidney, and her son, Mike.

It was Annie's job to make sure that new employees treated anyone who walked in the door as if they were family—no matter
what clothes they had on, how much money they had in the bank,
or the color of their skin. Georgia remembered Annie, her grandmother, saying: "I don't care if they're gay or straight." It's worth
noting that the restaurant's gay reputation had nothing to do with
a gay member of the Katinas family because, according to Georgia, there haven't been any.

Annie was the life of the party, Georgia noted fondly, "one
of these heavier people that was limber" who would "dance, no
problem," and was just as glad to be having a private conversation
as she was to be center stage, stirring martinis with her pinkie.
Annie, herself, said that her restaurant started attracting a gay clientele in the late '50s, but "they really adopted it as their home
in the late '60s."[5] As the story goes, Annie once spotted two men
holding hands under a table and told them they could do so above
it. In 1962, George renamed the restaurant Annie's Paramount
Steakhouse, given his sister's popularity with customers.

Annie once recalled that riots rocked Washington when Martin
Luther King, Jr., was assassinated in 1968. The restaurant was
forced to close, and the neighborhood turned into a ghost town.[6]

"When the restaurant reopened, if it weren't for the gay guys
who came in here regularly, we would have gone broke," she once
said.[7]

Gay men were drawn to Annie because she was a mother figure
who accepted people at face value, Georgia said. (Annie was also
a fixture behind the bar, where she was known for a heavy pour—
bonus points for thirsty gay people.) Annie was an especially welcome face for gay men who lived in Washington in the 1950s and
'60s and were estranged from their families, or were closeted at
the office after the end of World War II, when hundreds of gays
were fired from government jobs during a purge known as the
Lavender Scare. Georgia didn't have much of an explanation as

to why Annie was drawn to her gay customers, other than it was in Annie's blood to welcome everyone. If other family members didn't like it, Annie didn't want to hear it.

Gay life during this era was described in lurid but electric detail in *Washington Confidential*, a 1951 Washington tell-all written by Jack Lait and Lee Mortimer. The book singles out gay restaurants in "Garden of Pansies," a chapter devoted to how "the hand-on-hip set wins the battle of Washington."[8] The authors call gay men "wandering semi-boys" and "twisted twerps in trousers" who congregate at restaurants near the luxury Mayflower Hotel. "Fags also like a restaurant known as Mickey's, behind the Mayflower," they wrote. Lesbians, or "mannish women," frequent Kavakos' Grill in southeast D.C., and were said to "outnumber the pansies" at David's Grill, also by the Mayflower Hotel.

As they still do, lawmakers then regularly made outrageously offensive claims about gay people. But there's one speech about a gay restaurant that mirrors the antigay animus that many of Annie's customers had to put up with at the time. In 1950, Representative Arthur L. Miller, a Nebraska Republican, offered an amendment to a bill requiring background checks for employees of the Economic Cooperation Administration (ECA), in hopes of barring homosexuals from working there. Miller claimed that in D.C., there were places where homosexuals "gather for the purpose of sex orgies, where they worship at the cesspool and flesh pots of iniquity."[9] To be fair, he probably wasn't wrong. The combination of power, ambition, repression, and under-the-gun long hours makes it one hell of a freaky gay sex town. Trust me on this.

Miller's words—delivered to Congress—are too bonkers not to excerpt generously, spelling/grammatical errors and all, from the Congressional Record:[10]

> There is a restaurant downtown where you will find
> male prostitutes. They solicit business for other male

customers. They are pimps and undesirable characters. You will find odd words in the vocabulary of the homo-sexual. There are many types such as the necrophalia, fettichism, pygmalionism, fellatios, cunnilinguist, sod-omatic, pederasty, saphism, sadism, and masochist. Indeed, there are many methods of practices among the homosexuals. You will find those people using the words as, "He is a fish. He is a bull-dicker. He is mamma and he is papa, and punk, and pimp." Yes; in one of our prominent restaurants rug parties and sex orgies go on.

No wonder gay people turned to Annie for respite. Fortunately, Miller's amendment was rejected.

After I interviewed Georgia, she introduced me to Norbert Kupinski and Jay Penuel, two friends in their forties and longtime Annie's patrons, who were sitting at the bar. Norbert worked in hospitality, and lived so close to Annie's that he could see it from his balcony. He knew Annie, and he remembered her as "D.C.'s gay grandma."

"She took care of all of her little ones and it didn't matter if you were eighty years old or the eighteen-year-old who didn't know what they were doing," he smiled. "She made you feel like you're here and you're one of my little chicklings."

Jay, who worked for the city's board of elections, said Annie's was one of his favorite gay social spaces because it was less of a meat market than the nearby bars.

"There's something to be said about connecting with people over food and drink, not just drink," he mused.

Two days prior, in the upstairs dining room, Annie's had become a makeshift chapel, where Norbert attended a memo-rial service for a friend. As at other gay restaurants, memori-als were common at Annie's during the worst years of the AIDS crisis. Annie herself remembered: "We lost a lot of waiters, a lot of friends. HIV became obvious, but people kept it quiet if they had it. Then some night they'd have a few drinks at the bar and start crying, and they'd tell us. We lost a lot of nice boys. It was very difficult."

Norbert estimated that he had been eating at Annie's for about twenty-five years. On most nights, he could count on seeing a friend who would invite him to pull up a chair for dinner. It was evidence, he said, of what made a gay restaurant feel like a second home.

"Literally a block and a half from here there are two Michelin-star restaurants," he told me. "There you get a cold feeling, like *Oh, we're better than you.* Annie's is the complete opposite."

Annie died of congestive heart failure on July 24, 2013, at the age of eighty-five. Her obituary in *The Washington Post* called her restaurant "an early sanctuary for gay residents of Washington" that later became for locals "an unofficial social club."[11] Her survivors included her brother, George; her sisters Kitty and Mary; five children; nine grandchildren; seventeen great-grandchildren; and countless gay people who considered her their mom in spirit if not biology.

On May 24, 2024, just in time for Pride Month, a street sign with the words "Annie's Way" was installed outside the restaurant, over a decade after the D.C. Council and former mayor Vincent Gray approved the designation at the original address.

"It's incredible," Georgia said at the official unveiling. "It's a real reminder that she'll always be part of 17th Street and her legacy will live on."[12]

If only every city had an Annie, and an Annie's.

2

Tonight's Special

The Pioneers

America didn't get its first actual restaurants that weren't pubs or saloons with food until the first part of the nineteenth century. The steakhouse Delmonico's, which opened in New York in 1837, considers itself the first fine dining restaurant in the country.[1] Antoine's, a French-Creole restaurant in New Orleans, opened three years later.[2] Both are still in business.

I have no idea what the first gay restaurant was. How could I, when my contemporary understanding of what it means to be gay and eat out is nothing like that of same-sex-attracted people

14

during the Van Buren administration. But I do know this: Gay people have been going out in public to find one another since the country's earliest days, in parks and on the streets but also at commercial establishments, such as theaters and bars. Of course, they met at restaurants.

Unlike gay bars, of which there is a wealth of documented history, gay restaurants have mostly been afterthoughts to the keepers and chroniclers of American queer and dining histories. To research this book I read at least a dozen books about US restaurant history and dining culture—big books by big-name authors, about restaurants famous and not, great and small—and they barely mentioned where gay people ate. I did read some extraordinary journalism about America's gay dining past, including one of my favorites: "The Death and Life of America's Gay Restaurants," Mike Albo's delightfully observed essay about New York City eateries, including Paris Commune, where on a high school field trip I ate dinner before going to a performance of the Charles Ludlam farce *The Artificial Jungle*, where I saw, with eyes wide, my first drag queen, Ethyl Eichelberger. There's also "Your Fried Chicken Has Done Drag," Martin Padgett's ebullient essay on Atlanta's queer food scene, and a profile of Zuni Café and its pioneering gay chef, Billy West, that James Beard Award–winning author (and friend) John Birdsall wrote for *The New York Times* on the same day as my story on gay restaurants. Dr. Alex Ketchum's book *Ingredients for Revolution* is a must-read for anyone interested in the wave of lesbian-feminist restaurants and cafés that changed gay dining during the '60s and '70s.

But overall, the scholarship on gay restaurants wasn't as robust as I assumed it would be. I was especially surprised and disappointed to not have a much fuller picture of the gay and lesbian restaurant scene during World War II. Gays and lesbians ate out together in numbers that the country had never seen before, but the historical record of this shift when it comes to gay-welcoming restaurants remains underresearched.

By my definition, one of the earliest gay restaurants was opened by the editor of the influential nineteenth-century newspaper *The Saturday Press*. Henry Clapp Jr. was enamored with bohemians—artists and novelists, theater people, freethinkers, women with opinions and sailors' mouths—the kind of renegades he encountered during his trips to Europe.[3] Inspired by such maverick living, in 1856, Clapp opened the scrappy Pfaff's Saloon under Manhattan's Coleman House Hotel in hopes of drawing iconoclasts of various stripes, including underappreciated artists, such as painter Elihu Vedder and actress Ada Clare. There was a bar and a few tables on which waiters set out white cloth napkins. One Pfaffian called the overall ambience "a hole beneath the surface of the street, ill-lighted, ill-ventilated, and ill-kept."[4] The menu was not for the weight watcher: it featured hearty fare—for instance, beefsteak with onions, Limburger cheese, and Welsh rarebit—with steins of German lager to wash it all down.[5] Clapp hired a cook who specialized in *Pfannekuchen*, a thin German pancake served with fruit compote or butter and powdered sugar. The place was open late, often until dawn—the better to eat, get sloshed, and flirt.

Among the regulars at Pfaff's were gay men, most notably Walt Whitman following the publication of his poetry collection, *Leaves of Grass*, in 1855, back when "gay" meant lighthearted and the term "homosexual" was still years from being used to mean same-sex-attracted people. Justin Martin, a historian and the author of *Rebel Souls: Walt Whitman and America's First Bohemians*, told me that Pfaff's had such a gay reputation, it was essentially a "semi-gay bar"—not exclusively gay, but gay enough. Whitman probably first visited in 1858, and he spent time there almost weekly until around 1862, sometimes with Fred Vaughan, his younger lover. Whitman enjoyed holding court with other high-profile bohemians at a long table under the separate vaulted section of the saloon, where a seat was hard won.

"Whitman has a lot of descriptions in his letters and diaries of cruising," Martin said. "If he could meet men and have sexual liaisons, of course he would have wanted to find a bar where they could meet up."

In Whitman's lifetime, Pfaff's didn't consider itself a gay restaurant; the very notion would have been absurd. But if a gay restaurant is where gay men eat and drink, it was. After all, for my purposes, a gay restaurant isn't defined by how it advertises or who owns it or who cooks or serves the food. What makes a gay restaurant is who eats there.

"This was a place that was welcoming to gay men," Martin explained, "and they were comfortable."

Pfaff's advertised in the local press—"The best of everything at moderate prices," claimed an ad from 1859. Without television, radio, or the internet to help gay men find their way there, the restaurant's best friend was word of mouth.[6] Pfaff's was located on a stretch of Broadway near Bleecker Street that was a popular promenade, which made it easy for gay men to stroll by and pop their heads in to see whether their tribe was inside.

An expanded edition of Whitman's *Leaves of Grass* came out in 1860, featuring a new section called "The Calamus Poems" that delved into romantic and erotic relationships between men. Nothing like these poems had appeared in the first edition, from five years earlier.

The poem "Calamus #29," in which Whitman takes poetic license about holding hands with a young man at a bar, may have been set at Pfaff's:

One flitting glimpse, caught through an interstice,
Of a crowd of workmen and drivers in a bar-room,
around the stove, late of a winter night—And
I unremarked, seated in a corner;
Of a youth who loves me, and whom I love, silently
approaching, and seating himself near, that he
may hold me by the hand;
A long while, amid the noises of coming and going
—of drinking and oath and smutty jest,
There we two, content, happy in being together,
speaking little, perhaps not a word.

Pfaff's closed at its 647 Broadway location in 1864, and moved around a few times afterward. Perhaps Whitman found his way to those new spots too.

Pfaff's underscores my foundational premise that where there are booze, food, and men into men, there are gay restaurants. The gay bar as we know it today didn't begin to emerge in earnest until after the end of Prohibition in 1933 when, as sociologist Greggor Mattson explains, "the increased policing of alcohol had the perverse effect of encouraging gay-only" congregation.[7] Gay men turned existing bars and restaurants into spaces where they could gather with their gay friends to gossip and "ridicule the dominant culture that ridiculed them and construct an alternative culture," according to gay historian George Chauncey, even if it meant having to develop "elaborate stratagems to protect such places, precisely because they played such an important role" in their lives.[8] Prohibition, in other words, was the mother of gay invention.

With the increased availability of underground and word-of-mouth gay spaces came significant peril, considering that during this time, in many parts of the country, it was also illegal for gay people to congregate in public. Between 1923 and 1966, more than fifty thousand men were arrested for cruising in bars, streets, parks, and subway washrooms in New York City alone.[9] The Committee of Fourteen, a citizens' group started in 1905, acted like morality police by targeting saloons and whorehouses, eventually devoting manpower to keeping an eye on suspected homosexual men and women. Among its targets were restaurants frequented by gay men, including Enrico & Paglieri, a well-known Italian restaurant in Greenwich Village that Enrico Fasani and his brother-in-law, Paulo Paglieri, opened in 1908. A postcard from around 1910 features an expansive dining room filled with white cloth–covered tables and wall-to-wall plants and small decorative trees. The restaurant had become so well known among gays and lesbians that, in 1916, modernist author Djuna Barnes mentioned it as a gay hangout in her essay "Greenwich Village As It Is," not by name but by its address: 64 West 11th Street. If you knew, you knew.

In 1919, after learning that Enrico's had a reputation as a gay hangout, the committee sent an agent to surveil the restaurant. But the agent found no evidence that gay men ate there, even though she did report seeing two "extremely effeminate" young men.[10] During a later visit, the female agent saw girls whom she suspected of being lesbians even though they "made no definite motions or signs that they were such." Did the women moderate their behavior because they suspected they were being watched? Maybe, and for good reason. Code switching, as we would call such public behavior modification today, is a survival skill that has served gay people well for a very long time. Just ask any queer person who has butched or femmed it up during a holiday dinner with conservative grandparents in their red state Red Lobster. To blend in can be the safest way to eat out.

As the twentieth century dawned, gay people in New York City discovered a restaurant where their skills at going undetected came in handy, a place where meeting other gay folks could be as easy as letting a glance linger a few seconds longer than normal in a crowded dining room filled with straight families and businessmen going about their day. With it came flaky fruit pies and hearty beef stews. But first, you had to drop a nickel and open a door.

On January 14, 1937, Chauncey Miles sat down to eat a ham sandwich at an Automat in Greenwich Village. He was on break from his job at the Irving Place Theatre, a burlesque house where he entertained audiences by playing a flaming, comedic stock character called a nance. Long before Jack McFarland swished across Will and Grace's living room, nances pranced through movies, nightclubs, and burlesque houses during what became known as the Pansy Craze of the 1930s. To the delight of audiences, performers such as Gene Malin and Ray Bourbon portrayed exaggeratedly effeminate, bawdy male characters who were double entendre virtuosos. Some of the performers were straight, but some were gay but discreet, at least publicly.

There's a great example of nances prancing through a restaurant in John Francis Dillon's pre-Code film *Call Her Savage* (1932). ("Code" here refers to the Motion Picture Production Code, a 1930 self-regulatory measure that, in response to calls for federal censorship of the film industry, outlined what could and could not be shown on screen.) Nasa "Dynamite" Springer, a rich, wild child (played with bonkers energy by the silent film star Clara Bow) hires a dashing young man to show her around New York City. One night, he takes her slumming to a Greenwich Village restaurant where he says "only wild poets and anarchists" eat. There, a pair of pansy waiters dressed in maid's aprons wave around dusters in their extra-limp wrists. They flounce around the dining room entertaining folks with a flitty ditty about working as chambermaids on a battleship. After they swish away, Nasa gets

swept into a chair-swinging brawl. Nances like these were minstrel acts, for sure, but they were widely popular minstrel acts that
straight audiences devoured. Their prevalence should put to rest
any assumptions that femme queens and bitchy shade are only as
old as *RuPaul's Drag Race*.

But back to the Automat: Across the dining room, Chauncey
spots Ned, a handsome younger man who mixes ketchup with hot
water to make a thin tomato liquid, a common Automat work-
around for people who couldn't afford a proper bowl of soup.
Taken by his youth and good looks, and convinced that Ned is not
a cop, Chauncey strikes up a conversation with Ned without looking at him, lest other diners think they're flirting.

"One would almost assume that you had heard of this particular Automat," Chauncey says to Ned, "and of appearing at this
particular Automat at this particular time in the evening."[11]

Chauncey tells Ned there are only three things he ever talks
about: show business, politics ("I like mine Republican and conservative"), and "finding the places in whatever city I am currently
in where the boys meet the boys, of which this Automat is one."
After warning Ned that there was a raid the night before "at the
Childs on Fifty-Second Street"—referencing the popular lunch-
room chain—Chauncey cautions Ned, "We are being a little more
cautious. Do, but do be discreet, dear." Chauncey imperceptibly
slips the young man a dime, telling him to either take it and run
or use it to get a dessert and leave—a covert but still risky way for
Chauncey to signal that he's interested in the young man. What
Chauncey really wants is for Ned to pick the unspoken third
option: to have Ned enjoy a slice of the pie and a cup of hot coffee
by himself and then head to Chauncey's Hell's Kitchen apartment
for an assignation. Chauncey gets his wish when Ned leaves the
Automat and meets him.

Thus begins *The Nance*, Douglas Carter Beane's comedy
about a time when it was "easy to play gay and dangerous to

be gay," as the script describes. The play opened on Broadway in 2013, with Jonny Orsini as Ned and Nathan Lane in a Tony Award–nominated performance as Chauncey. The play received generally good reviews; writing in *The New York Times*, Ben Brantley called this opening scene "a terrific shorthand introduction to an underground culture, with its coded language and furtive signals."[12]

More than a glimpse at nance culture, the play is a slice-of-life dramatization of one of the most influential early types of gay restaurants: the Automat. Well before order-ahead apps and self-checkout fast food, the Automat was the *ne plus ultra* of casual dining in the first half of the twentieth century. Instead of ordering with a server, customers went up to one of many vending machine walls, inserted coins into a slot, turned a knob, and opened a small door to reveal hot or cold foods, everything from a hamburger steak with home-fried potatoes and a side of peas and carrots to a slice of fresh huckleberry pie. Signature foods were baked beans, Salisbury steak, ham and cheese sandwiches, creamed spinach, and an array of pies, including a chocolate pudding pie that one chain, Horn & Hardart, eventually sold as a whole.

Many Automat tables were communal, meaning patrons could have a meal with a stranger over light conversation or no conversation at all. Automats were quicker, easier, and cheaper than a traditional restaurant: You didn't even need to be able to read what was being served, since you could see the selection through the glass windows. You didn't need to be a Rockefeller to treat yourself. All it took was a penny at the hot water station for a spigot to release the perfect pour for a mug of tea.

The Automat concept first appeared in Berlin in 1895. The two biggest American Automat chains were Childs and Horn & Hardart.

William and Samuel S. Childs opened their flagship Childs restaurant in New York City in 1889 in the Financial District. By 1894, Childs had expanded to five separate locations, and eventually there were over 120 in thirty-three cities across the country, serving nearly a million customers a day. The Childs on 59th Street near Columbus Circle was nicknamed "Mother Childs," both for its prime gay location, between Central Park and the Broadway theater district, and because of its reputation as being particularly open to a gay clientele. A Childs in the Paramount Theatre Building, at Broadway and 43rd Street, also drew a gay crowd. Harlem Renaissance writer Richard Bruce Nugent recalled walking by a Childs restaurant and seeing "twelve young men—very delicate, very rouged, very elegant."[13]

The first Horn & Hardart opened in Philadelphia in 1902, the brainchild of business partners Joseph Horn and Frank Hardart. In 1912, Horn & Hardart opened a second location, in Times Square. There, the cavernous dining room followed a commissary model, packing in everyone from working-class men and women to more monied patrons who came dressed to the nines before nights on the town. The fixtures were made of shining brass and gleaming chrome, and the floors were marble. The street-facing windows were extra tall, allowing sunlight to wash over the tables where diners sipped hot cups of Gilt Edge, a darkly nutty mix of coffee and chicory, a Horn & Hardart house specialty. The spouts were in the shape of dolphins, inspired by Italian fountains. Automats served almost anyone who walked in, which made it a real dining democracy; in 1924, a newspaper columnist called the Automat "one of the melting pots of Broadway where all castes rub elbows and carry their food to marble-topped tables."[14] Automats also hired people of many races to work behind the scenes, although in the Automat's early years, cashier jobs were reserved for white women.

Anonymity, isolation, turnover: These are just some of the reasons Automats became gay. They offered cheap food, hands-off staff, and space to sit in a big city—a lot like today's gay coffeehouse culture but more elegant. At the Times Square Horn & Hardart, there were half-balconies, the better to keep an eye on the entire ground floor from a safe distance. Gay patrons knew to wear clothing or accessories in purple or lavender, considered feminine colors, to signal their same-sex attraction to other customers—the kinds of "instantly decipherable codes," as the scholar Lucas Hilderbrand put it in his book *The Bars Are Ours*, which gay people still use to find each other in mixed company. The same quest for self-identification happened much more openly later in the twentieth century with the Hanky Code, in which gay men, mostly, placed different colored hankies in their back pockets to signal a litany of sexual interests, from anal sex to water sports.

When the dining room was crowded, you'd have to sit next to a stranger, which came in handy for gay men on the prowl. Automats got gayer as the night went on, when gay men—horny and eager to be social—were more likely to be on the streets going to and from bars and theaters. If they got too drunk or belligerent or ostentatiously flirty or otherwise made straight people feel uncomfortable, they risked arrest. Horn & Hardart Automats were one of only a handful of restaurant chains in the early twentieth century where unescorted women were allowed to eat, making it easy for lesbian interaction.

Douglas Carter Beane, the playwright who wrote *The Nance*, grew up in Wilkes-Barre, Pennsylvania, outside Philadelphia. He often traveled to New York to spend time at the club Reno Sweeney, where such singers as Barbara Cook and Jane Oliver regularly performed.

"I would sit there and there wouldn't be someone my age, but there would be a very old gay man and I'd just ask him questions," he remembered. "That's how I learned about Automats."

Beane told me that the Automat's impact on urban gay culture in the early part of the twentieth century is impossible to exaggerate. Besides the history of pansy entertainment, part of his inspiration for *The Nance* was the idea that gay men once made it a habit to sit at Automats for hours on end, patiently and intently cruising and staking claim to a nongay space as their own—an idea "that put Edward Hopper in my head, of people waiting."

"I knew from my bar days, when I was young, of not being rich enough to get a second drink but milking one gin and tonic for three hours so that the ice would be melting and it would be just fine," he continued. "Waiting to find somebody or have a conversation—I knew the energy of that."

Some of Beane's favorite dining memories as a young gay man happened at Equus, a Philadelphia nightclub-restaurant that served food and attracted such performers as Karen Young, a bar singer whose disco hit "Hot Shot" packed the dance floor, and the insult comedienne Pudgy, "the fag hag Don Rickles," as Beane called her. Upstairs from the dining room there was a disco decorated with carousel horses, and "the minute they opened the door," he said, "you could smell the Pierre Cardin." One of its more popular meals was the steak teriyaki with rice.

Beane said he and many in his circle of gay friends miss the thrill of cruising at a restaurant under the radar of straight patrons.

"You knew when you walked into a place that, 'Oh, this is gay, here we go, I know what this is,'" he explained. "Now, you go on a website and find out. There was a game back then."

The Automat started to fall out of favor in the middle of the twentieth century as Americans' tastes pivoted away from elegant cafeteria-style dining toward a fast-food model. Horn & Hardart eventually raised its prices but also lowered the quality of the food it served, a move that sullied its reputation as a place to get a good meal at a reasonable price.[15] In one of the stranger pivots in gay restaurant history, in 1976, Horn & Hardart was sued by *Blueboy*, a self-described "national magazine about men"—i.e., a gay porn magazine—after the company decided not to partner with the publication on a string of gay discos across the country. The publisher of *Blueboy* thought he had a firm contract with Horn & Hardart to open a gay disco in Miami. "I'm dumbfounded that we're not open and operating now," he told the press.[16]

But the chairman of the board of Horn & Hardart sounded less convinced that a deal was in the works. "One of our people explored it," he said at the time, "but we're not entering . . . [the gay] market."[17] It never happened. (How I wish it had.) The last Automat in the United States, a Horn & Hardart in Midtown Manhattan, closed in 1991.

The Automat and other early gay restaurants were groundbreaking, in that they offered varying degrees of gay social permissiveness and conspicuousness, from a blind eye to tacit approval to a full-on embrace. Their openness to do so, even if they didn't know that what they were doing was enabling gay placemaking, was radical. They also set the stage for a new wave of gay restaurants where there was safety in numbers. But at these cafés, there was no reason to hide.

3

Bloodroot Revolution

Bloodroot, Bridgeport, Connecticut

To get to Bloodroot, I drove to the historic Black Rock neighborhood of Bridgeport, Connecticut. I turned down picturesque Ferris Street and parked in a gravel lot on the banks of a sweet little creek on Long Island Sound. A "feminist restaurant & bookstore with a seasonal vegetarian menu"—that's what the sign said. I walked up the flagstone path and opened the door on a time capsule set to 1977.

That was the year Selma Miriam and Noel Furie opened their restaurant, around the time that Mollie Katzen's game-changing *Moosewood Cookbook* introduced many Americans to animal-free eating. The Bloodroot dining room, once a machine shop, looked crunchy, lived in, *collective*. Patrons sat in mismatched chairs at sturdy wooden tables under vintage framed portraits. An oversize, multipatterned quilt was draped across the ceiling, its colors faded with time yet still vibrantly pulsing blue and green. To one side, a nook of shelves offered books for sale, including *Yarns to Dye For* and *What It's Like to Be a Female Union Electrician*. Bumper stickers promoting animal rights ("I Don't Eat Anything with a Face") fought for space on a bulletin board with bumper stickers for abortion rights ("Against Abortion? Have a Vasectomy"). A small sign in handwritten marker cautioned: "Because all women are victims of fat oppression, and out of respect for women of size, we would appreciate your refraining from agonizing aloud over the calorie count of our food." Two cats—Bella Abzug and Gloria Steinem—lounged in the sunlight on tall-backed chairs, steps from a loom.

Under a handwritten menu board, there was a wide pass-through window where the all-female kitchen staff stirred massive pots of soup and monitored the oven that filled the room with the smell of fresh, warm breads. The menu took David; his mother, Marian; and me on a world tour of flavors, ingredients, and temperatures. I paired a Caesar's Wife—a feminist vegan twist on the traditional salad—with an extra-creamy vegan "chicken salad" sandwich on cloud-soft bread. We split two hearty soups: cauliflower with Hungarian paprika and a Cambodian *kanji* with rice, potatoes, and cashews. For dessert, we paired fat forkfuls of a moist Jamaican rum cake with a surprisingly luscious bourbon-vanilla vegan ice cream. I washed it all down with a glass of magenta-colored Jamaican sorrel, made from hibiscus blossoms. It was a brisk Saturday afternoon in November 2022, and Thanksgiving was around the corner. I was tempted to return for the special holiday menu of mushroom soup, squash with chestnut stuffing, and cranberry kissel, a dessert of sweetened fruit puree.

Bloodroot has no servers or bussers, so we cleaned up our own dirty dishes and silverware. There's no head chef, either; rather, many cooks in the kitchen. I later learned that the four women cooking for us that day were immigrants from Honduras, El Salvador, Jamaica, and Haiti. All had found their way to Bloodroot through the Mercy Learning Center, a local school that provides classes and support services for women in need.

Bloodroot's collectivist management philosophies might be unusual and even untenable at most restaurants. But at Bloodroot, they're foundational and intentional, meant to flatten the wall between who makes the food, who eats it, and who cleans up. This ethos saturates everything the restaurant does, letting you know that you're on lesbian-feminist turf with working-class women at the center and capitalist resistance at play.

During my visit, I met P.J.—"like pajamas"—Schimmel, a Bloodroot regular. A seventy-year-old retired auto mechanic and printer-copier technician, she now works part-time at her late wife's business, teaching sewing.

"I'm not a big fashionista," she said, motioning down to her mom jeans and coral-colored sweatshirt. "But I can *sew*."

P.J. had just finished hosting her lesbian book club. A RESERVED sign marked the group's territory at the largest table in the room. Ten women had joined P.J. over slices of homemade parsnip spice cake for a discussion of *Yeah, I Said It*, Wanda Sykes's 2004 memoir. P.J. told me that her group—a "book club and lunch bunch," as she called it—had been meeting at Bloodroot for six years. They used to hold meetings at a nearby Panera, but decided they wanted their money to go to a local women-run small business that supported lesbians and aligned more with the group's progressive views, not a corporate chain.

"It's a feminist restaurant that's been around forever," P.J. explained. "It's independent and they let us sit and gab for as long as we want. It's a vegetarian restaurant, and I'm a vegetarian."

Besides, she said, when they used to meet at Panera, "occasionally we would read something racy with sex scenes, and we'd get animated."

"Nobody ever said anything to us when we were at Panera," she continued. "But that's not really their thing. Here, we don't have any problem."

Out since 1971, P.J. considers herself a lesbian feminist and an old-school butch. "It's like, yes, I am still a woman," she said. "I'm not going to be a man. I don't *want* to be a man."

She's not a huge fan of *they/them* pronouns or other outward markers of contemporary queerness.

"I respect other people's choices, but to me, all of that is a sign that the feminist message from the '70s did not reach into people's heads, that it's okay to be whoever you are no matter how you were born or whatever you look like," she sighed. "A woman can do anything and wear anything, and vice versa for a man. You can do any job, look any kind of way, and you're still a woman."

At the time of our meeting, P.J. was hopeful that Bloodroot would persevere despite the many pandemic-era challenges that most restaurants were facing: high food costs, a labor shortage, people's caution about eating indoors with strangers. (Bloodroot doesn't deliver.) Like other restaurants long set in their ways, Bloodroot has been slow to adapt to TikTok-era marketing; in its early days, Bloodroot regularly advertised in gay newspapers, but with those outlets all but dried up, the restaurant now relies mostly on Facebook to update its followers with photos of strawberry cream cheese pie, tomato fennel soup, and other meals from its seasonal menu.

"The older crew from the seventies, they all know about Bloodroot," she said. "But the younger folks, no. There's so much that the younger folks don't know."

Named after a Connecticut wildflower, Bloodroot is a culinary unicorn: It's the only lesbian-feminist restaurant that was founded during the 1970s in the United States and is still in business. It's one of the only lesbian-feminist restaurants in the country, period. Its sisterhood includes such restaurants as the beloved Bluestockings Cooperative, a queer, worker-owned bookstore and café that opened in 1999 on New York's Lower East Side. Like Bloodroot, it is a restaurant where politics is central to its mission, in this case on advancing "trans-affirming, gender nonconforming, and sex-worker affirming feminisms."

Bloodroot officially opened as an ecofeminist collective with several members. But the public face of Bloodroot for most of its history has been Selma and Noel, business and onetime romantic partners. When I met them in person in 2022, Selma was eighty-seven and Noel was seventy-eight.

"We began as radical lesbian feminists," Selma told me during a break in service, when she and Noel sat down to chat. "We wanted to have a place for people like us—outside the norm—which gave us the freedom to make decisions. A lot of people who started feminist lesbian things wanted to do them the way the patriarchy did them. We didn't. We wanted it to be vegetarian because we didn't want sentient creatures to be exploited." One of its purposes was to be "accessible and welcome everybody, whether straight or gay or Catholic or Muslim or atheist or whatever." Women's groups met there to mobilize as much as to socialize.

As we chatted, I watched two distinct but intertwined portraits of Selma and Noel emerge. One was of kindness and warmth and welcome, the same feeling I got when my grandmother Blanca and I shared leisurely early bird dinners together, just the two of us, at the Higbee's department store restaurant across the street from my high school, on days when my parents worked late. The other was of warrior strength, not like *Mad Max* but like Father Jim, a priest and my favorite professor during my undergraduate years at DePaul University, whose devotion to social justice included gay people and was manifested not in empty, condemning homilies but in a Catholic tradition of good deeds, such as soup kitchens.

Selma and Noel came across as caring but no-nonsense, the kind of women who will greet you with a bowl of hot lentil soup and a hand on the shoulder, but who will also put a bigot in their place faster than you can say "grilled tofu." They met as feminist organizers in the '60s, at local meetings of the National Organization for Women and other feminist groups.

"Selma knew all about cooking, and was the inspiration and the founder of this institution," Noel told me. "I met her at a consciousness-raising group, and when she decided to do this, I thought, 'I'm going with you.' That's how that got started for me. I'm really grateful."

To hear the two women describe it, the demands of heteronormativity were no match for the draw of feminism.

"I think a lot about fate and the fact that I met Selma at that time of my life," added Noel. "I was very unhappy about being a housewife and taking care of children. I was bored. The answers to a lot of my questions were answered by feminism."

The two became lovers. When I asked them to describe their romantic relationship, Noel smiled.

"We are business partners, and we did have a very interesting, very long-term relationship with many different aspects to it at different times," she laughed. I asked Selma whether there was anything else she wanted to add.

"Sex is temporary," she replied. "It's desirable. It has nothing to do with long-term relationships. What has to do with long-term relationships is having a shared vision, of really liking each other and getting used to each other. Usually the sexual relationships, something happens and they fade. It's not that there wasn't any sex but, let's face it, it was temporary."

She wasn't done. "I had some good sex, but that was not the measure of the relationship. . . . What we do together, what we build together is more important. The fact that we care about each other and that we have a lot in common, *this* makes a long-love relationship."

As young women, running a restaurant was not on their career radars. Selma was a premed student at Tufts University. Noel was a teenage model for a while because that's what her actress mother wanted; Noel later worked at the Playboy Club, where she met her husband. Neither woman had much experience running a restaurant. But when they decided to open one, both envisioned a women's café built on feminist ideals and business models. Friends in the animal rights movement convinced them to take meat off the menu. "If you're going to do feminist food, you're not going to be eating animals," Selma remembers being told.

The pair secured a mortgage in 1977 and bought the space for $80,000. Selma said her mother cautioned her to not put the word "feminist" in the name. She had good reason: In the 1960s and '70s, some straight feminists saw lesbians as a threat to the movement. In 1969, Betty Friedan, a feminist leader and author of *The Feminine Mystique*, used the term "lavender menace" to refer to mainstream America's perception of lesbians in the feminist movement. Transgender women weren't even on the straight feminist agenda's radar.

Selma didn't listen to her mother. When she opened Bloodroot, she defined feminist as being "interested in black equality, the problems of Spanish-speaking people, and we do feel that the largest number of people who are discriminated against are women."[1] The women hired only female attorneys, carpenters, and accountants, and got advice from friends who ran Mother Courage, a feminist, lesbian-welcoming restaurant in New York City. When they opened, meals were $5 (about $25 today).

"We're coming to this venture from a very political place," Selma said then, in a way that sounds a lot like now.[2]

Bloodroot's politics were tested in 2017, when the restaurant received threats of violence and accusations of transphobia after a transgender customer took to social media to claim that during a conversation with Selma and Noel, the women had made a distinction between transgender women and women assigned female at birth.[3] The customer eventually deleted her accusatory social media post, but the negative comments and one-star reviews had already piled up, leading Yelp to put a disclaimer on Bloodroot's page that it was monitoring the situation. In response, the restaurant posted a statement on Facebook, saying that it served everyone and always has, including trans people.[4]

Bloodroot's post also quoted a statement from the disgruntled customer at length: "I agree that the use of the word 'violence' to describe the Bloodroot owners was dramatic and out of place. I agree that folks (me included) tend to use the word 'violence' frivolously, which can dehumanize the person we are accusing and unwittingly cause real violence to occur. Also, most of the businesses that we shop at are probably owned by shitty cis men who do real harm to women, unlike the owners of Bloodroot." Not long afterward, the fracas quieted down. Transgender people continue to eat at Bloodroot.

The incident surfaced long-simmering tensions in the queer and feminist communities, between what makes a woman a woman and who should have access to women's bathrooms, sports, and other environments that have been separated under a gender binary. Many queer people consider gender to be resilient and fluent and unbound by a binary, and think that suggestions to the contrary are evidence of deep-seated anti-trans bigotry. But other queer people, including several elders I talked to as I researched this book, consider a trans woman a woman but not female—it's a belief in what cultural geographer Jen Jack Gieseking calls "stabilized notions of 'women.'"[5] For these folks, the male-female binary is fixed because DNA says so; the gender binary is far more heterogeneous.

This schism between old-line feminism and trans inclusion can be traced back to at least the '90s, a result of what sociologist Greggor Mattson calls "the rise of the binary-destabilizing queer identity."[6] It's a generational clash that can make intergenerational conversations uncomfortable.

But for many queer restaurant owners, making a space inclusive of as many people as possible is not just the right thing to do. It also makes good business sense: The more welcoming you are, the more customers you'll attract and the more money you'll make. For many queer folks, it's offensive to operate a gay-only or single-gender-only restaurant where transgender and nonbinary people might not feel welcome. From what I've heard on my travels for this book, at today's queer restaurants, this ethos is thriving. Queer restaurants of today and to come are embracing an all-inclusive customer base when it comes to gender, sexual orientation, race, and class. It's far removed from gender-segregated gay restaurants of the past, the kinds of restaurants where I ate as I came of age. In turn, and as the final chapter in this book explains, this new vanguard is forging queer spaces the likes of which American diners have never experienced.

The feminist restaurants that opened along with Bloodroot, in an era that lasted roughly from the late 1970s to the mid-1980s, *were* welcoming spaces: for cisgender women to eat, relax, socialize, and organize. They were especially much-needed safe spaces for lesbians, who were and are more likely than gay men to have kids and less likely to make as much money.

Lesbian restaurants blossomed across the country starting in the decade after Stonewall. They included Susan B in Chicago, where the menu featured an image of Susan B. Anthony, and Mother's Brew in Louisville, Kentucky, which boasted of having a "real cross-section of the womin's community," using a feminist-inspired "man"-erasing spelling of "woman" that was in vogue at the time in some lesbian circles.[7] In 1975, Los Angeles got one of its first feminist restaurants, the Los Angeles Women's Saloon and Parlor, which was sponsored by a Los Angeles feminist research and reading society and served vegetarian meatloaf and sandwiches. Tipping was not promoted, but waitresses were paid $3.50 an hour (a whopping $21 an hour today).

In the 1960s and '70s, the West Coast was a hotbed of lesbian dining. The Brick Hut Café—a lesbian-feminist restaurant that opened in Berkeley, California, in 1975—was small but mighty. It had only three booths and nine counter seats, but it was a hub for the gay community and a go-to spot for tofu sauté and a bottomless cup of coffee for 70 cents. Over the years, it earned several affectionate nicknames: Dyke Diner, Lesbian Luncheonette, the Chick Hut, the Brick Hug. The place was so popular that, in 1978, it inspired its own song by musician Mary Watkins, called "Brick Hut," on her album *Something Moving*. "If you're bored and need a change of pace stop by the Hut and meet a new face," Watkins croons, a fat bassline guiding her way through lyrics written by lesbian poet Pat Parker. The album was released on the lesbian-feminist label Olivia Records; to really drive home the influence of this particular eatery, the cover of the record features a photograph of Watkins sitting at the counter of the Brick Hut's original location.

Still, the Brick Hut's lesbian vibe wasn't everyone's cup of tea, even in liberal Berkeley. The restaurant was robbed and vandalized almost twenty times in the span of just eleven years. On one occasion in 1977, vandals threw bricks through the window after the restaurant displayed a poster announcing that it was boycotting Florida orange juice because of the Save Our Children campaign, spearheaded by singer Anita Bryant and other antigay activists who sought to repeal a gay antidiscrimination law in Dade County. For her efforts, Bryant was hit in the face with a pie during a news conference, in one of the more literally in-your-face acts of resistance in the history of gay civil rights activism and my favorite example of how to radically weaponize queer food. The Brick Hut persevered through two moves until 1997, when it filed for bankruptcy.

———————

Set foot inside Bloodroot today and the dining room looks like any other restaurant born of and holding on to a '70s attitude about feminist, meat-free dining. That's part of its charm. Bloodroot isn't in a high-traffic area, which means it's a true destination restaurant, not in an exclusive sense, but in a purposeful one. Lunch there made me feel that I was honoring women who charted a course forward in the restaurant business and who have stayed on the same ethical path despite shifts in how gay-welcoming restaurants are supposed to look and operate. Eating there made me appreciate how radical it was for Noel and Selma and other women, especially lesbians, to own, operate and cook at restaurants, their own and others'.

As David, Marian, and I took the last bites of our cake, I looked around at the gender diversity of Bloodroot's customers and wondered what it would have been like to eat there the year it opened. How I wish I could have been a fly on the wall, to see what it might have been like for a lesbian, newly out perhaps, to walk through the front doors and be welcomed into a sea of other women making and sharing food in a space free of men and their bullshit. How liberating it must have felt to be at a restaurant that finally aligned with your ethics, not just about feminism and vegetarianism but about how eating out can be an act of resistance, a culinary "fuck off" to America's male-dominated kitchens, to meat-and-potatoes menus and to all those forced-to-be-flirty waitresses in miniskirts. Unlike many restaurants in this book, Bloodroot wasn't queered, it was foundationally queer—although Selma and Noel (and P.J.) would probably prefer to say it was lesbian-friendly or, to be even more accurate, a women's restaurant that welcomed everyone, with delicious food and a devotion to progressive politics.

"I like this place," P.J. affirmed to me on my way out. "We all have a good time here. It works for us. I hope they're able to stay open."

In February 2025, Selma died just short of her ninetieth birthday, survived by her former husband, Abe Bunks; her children, Sabrina and Carey; Carolanne Curry, her companion of thirty-seven years; and, of course, by Noel. In an obituary, Noel said Selma's death was "like an earthquake," adding: "Her existence made such an impact on so many lives, including my own."

4

Two Lesbians Walk into Papa Choux, and Other Acts of Resistance

G ay restaurants can advocate for change in many ways. They can treat workers fairly and pay actual living wages. They can hang posters in support of causes and communities. They can serve animal-free meals, or donate money to food banks. They can also look hate in the face and respond not with peace but with a fight.

———

New York City was having one hell of a heat wave. It was July 2024, and my shirt wasn't thin enough and my shorts weren't short enough to keep me from sweating like your mom at a paternity test. I was thrilled to escape the hazy oppressiveness by walking into Julius, a gay bar at West 10th and Waverly Place in the West Village. I let out a sigh of submission as a frigid swoosh of air conditioning and the smell of freshly fried fries made me feel normal again.

"Erik?"

Tom Bernardin spotted me before I found him. He'd been coming to Julius since the early 1970s, more for the camaraderie than the food. (If he wanted to eat, he preferred a burger at the long-gone One Potato, not far from Julius at the corner of Hudson and West 10th Street.) Tom was seventy-five on the day we met. He's tall and lanky, with a head of silver hair and a set of mischievous blue-gray eyes. His résumé includes years as an ESL teacher and also as a tour guide and a cookbook author. We sat next to each other, he in shorts, too, at a banquette facing Julius's long and intricately carved wooden bar. He was there with a group of friends, gay elders mostly, whom he sees regularly for happy-hour shoot-the-shit afternoons. They sat on stools nestled closely at one corner of the bar, while other customers—gay men alone; a group of older women at tables in the back; a man who gave his lady companion a big, lingering kiss on the lips—nursed cold beers and bitched about the goddamn heat.

Julius's laminated menu—"CASH ONLY," it proclaims—features its signature burger for $12, including lettuce, tomato, and onion. There are bar food staples, too—hot dogs ($4), a BLT ($8), and chicken fingers ($9)—but also vegetarian options, including a veggie burger ($10), mozzarella sticks and onion rings (both $8). I opted for the grilled cheese, which arrived snugly nestled in a small, gingham-print paper basket and glistening with grease. I had watched it being made by Ray, Julius's short-order cook that afternoon, whose work station was a small grill that takes up a closet-size area in the middle of the space. I balked when Tom suggested I add some yellow mustard to my grilled cheese, but I'll be damned if it hasn't become a new favorite grilled cheese dipping sauce.

I met up with Tom because several friends said he knew a lot about Julius, and because, over the years, he's been featured in news coverage of the bar's storied history. I asked Tom why he thought Julius was such a special place. The answer, to my surprise, had to do with why he had made a woman cry there two weeks before.

"I'm there with my buddies and she comes in with her gay friend, and she's got a fucking margarita," he said, straight faced.

"She was so fucking loud," he continued, his voice rising. "I got up—my friends were complaining—I got up and went over and said, 'Would you please lower your fucking voice. What, they can't hear you in New Jersey?'"

He leaned forward, looking directly at me with a smirk that said: A read is incoming.

"Her gay friend, who was kind of hunky, gave me a big hug and said, 'Don't worry about it.' She went outside, crying. I'm like, 'Fuck you, bitch. Behave yourself.'"

The smile disappeared and he got down to business.

"You don't go to a gospel mass in Harlem in Bermuda shorts and then leave after the music, like tourists do," he explained. "You have to show respect for where you are. I don't care where the fuck you are—a gay bar or a church. Learn to look around. I assure you, that young lady is going to think *twice* before she cackles like that wherever the fuck she wants."

Tom isn't alone in his protective affection for Julius: On December 6, 2022, the bar was officially recognized by the New York City Landmarks Preservation Commission as a city landmark for its role in a 1966 protest against antigay discrimination in New York. (Even though, in the late '60s, Julius wasn't explicitly or exclusively a gay bar.) Mayor Eric Adams called the protest "a pivotal moment in our city and our nation's LGBTQ+ history," and dubbed Julius "a home for New York City's LGBTQ+ community."[1] New York City may not have a culture of bar-restaurants as do other cities its size and smaller. But when it comes to *this* category of gay restaurant, Julius is in a league of its own.

Built in 1826 at what was then the corner of Amos and Factory Streets, the building that houses Julius has been home to a bar since 1864. By at least the 1960s, it began attracting gay men with, among other temptations, a good burger. The tagline in a black-and-white illustrated ad from 1952 reads "the BIGGEST AND BEST HAMBURGER in N'YAWK!" to the left of a midcentury-style caricature of a chubby cook in a chef's hat, his hand outstretched and holding a burger on a fat bun with two little heat squiggles rising from it. Among the gay notables who visited Julius in years past were playwrights Edward Albee and Tennessee Williams and writer Truman Capote. Novelist Edmund White, too, who remembered a period "when we weren't allowed to face the bar but had to stand absurdly with our back to it to prove, I suppose, that we had nothing to hide."[2]

But in 1965, a plainclothes New York City police officer named Stephen Chapwick rattled the unspoken acknowledgment and acceptance of the gay customers who frequented Julius. As he scanned the narrow barroom, Chapwick was shocked to find men walking with "a mincing gait" and "waiving their wrists, very loosely."[3] He later reported his findings to the New York State Liquor Authority.

"There were a few males there and when they spoke, they spoke in a high shrill voice," he testified.[4] "There was one or two there. There was approximately four in a clique of males standing adjacent to the bar, had very tight clothes on with limp wrists. They were calling each other 'honey' and 'deary.'"

This wasn't an isolated incident. Between 1959 and 1966, New York law enforcement used undercover stings to entrap and arrest gay New Yorkers in bars and restaurants. The State Liquor Authority routinely revoked liquor licenses for establishments with gay customers, under the belief that their mere presence was disorderly.[5]

Fed up, on April 21, 1966, members of the Mattachine Society, the pioneering gay rights group, organized what became known as the Julius "Sip-In" to challenge the ruling and document discrimination in real time. It was led by three Mattachine activists: Dick Leitsch, a twenty-one-year-old Kentucky native and the president of the society, who wore a gray suit over a blue dress shirt and carried an attaché case; Craig Rodwell, a twenty-five-year-old from Illinois who was the chairman of Mattachine's young adult group; and John Timmons, a twenty-one-year-old Floridian who worked as a coding clerk and was a member of the group's public affairs committee. All three, accompanied by several reporters and a photographer who had been invited, went to a selection of bars, announcing that they were "homosexuals," and asking to be served a drink. To be formal about it, they read a statement:

"We, the undersigned are homosexuals. We believe that a place of public accommodation has an obligation to serve an orderly person, and that we are entitled to service as long as we are orderly. We therefore ask to be served on your premises. Should you refuse to serve us, we will be obligated to file a complaint against you with the State Liquor Authority."[6]

"There were certain places that weren't really gay places, like Julius, which was a mainly heterosexual bar but they had a lot of gay customers," gay rights activist Randy Wicker later clarified for me. "Once they had entrapment arrests, they didn't want to become a gay bar. You had to be with a woman, which is one of the reasons they didn't serve us. They were paranoid."

The group's first stop, the Ukrainian American Village Bar on St. Mark's Place, had closed by the time they arrived. Above the bar there were several signs: NO CREDIT, NO DANCING, and NO SPITTING ON THE FLOOR. Another, in hand lettering, read: "If you are gay, please stay away."[7]

They were served at their next two stops: a Howard Johnson's on Sixth Avenue at 8th Street, which had a famously cruisy men's room in the basement. The men got a corner booth and asked for the manager. Emil Varela, the relief manager on duty, greeted them, and they read their statement. Varela, a grandfather of three, was a "gray-haired amiable man of 55 in black horn-rimmed glasses," as *Village Voice* reporter Lucy Komisar described in her must-read first-person account of the protest.[8] Varela said the activists looked like "perfect gentlemen," and he ordered a waiter to "bring the boys a drink."

"It's pretty ridiculous that anybody should determine what anybody's sex life is," Varela told the reporters. "I think there's plenty of lawmakers whose sex life I could challenge, and they drink too."

The three men were served at their next stop: Waikiki, a Polynesian-themed bar on Sixth Avenue near 10th Street. The manager, who gave his name as "Mr. Urban," said he would "serve anybody as long as he doesn't annoy anybody."

At Julius, however, the activists got exactly what they predicted, and what they wanted: The bartender, a forty-something man who said his name was Jack, refused to serve them.

As Leitsch recalled: "When we walked in, the bartender put glasses in front of us, and we told him that we were gay and we intended to remain orderly, we just wanted service. And he said, 'Hey, you're gay, I can't serve you,' and he put his hands over the top of the glass, which made [for] wonderful photographs."[9]

After the protest, the head of the State Liquor Authority told *The New York Times* that regulations leave service to the discretion of the management, and that bartenders could refuse service to disorderly customers. (The article's headline was this doozy:

"3 Deviates Invite Exclusion by Bars.") But the city's commissioner of human rights, William H. Booth, later expressed opposition to the "denial of bar service to a homosexual, simply for that reason."[10] Eventually, the State Liquor Authority loosened its restrictions, giving gay people the right to be served.

———————

There were other significant gay uprisings at other bars and restaurants in the years leading up to Stonewall. On April 25, 1965, some 150 protesters staged a sit-in at Dewey's, a diner in Philadelphia's Center City, after its management instructed employees to start denying service to "homosexuals and persons wearing nonconformist clothing."[11] It was odd that such discrimination would happen at a diner that was so gay it was known as the "fag Dewey's," a slur-reclaiming sobriquet that differentiated it from a fag-unfriendly Dewey's. (Straight people probably also called it the fag Dewey's, and not in the slur-reclaiming way.) After more protests, Dewey's dropped its policy days later.

In Los Angeles, undercover police officers raided the Black Cat Tavern as New Year's Eve revelers welcomed in 1967, after having received reports of lewd behavior taking place there in plain view. The fracas allegedly began after police entered the bar and apprehended a person they thought was a boy dressed as a girl who had kissed another boy. They were almost right, as one local gay news outlet put it: "Patrons, most of them men dressed in girlish attire and definitely the effeminate type, took violent exception."[12] By the end of the whole ordeal, the police had arrested at least a dozen people, six of whom were charged with lewd conduct for kissing people of the same sex. On February 11, 1967, some six hundred people attended a peaceful demonstration outside the Black Cat that was organized by the activist organizations Personal Rights in Defense and Education and Southern California Council on Religion and the Homophile—at the time, the largest documented gathering for gay rights in the United States, two years before Stonewall. Six of the men arrested during the raid were convicted of lewd conduct and had to register as sex offenders.

The Black Cat eventually closed, but it has reopened several times in the years since, once as a disco and now as a tavern again. In 2008, the site was designated a Los Angeles Historic-Cultural Monument; in 2022, the California State Historical Resources Commission approved the site becoming a state historic landmark. In 2023, a bronze marker was placed near the front door in a small ceremony attended by local politicians, preservationists, and eighty-seven-year-old Alexei Romanoff, who helped organize the demonstration back in 1967. The Black Cat's queerness, once a risk and a liability, has now become a selling point.

Fast-forward to the '90s, and the spirit that drove activists to protest at Dewey's and the Black Cat returned to shake things up at Cracker Barrel, a Tennessee-based chain of Southern-inspired restaurants that announced it would discourage hiring gay people. (The company officially said it would not hire anyone "whose sexual preferences fail to demonstrate normal heterosexual values.")[13] When a Cracker Barrel location in rural west Georgia fired Cheryl Summerville in 1991 for being a lesbian, about four hundred people protested outside the restaurant. After a series of additional protests at locations across the South, Cracker Barrel eventually dropped its policy, and LGBTQ+ activists claimed victory.

In a turn of events that would have sounded like science fiction to those of us who remember the Cracker Barrel drama in the '90s, in 2023 the company came under fire from Christian conservatives for being *too* gay-friendly and for voicing support for Pride. "We take no pleasure in reporting that @CrackerBarrel has fallen," the right-wing Texas Family Project tweeted. The offense? A Cracker Barrel restaurant posted a picture of a rainbow-colored rocking chair on the main Cracker Barrel Instagram account, saying: "We are excited to celebrate Pride Month with our employees and guests."[14] As with a lot of these kinds of dust-ups meant to rile social media and create conservative outrage, the controversy over Cracker Barrel ran its course. A brand that was once synonymous with antigay bigotry is for a new generation of queer people a campy faux-farmhouse place to get gravy-smothered country fried steak and a slice of cinnamon roll pie.

In 2024, drag queen Kim Chi, a *RuPaul's Drag Race* fan favorite, disclosed on a podcast that Cracker Barrel was her favorite fast-food chain restaurant.

"No one makes pancakes like Cracker Barrel does," she said.[15]

In the case of one landmark gay protest at a straight restaurant, change was ignited when two women walked out the front door.

On January 13, 1983, Deborah Johnson and Zandra Rolón were looking forward to having dinner at Papa Choux, a posh, "prime rib and cocktails" kind of restaurant that opened in Los Angeles in 1971. (The blood-red ashtrays and matchbooks reminded diners, in elegant italicized script, that they were eating at a "Restaurant Exceptionale.") To celebrate their six-month anniversary, Zandra made a reservation for one of six booths in what the restaurant called the Intimate Room, which was saved explicitly for couples. Each booth was covered by sheer curtains for semiprivate dining and came with a server call button. Strolling musicians sauntered by, playing songs like "Stardust" and other "melodies from heartbreak hotel," as *The Los Angeles Times* put it. Valentine's Day was around the corner, and the women, both twenty-seven and LGBT activists, were in a romantic mood.

When Deborah and Zandra first arrived at the restaurant, the hostess escorted them to their booth. But as the women prepared to sit down, the maître d', realizing what lesbian drama was about to unfold, rushed over and pulled the table away from the women, a jarring act that caught other diners' attention. He informed the women that they would have to move to a different part of the restaurant because the booth they reserved was only for couples. They said they were a couple. He then told them that the booths were reserved for mixed couples. They replied that they *were* mixed: Deborah is Black and Zandra is Latina.

The women later claimed the manager told them, incorrectly, that a city ordinance prohibited him from seating two men or two women in the booths. He offered to seat them elsewhere and give them free drinks. Angered by the indignity, the women left "fuming," as Zandra later recalled.

The women sued the restaurant and hired famed civil rights attorney Gloria Allred, who filed a lawsuit that sought an injunction to force Papa Choux to seat and serve same-sex couples in its booths.

"This is a bias by businesses against homosexuals engaging in conduct which would be normal when engaged in by heterosexuals," Allred said at a sidewalk news conference outside the restaurant.[16] "Dining should be a delight—not a dilemma. We intend to end this dinner discrimination and give Papa Choux its 'just desserts.'"

The restaurant responded with an unapologetically homophobic newspaper ad.

"Papa Choux's will never allow this charade," it read. "It would certainly make a mockery of true romantic dining. Our policy at Papa Choux for that area only has been, is now, and will be in the future for mixed couples only." The announcement was signed "Very respectfully yours" by the owner, Seymour Jacoby, and the managing director, Walter Kulwitzky.

In July 1983, a Superior Court judge ruled that the restaurant's refusal to seat the two women in a private curtained booth did not constitute illegal discrimination based on sex. Superior Court Judge Bruce R. Geernaert visited the restaurant to inspect the booths "to judge the policy as a reasonable regulation of public homosexual behavior unacceptable to society."[17] The judge called the case "very, very close" when it came to determining whether the restaurant's uncurtained booths and regular tables were accommodations that were comparable to the curtained booths for couples. (Keep in mind that laws protecting gay people from discrimination weren't in place in California, or federally, at the time.) Eventually, it came out in court that Papa Choux let two presumably straight men sit together at the booths for business meetings. Zandra and Deborah were the first people to refuse to move when they were asked to sit anywhere but at the lovebird tables.

The case eventually made its way to the state Court of Appeal, which ruled against Papa Choux. The state Supreme Court denied the restaurant's petition for a hearing, which ended the case. In response, Jacoby took out *another* ad, lamenting that "true romantic dining died on this date": May 18, 1984. Days later, some one hundred Papa Choux loyals gathered there for a sardonic, up-yours "wake." The booths were covered in dramatic black mourning crepe.

In response, Allred defiantly told *The Los Angeles Times*: "This is not the death of romance. It is the death of discrimination." It also led to the death of Papa Choux, which closed for good around 1987.

"Nobody wakes up one day and says, 'Today I'm going to make history.'"

That's the first thing Zandra told me when I got on the phone with her and Deborah in 2023. Zandra had become a chiropractor and lived with her wife in the Santa Cruz area; Deborah was a minister and diversity consultant in Las Vegas. (The two separated around 1994 after fourteen years together.) Both women—they identify as lesbians—spoke about the incident at Papa Choux as if the indignity of their thwarted dinner date had happened the night before.

"What we didn't know was that we were essentially the national test case for the right to be out," Deborah told me, her voice sturdy and determined, as if she were delivering a sermon. "The logic that the restaurant was using against us was the same logic that was being used in the civil rights days about refusing service to Black people: our visual presence was offensive to the public eye and that was enough." Both women had been active in the gay rights movement prior to their dinner date at Papa Choux, and when the maître d' started giving them a hard time, Deborah remembered thinking, You are messing with the wrong people.

As a child born and raised in the South, Zandra said the Papa Choux incident hit hard when it happened. Her mother had relatives who lived two hours away from her family's home in Brownsville, Texas, and when Zandra's mother took them on road trips to visit, they only had a few places, including a Whataburger, where she could stop as a person of color.

My favorite photo of the pair is from 1984. Shot from below, the women stand in front of Papa Choux's big outdoor sign that encourages folks to "Take Dad to Dinner" in anticipation of Father's Day. They smile at the camera, arms around each other's waists and fists raised to the sky. Both women are wearing sports coats; Zandra has her sleeves pushed up, looking like a *Miami Vice* extra who is living out her cop show dreams.

The image is a stark reminder of how theirs was one of the first cases in which sexual orientation was deemed a civil rights issue on par with race and religion. Their activism drove home the point that the list of characteristics that should be covered by antidiscrimination laws was illustrative, not exhaustive.

"It set the stage for marriage equality and things that put sexual orientation under the rights banner," explained Deborah.

In today's political climate, Deborah and Zandra's legal win remains incredibly relevant, especially as an increasingly right-wing Supreme Court has made it easier for small businesses, such as bakeries and wedding photographers, to refuse service to queer people based on the business owners' religious beliefs. As a new wave of antiqueer legislation makes a path across the country, the women told me that they hoped their willingness to fight back decades ago will resonate with a new generation of queer diners.

America has never stopped pushing and pulling between secular values and religious convictions, a tug-of-war with dire consequences. That has especially been true for transgender people and where they go to the bathroom.

I saw a flash of fury when I brought this up with Jessica Jones, a transgender woman who, with her cisgender queer wife, Erica, owns Giant Jones Brewing Company in Madison, Wisconsin. I met Jessica and Erica in 2023 at their brewery, one of a handful of certified organic breweries in the country. Giant Jones had recently been featured in a local newspaper story about how Wisconsin's conservative building codes made it difficult for small businesses to designate gender-inclusive bathrooms. At the time, Wisconsin was using an amended version of the 2015 International Building Code which required, with few exceptions, that bathrooms be divided by sex. State legislators had refused to update the code to allow for more flexibility, having already rejected a major allowance for multiuse gender-neutral bathrooms. Jessica said when the building inspector visited in 2018, he pointed out that her two bathrooms were supposed to be divided by gender. "I'm not doing that," she remembered telling him. She stood her ground and eventually won, as I saw, myself, when I used the gender-neutral bathroom.

The subject of where trans people go to the bathroom has long been a source of contention, including at restaurants. In 1972, Francis R. Thompson, a transgender woman from Binghamton, New York, lost a case that she filed with the state's Human Rights Division alleging that a tavern owner had discriminated against her on the basis of her sex. Thompson alleged that Genesio Riccardi, the owner of Gondo's Restaurant and Lounge, which Thompson "frequented before her operation" (as the magazine put it), told her after she used the women's bathroom that she would no longer be served there if she didn't use the men's room instead.[18] (It's unclear how long she had been using the women's restroom before he made a stink about it.) When she officially launched her complaint, the agency found that the restaurant owner had not unlawfully discriminated against Thompson.

Gender-neutral bathrooms are not just about making transgender people feel comfortable or special. Such bathrooms are usually more private, which appeals to people seeking additional space or safety options, such as families with kids, disabled people, and caregivers. Opponents say updating codes to require existing bathrooms be retrofitted would be too expensive for small businesses, as would having to build several single-use bathrooms.

Jessica counters that such objections aren't actually about expense but about "discomfort with trans rights and making the world navigable for trans people."

"Trans people aren't trying to get away with anything," she said. "We're just trying to pee."

Jessica told me that gender-inclusive bathrooms are just one part of a larger agenda behind running a queer-identified brewery in a beer state like Wisconsin.

"People connect to me, a trans person, because they are drinking a beer," she explained. "People can come in and interact with a trans person and that changes things for them. There are plenty of our customers who have said that their understanding of trans people has really changed because they came to Giant Jones to drink beer."

———————————

As Bloodroot did for women and lesbians during the heyday of second-wave feminism, gay restaurants are taking on oppression today, wherever it is and whoever is in danger. Take Laziz Kitchen. When the restaurant opened in Salt Lake City three days before the 2016 election, it quickly became a queer oasis in an otherwise deep red state that helped elect Donald Trump (twice, eventually). Fear of a Trump presidency helped motivate Laziz's owners, Derek Kitchen and his then-husband Moudi Sbeity, to open the restaurant. In 2012, the couple worked out of their home kitchen, making Middle Eastern spreads, including hummus and muhammara, which were inspired by Moudi's upbringing in Lebanon. (He evacuated from there as a consequence of the 2006 war.) The couple sold their food at farmers' markets, Whole Foods, and other local stores, to rave reviews. Their adorable "Hummusexual" T-shirts were a hit too.

From its earliest days, Moudi and Derek made sure customers knew they were eating at a restaurant that centered queerness and progressive social justice causes. The bathrooms were gender neutral, and outside a trans-inclusive Pride flag swayed not far from a poster that designated Laziz as a place that welcomed refugees. Such hospitality tracked with the restaurant's name: In Arabic, *laziz* means "nice and lovely, like a sweet person"; Derek said he told customers it meant "tasty and enjoyable," akin to *rico* in Spanish.

An early regular at Laziz was Nan Seymour, a self-described "pansexual, postmenopausal woman who adores her husband and abhors labels." When I spoke to Nan over the phone in 2021, her voice broke as she told me how much Laziz meant to her and her trans daughter after Trump was first elected.

"The default in our current culture is cisnormative, heteronormative white supremacy, and it's not safe for people who aren't in those majority privileged groups," she said. "It's essential for us to know that we can be at a restaurant and not worry about how it will go for my daughter when she goes to the bathroom." Moudi, she added, was "exceptional in his willingness to be seen and take what is a significant risk."

I visited Laziz in 2022 with David and our good friend Diana, whose family is Jordanian and who has an expert palate when it comes to Middle Eastern food. ("We can order the grape leaves," she said as we looked over the menu, "but my mother's are better.") We sat in soft orange seats in the light-filled dining room and ordered almost everything on the menu that was vegetarian, including a deliciously seared halloumi. There was still a sign on the door that welcomed refugees, only now it offered support for Black Lives Matter too. Near the bathroom, I spotted a commemoration of Laziz's being named as a James Beard semifinalist in the "Best Chef: Mountain" category in 2020.

After we had lunch, I sat down with Derek, a soft-spoken man with an easy smile, neatly kept scruff, and a trim physique honed from regular treks into in Salt Lake's Wasatch and Oquirrh Mountains. Derek was elected to the Utah State Senate in 2018, five years after he and Moudi and two other same-sex couples won their lawsuit against the state of Utah and then-governor Gary Herbert that challenged Utah's constitutional amendment defining marriage as between a man and a woman.

Derek said that in its first year, Laziz became a shelter of sorts.

"We had people coming in sobbing, coming in for a hug or cup of coffee or a warm meal," Derek told me. "It started out as that safe space that we need as queer people."

But when I visited, Laziz didn't look that queer to me. David and Diana agreed with me that the dining room was filled mostly with opposite-sex couples and groups of coworkers on lunch breaks—what you'd see in *any* fast-casual style restaurant. I asked Derek whether he still considered Laziz a queer restaurant.

"My hope is that we retain the queerness in the sense that it's a place for everybody, especially if you're an outcast or somebody that has historically not felt welcomed," he explained. "But also, it's for everybody too, so it's not specifically a queer restaurant. It's a place for the LGBT community to come and feel safe. It's our roots, you know?"

Something else was missing from Laziz the day I ate there: Moudi. He and Derek divorced in 2019 right before the pandemic hit. After operating the business together for years, Moudi wanted to pursue a career in social work. Derek said he bought Moudi out "so that he could be free to do whatever he wants." The two still talk, and according to Derek, they "still hold each other in high regard."

In 2022, Derek came up short in the Democratic primary for the Utah Senate's new ninth district, the boundaries of which the Utah Legislature reapportioned after the 2020 census. But he's still in politics: In April 2023, he was appointed to the Biden-Harris administration as the director of intergovernmental affairs at the Export-Import Bank.

Derek said he enjoyed living and working in and representing Salt Lake City, where today lots of straight bars and restaurants are gay-friendly even if they don't fly a Pride flag out front. Far from being invisible, the queer community in Salt Lake City is simply more integrated than it once was.

"Going forward, deep assimilation is the future for the queer community," he said, adding that in Salt Lake City, "you go into any coffee shop or any bookstore or restaurant and you will have just as many gay people as you will straights. It matters less and less."

When I caught up with Moudi in the summer of 2024, he was studying mental health counseling at Naropa University in Boulder, Colorado, and was working on a book about his journey from

war-torn Lebanon to the United States. Laziz, he told me, "represented the culmination of all those years trying to find my place as
a stuttering queer Lebanese-American who still believed in shap-
ing a world inclusive of all.

"When I consider what it means to be a queer dining establishment, I think of the way we opened our doors to anyone who walked
through, without ever questioning their deservedness to be there," he
said, adding that it was part of a "guiding principle inherited from my
lineage which says feed any stranger that shows up at your door."

———————

Is Laziz still proudly progressive? Yes. Concerned with social justice? Absolutely. Queer-welcoming? No doubt. But is it still queer
if the dining room doesn't look or feel queer and if the people eating there aren't predominantly queer? By the definition that has
guided my understanding of gay restaurants, the answer would
be no. But that's not a problem. Because at today's queer restaurants, queerness is just one of many foundational identities. Black
Lives Matter, climate change, abortion: a queer restaurant could
certainly keep quiet about these issues. But for many queer restaurants, being queer is inherently political, and to remain quiet is
to risk alienating customers who want to make sure their values
align with those of the restaurant they're spending money at. To
remain neutral or advocate for a both-sides approach to politics
could negatively call into question a queer restaurant's responsibility toward and investment in intersectional social justice.

Take what happened in 2023 at Lil' Deb's Oasis, a restaurant in
Hudson, New York, that I featured in my *New York Times* article. Run by the queer chef Halo Perez-Gallardo (who went by a
different name when I interviewed them), the restaurant is located
on a quiet street not far from the train station where Manhattan
gays come and go to weekend and play in the Pink Belt, the term
given a queer stretch of the now-pricey Hudson Valley. Inside, Lil'

Deb's is bathed in bright pinks and citrus, with a look that lands somewhere between Caribbean day-at-the-beach and '50s suburban kitchen. The menu on my visit in 2021 was a Latin-Caribbean mélange: I had golden brown, sugar-sweet plantains; hearty rice and beans like my Colombian grandmother used to make; and a phenomenally moist tres leches cake. Even the cocktails had a queer sensibility, with such names as "Don't Have to Be Rich to Be My Girl" and "Garden Orgy."

In 2023, about two weeks after the start of the Israel-Hamas war, Lil' Deb's posted a message on Instagram in support of "the liberation of Palestine" and the return of Palestinian "occupied land" after "75 years of beautiful resistance" in the face of Israel's "colonial destruction."

"Hamas is an Israeli-funded terrorist organization," the restaurant wrote. "Israel is a US-aided colonialist project supported by US dollars and military." "To those who would charge us with anti-Semitism," it continued, "we refuse to conflate the settler colonial project of Israel and the racist project of apartheid against Palestinians with supporting our friends in the Jewish faith."

Comments on the post landed almost down the middle between supportive exuberance and pure fury. "Because Hamas absolutely loves queer people that['s] why they murdered, kidnapped, and raped a bunch of liberal ravers at a music festival," wrote one commenter. "Respect y'all for putting your neck out to speak up for justice and stand against genocide," said another. Several commenters posted Palestinian flag emojis with the words "From the river to the sea," a slogan that to some is a call for Palestinian self-determination, and to others, a hope for Israel's eradication. In a follow-up Instagram post, Lil' Deb's claimed the original post cost them two thousand followers overnight.

This kind of public political stance isn't the norm at most gay restaurants, which tend to fill their social media feeds with hot young able bodies in bathing suits and ads for appearances by

Drag Race winners. If they get political at all, it's with generic messages in support for queer equality.

Lil' Deb's was more direct, and that was the point. It would have been one thing for the restaurant to support human rights generally. But fresh into the war, it called Israel an oppressor knowing that the message would result in some of its customers and neighbors being offended. The owners knew that such a stance could end in the kind of backlash that soon roiled colleges and other cultural institutions that were debating how to respond to the war.

The first thing Halo told me when I called to talk wasn't about the Instagram post at all, but about how COVID-19 and inflation had done a number on their business. They were hopeful about the future, though, even as the profile of their perceived target customer had changed.

"We want the space to be for everyone, but we have had an increase in wealthy, white straight customers, and that's largely due to the fact that we have had to raise our prices," they explained. "Trying to be accessible and values-aligned becomes hard and changes your demographic."

Halo said they didn't anticipate the vitriol the post would cause, and they were unprepared for the pushback. "I speak from the heart often and I wrote that post, and in my mind, I thought our audience will understand," they said. "But I was underestimating how divisive this issue is and has been."

Halo had no regrets about the original post, even if it meant losing customers who wished Lil' Deb's would just stick to being a restaurant.

"It was not an option to stay silent," they said. "In the age of social media, we have power and word travels fast. I think that it's important to stand up for things that you know are just when you have a voice." Halo said they hoped that queer spaces "don't forget to be intersectional and not just have fun gay parties but stand up for other oppressed people."

They paused for a few beats.

"I don't have a solution," they finally said. "There might have been a time when I did. I hope we get there."

Eating at any restaurant (including a gay one) that's invested in social justice causes comes with risks, and always has. For many customers, discovering that an owner's politics don't align with their own may be a deal breaker the next time it comes to deciding where to make a reservation. I know gays who will never again eat at Chick-fil-A because Dan Cathy, the company's CEO, came out personally opposed to marriage equality in 2012. The company has since said it would no longer contribute to the Salvation Army and other organizations that have lobbied against same-sex marriage, but that doesn't matter to some queer people who want their dollars to match their politics. On the other hand, every time I pass by Chick-fil-A locations in New York City, where there were once calls for the chain to be banned, the place is usually packed. I know at least one gay who eats there, but he didn't want to talk to me about it out of fear that he would be seen as preferencing a delicious chicken sandwich over the queer community. I bet there are some older gay men who would never set foot in a Cracker Barrel after what the company put gay workers and customers through.

The question for customers, then, is this: Do you eat at a restaurant that publicly takes a stance you abhor? Or do you take your money elsewhere? I can't answer that, and I wouldn't want to. Gay people should spend their money, or not, at whatever restaurant they want.

But Zandra Rolón has advice for anyone, especially young queer people, who wants to see justice served, whether it's at a queer restaurant or elsewhere.

"The ball's in your court now," Zandra told me. "It's your turn to be vigilant. We did it in our twenties. You can do it in yours."

5

Myth America

What Happened at Cooper Do-nuts?

Late one night in May 1959, a small group of LGBTQ+ people fought back against the Los Angeles Police Department at Cooper Do-nuts, a donut shop in a seedy part of Los Angeles known as the Run. Fed up with police harassment, the assembled queers—including drag queens, transgender women, and street hustlers—pelted the cops with hot coffee and glazed donuts. Outnumbered, the police called for backup, and made arrests. In *City of Night*, a 1963 landmark of gay literature, author John Rechy recalled seeing coffee cups fly through the air. All this, ten years before the Stonewall riots.

Or so the story goes. Like trying to distinguish who threw the first brick at Stonewall, what I've discovered about researching the so-called uprising at Cooper Do-nuts is this: It is a frustrating and futile exercise to try and definitively determine what happened between queer people and the police at a Los Angeles donut shop in 1959. Memories are unreliable. Most of the people who may have lived it are not alive to talk about it. There was no coverage of a Cooper Do-nuts riot in local newspapers or on television, which seems strange for a major metropolis with a healthy tabloid press that likely would have jumped on a story about queer deviants violently rampaging against the police to the point of arrests and property damage. There are no arrest records either. The family behind Cooper Do-nuts, a beloved chain of Los Angeles–based shops that operated in several California locations from 1952 to 1995, won't vouch for the riot that has long been associated with its brand.

"We don't have concrete proof," admits Jacquie Evans, who runs CooperDonuts.com, a website that keeps the memory of the donut shops alive. And she, of all people, should know: She's married to Keith Evans, whose family owned and operated Cooper Do-nuts.

There is almost no evidence that the Cooper Do-nuts riot—labeled as such by historians, academics, the press, activists, and students of queer history for decades and today still—ever happened.

I have similar questions about what allegedly happened in August 1966 when a group of trans women, drag queens, and other queer people were said to fight back one night against police officers who were harassing them at Compton's Cafeteria at Turk and Taylor Streets in San Francisco's seedy Tenderloin district. A month earlier, members of Vanguard, a trailblazing and militant LGBTQ+ activist organization, picketed the twenty-four-hour diner—a burger, fries, and slice-of-pie kind of place—claiming that the management was giving peace-abiding queer customers a hard time. (The economy of the Tenderloin then was fueled by sex workers, many of whom used Compton's as a gathering place despite attempts by the city's vice squad to crack down.) Black-and-white news footage of a Vanguard protest in July 1966 shows a line of activists picketing outside the restaurant in opposition to police harassment.

But the exact August date of the Compton's Cafeteria uprising or riot, as it is alternately referred to, is uncertain, even by those who say they participated. There was no coverage of it or its aftermath on television or in newspapers—a surprising omission, considering that there is footage of a peaceful protest at Compton's a month before. There don't appear to be any records of arrests—to be fair, that wasn't unusual in the 1950s and '60s, when law enforcement wasn't diligent with its record keeping. Most of the information about a Compton's riot comes from Dr. Susan Stryker, a trans woman and an academic whose fascinating documentary *Screaming Queens* includes interviews with queer and trans people who said they were there and fought back against police with flying fists and lobbed sugar shakers. In several interviews, Stryker has recounted how she was at the Gay and Lesbian Historical Society archives in 1991 when she came across a timeline that referenced how drag queens protested "police harassment at Compton's Cafeteria." But a city archivist later told her that there were no arrest reports and that the "records have been disappeared."[1] Stryker's own conclusion is that the uprising likely happened on August 27, 1966. I reached out to Stryker during the course of my reporting to hear more, but I did not hear back.

There is evidence that perhaps *something* happened at a Compton's restaurant. The only surviving contemporary record of the incident is in a brief article for the 1972 San Francisco Pride Parade program, six years after the alleged riot. It was written by Reverend Raymond Broshears, the gun-carrying clergyman-leader of the Lavender Panthers, a group of Black Panthers–inspired vigilantes who organized the first documented US gay militant street patrol. There's also a letter to the editor that a drag queen named Sandy Green wrote, which said that if people thought Stonewall was something, "they should've seen what happened at 'Turk and Taylor [the cross-streets of Compton's] in '66.'"[2] Most of the best evidence of a Compton's riot rests in the oral and written testimonies from people who said they were there. Such accounts are nothing to dismiss out of hand, and I'm not saying the riot never happened as they claim it did. I hope it did.

But as a longtime journalist, I wish that evidence were rock solid. In any legitimate newsroom, reporters and editors would need more than firsthand testimony, no matter how ample, to publish a story saying definitively that an honest-to-god riot occurred, especially in the absence of arrest records and media coverage. In 2023, San Francisco's ABC station aired a news segment about the alleged uprising, and the reporter was careful with his language, using the phrases "likely happened" and "believed to have happened" to describe that night. Stryker is also interviewed, and even she says: "It seems like the riot took place in the weeks after that picket."

A skeptic would say there's a reason the Compton's and Cooper Do-nuts uprisings aren't as well known as Stonewall: There's just not enough evidence that they happened. Still, their narratives endure. Hearing from people who claim they participated in such uprisings lay bare the tensions that built between gay people and the police before Stonewall. The stories offer instructive if cautionary lessons in how gay history is retold, remembered and honored. And verified.

So, did the Cooper Do-nuts riot happen or not? It comes down to what you mean by Cooper Do-nuts and whose memories about that night you believe.

On a sunny October morning in 2023, David and I met Jacquie and Keith at the Latte Shop, a coffeehouse in the Little Tokyo neighborhood of Los Angeles. We sat at metal tables outside, getting to know each other over gooey egg-and-cheese breakfast sandwiches and iced oat milk lattes. Jacquie has dark brown hair and big brown eyes that light up when she lets out a hearty laugh, which is often. Keith has light brown hair just this side of going gray at the temples. He's tall and lanky and looks as if he grew up surfing. He's quieter than Jacquie, who did most of the talking. She is a proud bisexual who was married to a woman before she married Keith.

Jacquie told me her interest in keeping the legacy of Cooper Do-nuts alive was about more than just being married to an heir. She believes that Cooper Do-nuts welcomed queer people at a time when doing so would have been bad for business. Her efforts to preserve this history came from her desire to reframe our understanding of the queer past.

"Any other business, as soon as they found out you were anything other than straight and white, you were shown the door," Jacquie said. "At Cooper Do-nuts, they served the cops, too, along with veterans and transients and LGBT people. It was welcoming to everyone."

Jack Evans, Keith's grandfather, grew up on a farm outside Chicago and moved to California during the Great Depression. Trained as a chef, in the 1940s Jack opened two Evans Cafeteria locations in Los Angeles, where in addition to such diner favorites as cheeseburgers and pancakes, he sold a variety of Cooper Do-nuts's desserts: traditional glazed; chocolate bismarks; Long Johns; and Persian rolls, a type of cinnamon bun. After a few years, once Jack realized

how profitable the donuts were compared to the rest of the cafeteria, he bought the ownership rights to Cooper Do-nuts from its
creator, Richard Cooper, for $50,000. (Marge Evans, Keith's grand-
mother, designed the logo, which incorporated a bite out of a donut
to create the "C" in "Cooper Do-nuts.") At one point there were
thirty-three Cooper Do-nuts locations across California.

Keith remembered his "grandpa Jack" as a quiet man who was
kind and generous, and who would have been pleased by the attention Cooper Do-nuts was receiving. "He loved his workers and the
people who came into his shop," Keith smiled.

Among the gay people who ate at Cooper Do-nuts was Nancy
Valverde. Nancy was born in Deming, New Mexico, and grew up
poor in East L.A. ("I didn't know about lesbianism or anything,"
she once told an interviewer. "I just knew I was comfortable in
pants.")[3] In the 1950s, Nancy and her friends Audrey Black and
Delores Newton were cosmetology students at Moler Barber College at 265 South Main Street, a few doors down from a Cooper
Do-nuts at 213 South Main Street.

"The minute we got a dime for cutting a head of hair, we'd go
there and enjoy each other's company," Nancy remembered.

A Chicana lesbian and a masculine-presenting woman, Nancy
told me she was routinely arrested for violating a citywide ban on
cross-dressing between six p.m. and six a.m. (In other interviews,
she said her first arrest was in 1949, when she was seventeen.)
Nancy was jailed in a section known derisively as the "Daddy
Tank," reserved for women suspected of being lesbians.

"The cops would stop me for wearing male attire and they
would tell me, 'Do you want to be a man?'" Nancy told me over the
phone in 2023, when she was in hospice at the age of ninety-one.
"I'd say 'No, I'm a lesbian.' And they'd say, 'We want to see you in
a dress.' And I went to jail. They made my life miserable."

On March 25, 2024, a few months after we spoke, Nancy died
at ninety-two. But her legacy was cemented in June 2023, when

the Los Angeles City Council installed street signs commemorating her activism and Cooper Do-nuts for its "ongoing work to make Los Angeles a more inclusive place." In large, simple script on a beige background are the words, COOPER DO-NUTS/NANCY VALVERDE SQUARE. Below that, in all caps, there's a vague explanation: HONORING THEIR COMMITMENT TO AN INCLUSIVE LOS ANGELES. There are no rainbows or other markers designating the sign as queer-related.

The record of what happened at Cooper Do-nuts comes down to one person: John Rechy. It's no surprise that Rechy, a trailblazing gay writer, would recall in one of his books an uprising that took place at a donut shop where he hung out with friends.

When I corresponded with Rechy via email in 2023, he was ninety-two and had just finished his eighteenth book. I asked him about the reference to a donut shop uprising that he included in *City of Night*. He told me he was almost arrested there one night after queer folks pelted the police with "catcalls, curses, taunts and then objects." Nothing about the incident appeared in newspapers, but, according to Rechy, "that was not rare."

"During those years, gay people were aware of police hostility as a part of one's life," he added.

Rechy said that this specific uprising occurred at a donut shop at 500 Main Street in Los Angeles. He clarified that the shop in question wasn't a Cooper Do-nuts after it was pointed out to him that there was no Cooper Do-nuts on the 500 block of Main Street.

Contrary to what had been widely repeated as fact, the words "Cooper Do-nuts" are not in *City of Night*. Cooper Do-nuts is, just by a different name. Here's why: Rechy shared with me that he was asked to change some of the place names in his novel "because of possible trademark issues." As a result, Harold's Bar became "Harry's" and Cooper Do-nuts became "Hooper's,"

which in the book he describes as "an all-night coffee shop" frequented by police who harassed the "scattered army" of "male
hustlers, queens, scores."

At the time, Rechy explained, there were so many Cooper
Do-nuts locations in the city that "Cooper's" became shorthand
for "donut shop"—the equivalent today of using "Walgreens" to
mean "drugstore."

"Everyone, including me, who frequented that [particular] shop
called it Cooper's," he explained.

Rechy was baffled by the "hostility that has persisted" surrounding his account of what happened at a donut shop, calling it "undeserved, incorrect, malicious, infuriating and, yes,
saddening."

In response to my questions, Rechy wrote a deeply emotional
five-page letter. I asked him whether I could reprint some of it in
this book, and he agreed. I'm excerpting it here at length because I
admire how he describes, with his signature elegance and defiance,
what he remembers about that night:

> The shop on Main Street was a gay gathering place,
> open, I believe, 24 hours. At night and especially after
> 2:00 a.m., when nearby bars closed, their patrons
> moved into the street or into Cooper Do-nuts—hustlers,
> queens, "night people." It was a noisy, busy place, coffee
> and donuts on the counters. It was, too, a main site for
> the cops to harass—and harassing was their main objec-
> tive: Cops would park in front, an implicit warning.
>
> Two cops would enter, march about the horseshoe
> counter, questioning customers randomly for I.D., etc.
> Then they might walk away or they would pick one or
> more people out for further interrogation, often out-
> side the shop, to harass and implicitly warn. At times,
> they would choose one or two of the people and take

them to "the glass house," the jail nearby. Fingerprinted, interrogated—illegally since you had to be charged before that was done—but cops in Los Angeles were free to act on their own.

On one such night, two cops completed their round of the coffee shop and then told me and another young man to come out with them—no reason given, just intimidation. That night, the atmosphere changed. A drunk man inside started cursing the cops. What followed was a chorus of taunts and curses. All at once, there was a drag queen along with us outside waiting for whatever the cops decided and sassing the cops. The people in the coffee shop rushed out, and others leaving bars joined. The atmosphere changed, catcalls, curses, taunts, and then objects—cups, trash—were flying at the cops. We had not been handcuffed, I and the two others broke away from the squad car. It all blurred into one thriving mass. I heard a siren and saw a squad car—perhaps two—approaching the churning crowd, and one squad car stopped at the entrance, restricting traffic. Nothing appeared in newspapers, and that was not rare. Those arbitrary raids and "roundups" were invisible to everyone except those involved, and they occurred frequently throughout the city and Hollywood, in Pershing Square, the bars, the streets.

Rechy ends his letter by reminding me of something that every student of queer history should hold dear: Any claim about the Stonewall uprising as an event that "started" or "launched" or "began" the LGBTQ+ civil rights movement is lazy bullshit. Queer people had long been pushing back against discrimination in all its forms long before Stonewall, whether at a donut shop or anywhere else, in big cities and small towns. And that spirit of resistance, even with no evidence to back it up, needs to be honored. Rechy continued:

> A negative effect of focusing on Stonewall is that it divides our history into two periods: "Stonewall," synonymous with resistance and liberation; Pre-Stonewall, implicitly a time of passivity, acceptance. That denigrates the brave warriors on the front lines when a "homosexual" encounter exposed one to imprisonment for five years. It was a dangerous time that nevertheless gay people defied, simply by being gay.

Jacquie and Keith aren't entirely willing to say there was *never* a queer uprising at a Cooper Do-nuts; the commemorative signage they successfully fought for is predicated on the possibility that it did. On the Cooper Do-nuts website and Instagram account, Jacquie, a marketer, has posted several archival photos and explained that the incident was indeed a pre-Stonewall uprising, if "accounts are accurate." There is no dispute that there was a Cooper Do-nuts blocks from where Rechy claimed the uprising happened. The small building—in the same prefab design of other Cooper Do-nuts around town—is still there. It's an office for an immigration attorney.

Nathan Marsak is confident about his doubts. An author and a historian of downtown Los Angeles, he is not a fan of attempts to center Cooper Do-nuts in queer history, although he considers himself an ally to the queer community. His objections fall in line with what writer Ryu Spaeth has called "retroactive gestures at diversity"—in this case, an attempt to frame and understand our queer present within the context of the queer past.[4]

"The history of any minoritized people is important, and it is crucial that that history be fastidiously accurate," Marsak shared with me in an email. "It lends credence to those who would marginalize a group when the historical method is abused, and facts are trampled in favor of fiction, no matter how exciting and uplifting that fiction may be."

He went on to call it "heartbreaking and hurtful" that the LGBTQ+ community could be "disserved by members of its own, who in inventing and promulgating the patently false Cooper Do-nuts narrative, felt a *myth* was necessary to give its people power, when there exist so many *actual* stories of bravery and triumph. There is neither honor nor uplift in the City's memorialization of Cooper Do-nuts; it is, inarguably, a sad and ugly slap in the face to reality in general, and the LGBTQ community in particular."

I asked him about Compton's too. He agreed with me that *something* may have happened. But he found it "highly dubious" that there are no photographs—no record whatsoever—of rioters smashing the restaurant's windows, chasing police into the street and destroying a patrol car before dozens of people were arrested, as has been reported.[5] If the city met with protesters because of the riot, as has been claimed, that meeting would have left a trail of some kind in the city's archives. It's possible those records were destroyed or lost. Even if the city met with protesters, he wrote, "that doesn't mean there was a *riot*."

Ultimately, Jacquie told me, whether a riot did or did not take place at a Cooper Do-nuts is beside the point.

"I'm so tired of hearing about whether or not a riot happened," Jacquie sighed. "I really don't care. The bigger story is that there was this family that had twenty-seven donut stores all over Los Angeles and six in Northern California and they were so accepting and welcoming and were a ray of light in what wasn't the best part of town.

"There's a sign there now that's acknowledging more good in the community than just what may or may not have happened," she continued, leaning forward and raising her voice slightly. "You can't dispute the good part."

Humans can't get enough of fables and legends. Gay people are no exception, especially when it comes to a time before personal cameras were able to capture heroic acts. We want to know who threw the first brick at Stonewall, even though that's almost impossible to discern. We want to know whom we can blame for AIDS, since a disease just couldn't have randomly showed up to decimate an already vulnerable community. We want to proclaim that a group of angry queer people threw donuts and hot coffee at the cops who were harassing them, because it means that queer people were powerful despite being made to feel powerless. But it's more honest to say we don't know. Fiction that feels good is called faith, not a fact.

Yet: We need these stories, don't we? That's why the Cooper Do-nuts and Compton's Cafeteria narratives have staying power. They serve essential purposes: to remember, to celebrate, to commemorate, to inspire. Historian Lillian Faderman put it best when she described to me what happens when heroic events take on "a life of their own."

"They're not necessarily accurate," she said. "But they're stories of beautiful myths."

6

The Trans Nexus

Napalese Lounge and Grille, Green Bay, Wisconsin

I've had delicious meals at disgusting restaurants. I once ate three vegan Beyond Burger brand cheeseburgers at an A&W convenience store in Toronto at five a.m. after a night of partying. I've also had soul-sucking meals at fancy restaurants. One of the most horrific single dishes I've ever had was an overpriced and revoltingly dry mound of plantains one Christmas Eve at a James Beard Award–nominated restaurant.

I learned early that decor, location, and price have nothing to do with a restaurant's quality. One of my late father's favorite indulgences was a hot dog with mustard from Hot Dog Inn, a beloved hole-in-the-wall luncheonette on Cleveland's West Side. I was probably ten years old when, on one dark night, from the safety of our locked car, my mother and I watched a man stagger out of Hot Dog Inn and into the street with a knife sticking out of his head. My mother leaned hard on the car horn, but my father, undeterred, ignored it until the counterman put a steaming hot little wiener in a bun into his hand. My mother screamed bloody murder when my father got in the car and, ignoring her, took the last few bites. After almost a century in business, the Hot Dog Inn closed in 2020, after a new owner gave it a new name: Old Fashion Hot Dog.

Hot Dog Inn wasn't a gay restaurant, and what happened that night could have happened anywhere. But it had the qualities of the type of mom-and-pop restaurant—uncelebrated, locally cherished, noncoastal—that piqued my curiosity the most as I decided which gay restaurants to visit in person to write this book. I really wanted to know where gay people eat beyond monied enclaves where wearing the wrong Speedo will get you blacklisted. I wanted to know where small-town queers ate when there were no gay bars for miles around. I was for sure interested in big-city restaurants that were popular with gays. But a restaurant where muscle boys eat chicken breast in Provincetown? Yawn. A Miami restaurant run by a hotshot lesbian chef? What else is new? A café in West Hollywood where anybody who's anybody meets for brunch? . . . And?

What I really wanted to know what it was like to be a transgender person and eat out with other transgender people in towns and states where being transgender was more dangerous and politically volatile than in New York or California.

That's why, on a sunny afternoon with an overnight bag and a jonesing for cheese curds, I got on a bus to Green Bay, Wisconsin, to meet Martha at a place called Naps.

Napalese Lounge and Grille sits on Cedar Street in a sleepy stretch of downtown Green Bay. Naps, as locals call it, is in the quaint Olde Main Street Arts District, where its neighbors include national chains like Family Dollar and Dairy Queen but also small businesses like The Attic, a homey coffeehouse and used bookstore, and Taqueria El Local, where tacos come in tongue and tripe. It's mostly mom-and-pop territory, a far cry from the big-money opulence of Green Bay's biggest tourist draw: Lambeau Field, home to the beloved Packers football team and the anchor of a neighborhood where on game days, fans worship at the feet of a towering statue of storied coach Vince Lombardi.

At first, you might assume (as I did) that Napalese serves food from Nepal. It does not.

Arnold "Butch" Pendergast and his partner, Stacy Desotel, bought the property in 2012 and kept the name, assuming it had something to do with the dead owner's heritage. Butch, a straight shooter who works as a jeweler by day, is still not sure what the name means, not that it matters to him or his customers.

"Unless we have a séance, we won't get an answer," he shrugged. "But I have enough spirits around me. I don't need another one hanging out."

At one point, a visitor to Green Bay who drove by Naps might not have recognized it as a gay bar-restaurant from the plain brick siding and black script logo on its boxy exterior. But not long after it opened, some people did figure out Naps was gay, and it wasn't gays: For a while, some assholes kept throwing fireworks and trash through the street-facing front entrance. The vandalism forced Butch to keep that door closed and let people in only through a monitored side door off the parking lot.

Naps might have stayed under the radar if it weren't for what happened on a sunny day in August 2021, when Green Bay's mayor and Wisconsin's lieutenant governor gathered at the restaurant to unveil the city's first LGBTQ+ public mural. Created by Loschue "Chue" Lo, a queer Hmong artist and Oshkosh, Wisconsin, native, the mural became a striking visual marker of queer space. In bold letters, it features the words "We Will Be Seen" next to oversize portraits of transgender activists Marsha P. Johnson and Sylvia Rivera, who stand before the colors of the inclusive Pride flag. The mayor opened the front door and let people in that day, and since then, that door, no longer the security risk it once was, is an entrance once again.

Butch, a native of Eau Claire, Wisconsin, turned what was a shot-and-a-beer kind of pub into a bar-restaurant with a style I'd describe as bordello camp. The wallpaper, the comfy upholstered chairs, the small lamps that dot the main room: They're all covered in deep shades of red. Portraits of Dolly Parton and James Dean hang not far from a small stage where Kelli Jo Klein and her Green Bay Gals regularly host drag shows. Patrons can play darts or pool or shoot the breeze at the outdoor patio.

Napalese's menu is Wisconsin-style comfort food: Sam Adams beer–battered shrimp; deep-fried green beans; cheese curds in white, yellow, spicy, or bacon flavors. Good luck getting a seat for a Friday Fish Fry, a Wisconsin tradition with Catholic roots that now crosses religious, sexuality, and gender-identity boundaries. The Naps version lets you pick perch, walleye, or a combo, and with it you get rye bread, coleslaw, and a choice of potato salad or one of four kinds of fries. Dinners cost around $10, but for $18.75, a hungry homo can double up on the fish. On the night I visited, I sat at the bar with a red plastic basket piled high with bite-size white cheese curds that scalded my fingers. I popped those babies in my mouth one by one, savoring the one-two punch of crisp breading and wet, squeaky cheese—a Wisconsin orgasm.

I found myself at Naps not by chance but by the grace of Martha. I had interviewed her when I wrote my gay restaurants story for the *Times*. On the phone, I took quickly to her warmth, mirth, and sense of humor, a trifecta you hear in her from-the-gut laugh. Her friend Maggie calls Martha—a married parent, former bigwig in the Catholic diocese, devoted social worker, avid Harley Davidson rider, mama bear fairy godmother—"the guardian angel of our little trans community."

It was June 1, 2023, when I took a bus from Chicago, where I had been visiting friends, to Green Bay's lonely bus terminal on an industrial stretch of University Avenue. Martha picked me up, and I'll be damned if at seventy-two years old she didn't look chic as hell, as if she was about to go on a Chanel spending spree in Palm Beach. Her oversize sunglasses matched her black, chin-grazing pageboy, and her blue and white floral print blouse complemented her crisply ironed white slacks and strappy sandals. Her lips were a precisely applied crimson.

"Well, hello," she smiled, standing on her toes to wrap me in a hug.

As she showed off Green Bay through the windows of her white SUV, I quickly learned that there's not much quiet time in conversation with Martha, not because she monopolizes or monologues but because she's an astute observer with strong opinions, especially about being transgender. Martha told me the best way to describe her identity is "dual-gender," but gender fluid and gender diverse will do too.

"I have a male side, but I also have a strong female side," she said. "Both sides of me have to present in my life to be authentic." (Though she has always interacted with me as the feminine Martha, she also uses a masculine name.)

For over forty years, Martha was in the closet as she became a nationally recognized lay leader and full-time employee at diocesan offices in the Catholic Church. She served seven different bishops and co-authored a pastoring book that's still published and used in seminaries. As her "male self," as she put it, she met Pope

John Paul II, and as Martha, she and a group of other American Catholic transgender women chatted briefly with Pope Francis in 2024 in St. Peter's Square at the Vatican.

During Martha's many years of service for the Catholic Church, she lived in fear of being outed as transgender and getting terminated from working on behalf of a religious tradition that taught its believers that being transgender was an affront to God's plans for humanity. After retiring from church ministry in 2017, she came to accept that there might be a reason God made her who she is.

"I believe that the gift of my transness has been given to me to use to reach out to one of the most oppressed minorities in the United States today: the many people in the transgender community," Martha wrote to me after I left town. "I think that God has indeed continued to work with and through me to provide safe, caring, and compassionate places for trans adults and youth."

I timed my visit so I could sit in on the monthly transgender meet-up Martha organizes at Naps, the better to understand what it was like to live as a trans person in a county that Donald Trump won in 2020 and 2024. Martha said that when she retired, one of the things she did first was ask Butch whether she could rent a room in the back that could accommodate a small group of trans people for regular meetings. He agreed and gave it to her for free. The first one attracted just four people whom had met Martha online; there was no formal program, just a chance to meet, drink, and eat. It was what Martha called a "no-guilt group," meaning "if you don't show up, no guilt."

Martha tells newcomers that they don't have to check in when they arrive, because she and her regulars will know they're new and will make them feel welcome. Often, she will chat online for a year or more before convincing someone to visit Naps, only to have them back out at the last minute. The meetings aren't as secret as they once were, thanks to social media and word of mouth. Not a day goes by that Martha doesn't hear from transgender people from across the country inquiring about when they can visit Green Bay.

"I always have to battle [this idea] that they're guilty they didn't show up," she explained. "I follow up with: 'We're missing you, but it's no big deal.' We're like the old Motel 6 commercial. 'We're leaving the light on for you.'"

Martha now has contact information for about four hundred people, mostly from northeast Wisconsin but also from the larger region, including Michigan's Upper Peninsula, a three-hour drive away. Each mixer attracts dozens of transgender people plus cisgender allies, family, and friends. On average, there are two to four first-timers a month.

Fear, Martha said, is what keeps more people from coming. She's lost count of how many times she's received a call or text from someone who made it to the Naps parking lot only to be so frozen by fear that they were unable to walk in the door. A few have driven to Naps but gotten so scared, they turned around and went back home after anxiously texting Martha from their car.

"In many instances, they have spouses or family who don't know, and this is the only time and place they can come out," she continued. "My fear, too, when I started going to Napalese, was, What if a coworker or neighbor walks in? Even though people say with the wig and makeup, there's no way they'd recognize me, I have a weird laugh."

But it's not always so despairing for newbies. There was the night in the middle of winter when a young trans woman made it into Naps, shaking from both the cold and nerves. After chatting for about forty-five minutes, the young lady casually mentioned that because she didn't drive yet, her mother had driven her and was waiting outside in the car. She wanted to know, could her mom come inside? Martha went right out and introduced herself.

"The mother was wonderful," Martha remembered. "It's such an honor to be able to do that kind of stuff." She bought the mom and daughter their first drinks.

For Martha, hosting at Naps is more than a social gathering. It's a calling.

"I want to work with the most hurting people, and who's more hurting than the trans community," she told me.

It wasn't a question.

What Martha is doing for her transgender chosen family is part of a long tradition at restaurants across the country. Her meetings have roots in the underground network of transvestite, cross-dressing, and transgender women who in the 1950s and '60s met at restaurants dressed *en femme*, as they called it, to live as the women they were, even if it was just a weekend at a time. Back then, gender rules were strictly enforced socially and, in many parts of the country, legally. To get around being arrested for wearing clothes of "the opposite sex" in public, these pioneering women and men met through printed guides that offered listings of bars and restaurants where they would be welcome. *Transvestite Magazine* regularly chronicled the goings-on of such groups as the Salmacis Society, a national social cooperative, most active in the '70s, "that specializes in bringing she-males openly together with bisexual and feminist women" as well as "fellows who like to be feminine." The group had chapters across the country, in New York and Los Angeles, Cleveland and Detroit, and regularly held events at restaurants, although the magazine didn't always say which ones, the better to protect the owners and customers from threats of violence. (One issue of the magazine reported that an event was held "at a restaurant hotel in the Western section of San Francisco.") In 1980, the magazine *Femme Mirror* held a convention in New Orleans, where several cross-dressing men ate dinner at a restaurant called Anything Goes. "They loved us at the restaurant," wrote Cindy, one of the attendees who was quoted in the magazine's postconvention feature. I loved reading about Cindy's experience, because it reminded me that, even though the transgender community has faced and continues to face inordinate amounts of hate and violence in this country, there were nights like this—one dinner, for a group of friends who didn't conform to what a man or woman should be or look or dress like—that made life a little better.

To be clear, the people who read these magazines were probably straight white men who identified as cross-dressers or transvestites; they probably weren't gay and might have reacted with hostility if anyone had suggested they were. Many liked to dress in women's clothes, but they did not necessarily identify as women when they went home and took those clothes off. Regardless of how these customers self-identified, the point is that many restaurants were safe spaces where their identities as men and women weren't shunned or regulated but rather embraced and normalized.

To help ease any nerves transgender women might have about going out in public dressed en femme, magazines like *TV-TS Tapestry* and *Femme Mirror* offered advice columns on how a lady—a decidedly heterosexual and high-femme lady, to be clear—should act when eating out. In 1980, *Transvestite Magazine* offered helpful tips in an article titled "How to Build a Basic Wardrobe," detailing what to wear in order to pass when going out to restaurants.

"If you are lunching at a good restaurant in a city environment, any kind of wrap jersey dress, a shirt-waist dress, a suit, a silky shirt and skirt, a blazer, shirt, and skirt will do beautifully," the writer advised, adding: "A satin blazer and a skirt or dressy tapered-leg pants would be a nice look for a dressy dinner."

There were fashions of many varieties, from body-squeezing tunics to T-shirts, jeans, and sneakers, at Martha's "Cross

Dressing/Transgender Social Gathering," as the Naps website bills it. The Naps community room, a private space, is bordered almost entirely by mirrors. On the night I visited, some forty transgender folks, self-described cross-dressers, and a handful of family members and allies lined the periphery of the space. (Martha later told me that several of the women were living in homeless shelters—one key reason why the mixer is free and why it's held at Naps, where the food and drinks are cheap and people are willing to buy a stranger a drink.) The meeting lasted about thirty minutes. Topics included forthcoming Pride events across Wisconsin, a report on a local high schooler's trans-inclusive prom, and a call for donations to a trans clothing swap.

Martha then adjourned the meeting to let the real fun—cocktails and socializing—begin in earnest. I ordered a basket of smiley fries and sat down with Maggie, an art and special education teacher who identifies as trans-feminine. On this night, she wore a blousy brick-colored top underneath a fitted and distressed jean jacket and a pair of tight blue jeans, an outfit that looked especially chic against her long brown hair and blue-gray eyes. At Naps, she usually orders the chicken fingers or fries if she doesn't want to get messy, but if she's feeling gutsy, she'll get the quarter-pound "Gay Burger." Martha dipped into my conversation with Maggie to explain the burger's appeal was not just the price—$2 at certain times of the week—but how it's made on Butch's tacky grill.

"They turn it up so you get the good char, and it keeps all the juice," Martha clarified. "The meat they use is good and greasy, and I get it with fried onions, absolutely."

After Martha left to mingle with other guests, Maggie told me that she is married to a supportive cisgender woman, and together they parent a sixteen-year-old daughter in Neenah, Wisconsin, about a 40-mile drive from Green Bay. One of six kids, Maggie used to dress in her sisters' clothes growing up, and now shops in the women's department. At school, she wears women's jeans, tops, and gym shoes, along with mascara and earrings—an appearance, she said, that's "pushing the boundary a little bit" of what's socially accepted at her workplace. That's one of the reasons she's a regular at Martha's mixers, even though like other long-timers—she's been going for over seven years—Maggie admits she could stop attending because she now feels comfortable being openly transgender in her public life.

"I've got to keep coming because I want to be helpful and be a part in case people need community," she insisted. "I feel I still need it."

What struck me about Maggie and the other trans-identified people who showed up for Martha's mixer was how much they represented a cross-section of America. I met teachers, retired military and law enforcement, blue-collar workers and corporate executives, ranging in age from young Gen Zers all the way to the Stonewall generation. Maggie and almost everyone I spoke to was white, but in terms of their identities as transgender people, there was pronounced diversity. Most of the men who identified as cross-dressers were cisgender and straight, in their fifties and older; the transgender women tended to be younger. I didn't meet any transgender men, at least not that I was aware of. I also met younger attendees who identified as nonbinary.

One of the younger transgender people I talked to had gotten to know Martha online, and had flown from Tennessee to Green Bay just to be there that evening. She didn't want to tell me her name or say much about her life, other than that by day she sold guns in her conservative rural community where, if she wore a dress, she would probably get run out of town. She had on a cream-colored sequined gown and matching chunky heels—the first time she had dressed so in front of anyone, ever. Through a nervous smile, she told me that the experience was thrilling. I offered her some of my cheese curds, but she declined and politely excused herself.

I met seventy-six-year-old Marg, who lived near Madison and was a fan of Naps's burgers. Not only was she the only intersex person I met that night, but she was also the only intersex person I'd ever knowingly met, period. I asked her to define what intersex was.

"It's real simple: Intersex people are people who are different internally or externally from what the normal population understands as a male or a female," she explained, adding: "I'm like a natural trans."

Then there was Keri, dressed in a striped zebra print top and black skirt, with black tights and flats to match. Her hair was a dark rust color, at least from what I could tell under the bar's red lighting. She was also in town from Tennessee, where she was a psychology professor, but she had spent many years living in Wisconsin, and sometimes stayed in Manitowoc, about a forty-five-minute drive away. Travel time, gas expenses, traffic hassles: None of it mattered to Keri, because the draw to Naps was too strong. Besides, there was nothing quite like Martha's meet-ups where she lived, and being so far away from home provided her an extra layer of anonymity.

Real quick, I could tell Keri was not a person to be messed with, especially when she got on the subject of labels. Keri fluctuates between identifying as gay and bisexual, although she's more drawn to men, and between calling herself "a sissy, a transvestite, cross-dresser" and a "transsexual cross-dresser." Even so, she doesn't identify fully as a man even when she's not dressed in feminine attire.

"If I want to be a transvestite, I'm going to be who I want to be," she said, her voice rising. "You're not going to fucking tell me." She continued: "Some people don't like a lot of these terms, but I decide who I am."

At fifty-two, Keri had been cross-dressing for about fifteen years, starting with lingerie and panties that provided anxiety relief and the chance for her to express "feminine attributes, like caring for others." She liked being submissive, a "bottom-type position," and to her that meant pleasing, sometimes sexually, cisgender females or other cross-dressing males regardless of sexual orientation.

"If there was a CD here," she said, using an abbreviation for "cross-dresser," "I'd be attracted to her if I was dressed as a male."

Later, Martha found me and made a point of telling me how spoiled she was to have Keri, Marg, and other friends come to Napalese to make it a community hub. Not all Green Bay restaurants have been quite so welcoming. She recalled a sports bar where she and some trans friends had dined and felt welcome, especially by their friendly masculine-presenting waitress. But on a return visit, that waitress wasn't working, and the people in Green Bay Packers gear jammed around the bar didn't take to Martha's party.

"We were in the back and there were just too many people sitting around the bar doing those side looks and chatting and pointing," she recalled. "You could tell the conversations: *I think those are guys. Look at the hands on that one. The tall one, there's no way. What the hell are they doing in here?* It had an uncomfortable feel to it." Martha never returned there.

Martha and her friends aren't snickered at when they go to Napalese, so she figures: Why would they put up with that somewhere else? Besides, where else can you get a generously poured Manhattan for $7?

"Normally, I drink Diet Coke and Malibu, a nice tall one so I can nurse it along and not get sloshed over the course of the evening," said Martha. "But at about midnight, I order a Manhattan, and Butch knows it's the end of the night. If I have one earlier, he knows it's really been a rough day."

I joined Martha and about a dozen of her friends for lunch the next day at Mackinaws Grill & Spirits, a homey log cabin–style restaurant decked out with portraits of beavers and sturdy booths made from Norway spruce pines. It was there that I got to know Rochelle, who identified as dual-gendered but also trans-feminine, and presented as feminine in her life about a quarter of the time, when she wasn't working as a geologist for a local engineering company.

"There's a fair number of geo scientists who are trans or dual-gendered," she told me. "I don't know if there's anything to that."

I also met Rachel Maes, a lesbian trans woman and the assistant city attorney for Green Bay. She was there with her second wife, Danielle. Rachel got excited as she told me about the uniquely Wisconsin tradition of the supper club: a restaurant that's usually decorated in knotty pine with deer heads on the wall and a small menu that almost always offers a Friday Fish Fry, Saturday prime rib, and Sunday roasted chicken, accompanied by relish and dessert trays and a large build-your-own salad bar with cheeses, fresh breads, and various dressings, including a hot bacon dressing. Brandy sweet old-fashioneds are a staple cocktail; grasshoppers are the dessert beverage. Grandparents love it for the old-fashioned meals and the all-in-one dining experience. (Their kids and grandkids do too. Sometimes.) Plus, supper clubs will get you home for a ten p.m. bedtime.

Rachel recalled that when she and Danielle have eaten at supper clubs with their kids, most of the time the server asks them whether the bill should be calculated together or separately, as if two women eating together couldn't be anything other than friends.

"If you had a straight couple with kids, I don't think there would be a question," said Rachel.

And that's when I put my foot in it. We got around to talking about whether transgender people might engage in civil disobedience if anti-trans laws about bathrooms and locker rooms are actually enforced and not just used as political saber-rattling.

"I'm not a trans person," I started to say, "but I think there should be some ballsy trans people—"

"We don't know any of them," Martha said, straight-faced.

"You know a *lot* of ballsy trans people," I said to her.

". . . I don't have those anymore," said Rachel.

I realized my faux pas and my face turned bright red.

"I'm so sorry!" I exclaimed. "That's not what I meant *at all*. I meant *gutsy*."

I felt like an idiot, but everyone else at the table was laughing, Martha loudest.

"That was precious," said Rochelle, a small grin spreading across her face.

Rachel later told me that in Green Bay she had never experienced much anti-trans discrimination at a restaurant, other than overhearing "grandmas talking." Even a local Dave and Buster's donated to and hosted LGBTQ+ events.

"We don't have a huge LGBTQ population," she said. "But when we get together, we all support each other."

One person I didn't meet during my visit was Martha's wife, who I got the impression was not particularly a fan of Martha's transness. (Martha described her as "semisupportive.") I didn't push it. Martha said her three daughters took the news pretty well, as did her son, a former Marine Corps sergeant who, after quietly listening to Martha come out to him, said: "I was wondering if you were going to croak before you told me." That was the last story Martha told me before I left Green Bay.

When I called to catch up with Butch in the summer of 2024, he was driving to his day job at Kessler's Diamonds in Appleton, Wisconsin, where he had been working for over twenty years. I asked how things were going at Naps, and he sounded sad. Despite a robust presence on social media, including regular Instagram updates and ads, he told me that he's having a hard time attracting younger generations. Local straight sports bars and mom-and-pop bowling alleys have become gay friendly, and are hosting drag nights that attract people of all sexual orientations and gender identities.

"That's how mainstream being gay is, and it's coming back to bite us in the butt," he lamented. "We have to keep striving for acceptance, but we also have to work hard to make sure that people understand how much we fought and fought and fought for that dream."

Butch is trying to attract more and more straight people, to help keep the lights on at Naps—a striking reversal of queer placemaking that's changing gay socialization at gay bars and restaurants everywhere. If Naps were to close down, it could deal a blow to not just Green Bay but to queer people throughout the region who consider it a haven. Despite the challenges, Butch is confident Naps will persevere.

"We are struggling," he admitted, "but we are keeping our head above water." If my visit was any indication, I'm confident Naps will have a long life in Green Bay.

Safety is one of the most crucial, life-saving reasons why queer people seek out a place like Naps. But queer people have also flocked to restaurants for decades for something delicious and very much *not* on the menu.

Let's talk about sex.

7

Bread and Butt

Sex, Entertainment, and Other Temptations

Federico Santi didn't know what to expect one night in the early 1980s when he and his partner, who were visiting New York City from Massachusetts, opened a door and climbed up a long staircase. They were entering the Gaiety, a dirty movie theater at 201 West 46th Street, right next door to Broadway's Lunt-Fontanne Theatre, where the Duke Ellington musical revue *Sophisticated Ladies* had recently become a hit.

The Gaiety was a movie theater that doesn't exist much anymore. It was a place where mostly gay men sat before a medium-size screen to watch raunchy gay sex movies with Kip Noll or Al Parker or other big porn stars of the day. Legally, sex wasn't permitted on the premises, but nobody paid attention to that. Guys played with themselves or got it on with other men in the seats. Some cruised a side area and had anonymous sex with strangers or watched strangers have anonymous sex with other strangers. Once you paid to get in, you could stay as long as you wanted, as long as you didn't cause trouble. From the 1960s to the '80s, theaters like the Gaiety were common in New York and other big cities, but today they're almost gone, done in by the digital age of porn and by apps that will bring sex, or strippers, directly into your home.

The Gaiety, the Adonis, and other sticky-seedy porn theaters in pre-Goofy Times Square also offered stage shows. From early afternoon to early morning most days, go-go boys and erotic dancers took to a small stage in front of the movie screen and performed sets that got raunchier and more naked as midnight neared. Sometimes, the dancers were honest-to-god porn stars, back when porn stars were literally marquee names. Sometimes, the dancers were handsome young men fresh off the Greyhound bus, maybe gay but probably straight, and usually broke.

The lights would come up and three or four male dancers—two, if not everyone showed up that night—would get onstage under the spotlight and gyrate their hips to prerecorded dance tracks, making sure to highlight their perky butts and plump crotches. As the set continued, the dancers would jerk off onstage and, if they were feeling particularly brazen, position themselves under the spotlight to make sure the audience got a good look at their flying cumshots. The dancers exited to applause, usually, and the lights were lowered again so that the porn movies could start back up. About ninety minutes later, the dancers returned to the stage and did it all over again.

Historian Jeremiah Moss described a night at the Gaiety in poetic prose: "The dancer would emerge fully erect, the audience would applaud his hydraulic achievement, and the dance would go on. If you were next to the runway, for the price of a dollar tip, you could sit like Tantalus beneath the fruit tree as the dancer dangled his family jewels over your upturned face, just out of reach. After the performance, you could take a break in the snack room, where boys leaned against the vending machines and chatted while munching bags of Doritos."[1]

I went to the Gaiety a few times. I only knew about it as an NYU student, from 1989 to '91, because I'd seen ads for it in the *Village Voice*, back then a weekly go-to bible for what to do in the city. Gaiety ads were small but effective little boxes that doubled as $1 coupons, and promised X-rated movies like *Centurians of Rome* along with free snacks and refreshments. Later in my twenties, when I visited New York, the Gaiety was an infrequent but thrilling treat. On one Saturday afternoon, I went there between a matinee and an evening Broadway show.

So, what does this have to do with gay restaurants? *Here's* what: Strippers and go-go boys get hungry. Steps away from the Gaiety, at the corner of 46th Street and Seventh Avenue, was a Howard Johnson's, one of three Times Square locations of the popular diner-inspired restaurants that opened across the country after World War II. Built in 1955, the chain was famous for its fried clams, its many ice cream flavors and, according to Joseph Sherry, the manager of the 46th Street location, its hot dog *and* hot dog buns—"the talk of the town," as he called them.[2]

Stu Schwartz was a regular there, not because he loved the food, although he did, especially the hamburgers and fries. The main reason Stu frequently ate at this HoJo's was because he was a dancer at the Gaiety, under the stage name Eddie G. Lots of Gaiety dancers grabbed a bite there, although they rarely lingered.

"I don't think I ever did a sit-down meal" at Howard Johnson's, Schwartz told me. "I'd gobble it down and get back to the theater."

Gaiety dancers were easy to spot: They were the young men removing singles from their short shorts to pay for a patty melt and fries. Often, they ate at one of the restaurant's signature orange booths, but sometimes, like Stu did, they dined alone at the counter. The staff knew that there were gay people and erotic dancers eating there, but nobody cared as long as they paid their checks. Nothing ever turned violent, Stu assured me, despite the restaurant's location in what was then one of Manhattan's seediest neighborhoods.

"There were some drag queens who would come in and be loud and yell across the tables," he remembered. "But I don't recall anything bad or anything that involved the police when I was there."

In those days, Stu drank Coke but not alcohol, the better to maintain a boner and get more tips. Giving a sloppy, barely hard performance could mean going home without enough cash to pay the bills.

"I had to be cautious to not eat too much," he told me, "because I'd be dancing and jacking off in another thirty minutes."

When we chatted on the phone in 2023, Stu was happily married to a man, living in San Diego, and had a boyish voice that made him sound decades younger and randier than his seventy-six years. He had been stripping since he was nineteen and lived in Philadelphia, when an older acquaintance helped him get his start as an erotic performer on the East Coast at places like the Chesapeake House, a gay strip club in Washington, D.C., at private home parties, and in membership-only theaters including Boys Boys Boys on the Lower East Side in New York, where he had sex on stage with other young men. There, dancers were paid rather well and there were always filled tip containers to be split after the shows. He got his biggest tips performing in smaller towns where having a naked dancer at a bar was rare.

The Gaiety was Stu's most reliable paycheck: $20 to $30 a night on average from approximately 1963 to 1971, when he was dancing there regularly. For a man in his twenties who lived on his own in Philadelphia and worked the East Coast stripper circuit, Gaiety money was pretty good, although the money was better at other venues.

"It was enough to take the train from Philly to New York and spend money in a rooming house and get some food and get back on the train to Philly, and I was still ahead," he pointed out.

Much like the Automat in its heyday decades before, HoJo's was queered by the clientele and by the hour of day, the type of queering that happens still at all-night diners in gay neighborhoods. Another draw for Stu and his fellow Gaiety dancers was that at HoJo's the service was fast. He got to know some of the wait staff, who knew him to be good for his bill, unlike the hustlers who would dine and dash.

"The waitresses typically were older women who'd say, 'What are you doing tonight, honey?'" he said. "I'd say, 'Dancing at the Gaiety' and they'd say, 'Oh, you're one of those boys.'"

This particular HoJo's was also a go-to for Scott Blount, a female impersonator for thirty-two years and the winner of the 1985 Miss Gay World pageant. (You might also recognize him as a female impersonator in the Arnold Schwarzenegger film *Raw Deal*.) When Scott and his friends visited New York in the '80s, they usually stayed in Times Square and, as budget conscious queens in their twenties, ate at Howard Johnson's after taking in a Broadway show or to sober up after a night on the dance floor at the Limelight.

"As long as that Howard Johnson's was open, we'd go," said Scott, who was sixty when I talked with him in 2023.

Scott was partial to the pancakes and omelets at Hojo's and to the orange bar stools at the counter when he couldn't snag a seat in one of the signature orange booths that offered killer views of

Times Square. The decor "was very retro for 1985 and it still screamed early seventies," he told me. "It had probably never been remodeled."

Starting around ten p.m., he'd see "a little bit of everything, a hodgepodge of gay and straight and bisexuals and trisexuals." He only saw a couple of gay outbursts, such as the time a man cruised another man who didn't want to be approached. "The waitress said [of the rising tension], 'Take it outside or you'll get arrested,'" he recalled.

Scott, whose stage name was Scarlett Dailey, remembered a charming night-shift waitress there whom people used to call "Mama." When he asked her why they called her that, she replied: "Because I love my gay kids."

Unfortunately, not everyone was as accepting as Mama.

"It was right across from the Marriott Marquis, and you would see people walk in who would not know what they were walking into and would exit quickly," he explained. "They would be like, 'Henry, we are in the wrong place. Grab the kids and let's go.' I always chuckled at that."

The Gaiety survived despite changes in how gay men watched porn and met other gay men, and despite strict zoning laws in Giuliani-era New York. Before it closed, the venue gained main-stream attention after Madonna and some of the club's dancers took photos there for her 1992 book, *Sex*. Parts of her "Erotica" video were shot there too. And she wasn't the only celebrity who walked those stairs for the thrill of it: So did John Waters, Andy Warhol, and Shirley MacLaine, among others.

When the Gaiety shut its doors on March 17, 2005, it was New York City's last remaining male burlesque house. A small, hand-lettered sign on the door simply read: "The Gaiety Theater is closed. Thank you for your patronage. The Management." In a sad attempt to keep its patrons' hopes up, it added: "Please see the

G. publications for possible relocation address," using "G." as a strangely closeted abbreviation for "gay."[3]

John Galanopoulos, who operated a nearby hot dog stand at 46th Street and Broadway, told *The New York Times* when the Gaiety closed: "I've seen a lot of customers standing there in shock. They're almost talking to themselves, like, 'What am I going to do now?'"[4]

After forty-six years, Stu's favorite Howard Johnson's closed on July 8, 2005. Glass towers and megastores had dwarfed the restaurant's squat dimensions, and the "venerable old institution," as *Playbill* put it, "looked like an anachronism."[5]

A burger at Howard Johnson's, a scratched-up porn film, a stranger's dick in your face—this was just another Tuesday for many gay men who lived in New York during the heyday of the gay adult movie theater. As the sexual revolution kicked into high gear, meals and gay sex were companions like never before.

One of the most notorious spots was the Eagle, located a few neighborhoods south of Times Square. The space originally opened in 1931 as a longshoreman's pub called the Eagle Open Kitchen at Eleventh Avenue and 21st Street. Then, in 1970, a gay New Yorker named Jack Modica turned it into a leather-and-Levis bar that besides booze and the sex, sold "Eagle Burgers" for 50 cents on Saturdays. Food was a common amenity at New York gay bars in the '70s; the Eagle competed for hungry gay mouths with the Ramrod and the Spike, two other cruise bars that offered free buffets to go with flirty conversations and bathroom quickies.

At some point in the '70s, the Eagle also began serving more upscale fare, such as an 18-ounce Kansas City sirloin steak and roasted stuffed Long Island duckling in orange sauce, plus salad, rolls, a choice of mashed or baked potatoes, and vegetables du jour—all for just under $4. On Wednesdays, dinners came with a free slice of baked Alaska. The restaurant took reservations, and enforced the hours of its dinner service: seven p.m. to eleven p.m. from Tuesday through Thursday and from seven p.m. until ten thirty p.m. on busier Fridays and Saturdays. (The dining room was closed on Sunday and Monday.) That way, the restaurant's dozen or so tables and chairs could be cleared out to make more room for sweaty bodies and popper sniffing on the dance floor. The New York Eagle is still in business, now on West 28th Street near Eleventh Avenue, in the heart of what horrible people would call Hudson Yards but I will forever call Chelsea. The restaurant is long closed.

If there's been a constant at gay restaurants besides food, it's not sex but the promise of sex. Gay men who lived in Philadelphia in the early 1960s, for example, knew there were better and more chic restaurants to go to, including gay ones, than Venture Inn on Camac Street. (The restaurant's older clientele helped earn it a cunty nickname: Denture Inn.) The dark wood paneling and dim lighting probably helped make Venture Inn an extra-flirty place, as did the pitchers of screwdrivers and Bloody Marys that came with omelets and biscuits for brunch. A-listers rarely ventured in to Venture Inn. As *Philadelphia Gay News* put it in 1981: "No one here gives out attitude because either they are rich and successful and don't care or because they have wearied of the attempt to be glamorous and witty and have come here to relax in a less competitive atmosphere."[6]

But Venture Inn was the kind of place where waiters knew to flirt with customers, because it was safe to assume that if a man was there, it was fine to get fresh. Customers got a warm smile, a sexual rush, and maybe even an arm around the shoulder from male servers with whom they were on a first-name basis. Servers, in turn, whether gay or straight, got good tips, and maybe even got lucky, for free or for a fee. When I'm at a gay restaurant, you better believe I want my server to flirt like his tip depends on it.

———————

Before TikTok and local gay newspapers, gay men had to turn to under-the-radar print sources to learn the best places to flirt and find a trick with dinner. In 1966, Grove Press published *New York Unexpurgated*, a book that promised it was an "amoral guide for the jaded, tired, evil, non-conforming, corrupt, condemned and the curious." (It was allegedly written by a woman who went by the name Pretorious.) There are chapters on "The New York hooker," "The dirty old man" and "The New York orgy." My favorite chapter is called "The fag world." In it, Petronius claims that New York "has never been gayer!" and that "New York's fags move in very impressive, exclusive company" that includes "doctors, designers, architects, pig farmers, flower arrangers" and other occupations. A few "ugly faggots manage to exist," she claims, but there "are practically no fat faggots!"

"New York's male homosexuals are the smartest, best-dressed, most glamorous, jaded, wittiest, most attractive, most successful, vicious, shrewd, influential and desirable queens in the world," she writes. "They are also the sickest, most desperate, most ridiculous and dullest in the world." This is my kind of gal.

Petronius, named after the Roman courtier, I assume, then goes on to list gay bars, stores, cruising grounds, and bathhouses where gay men, lesbians, and "fops" should visit. Gay restaurants and cafés too—seventeen in total.

Most of the restaurants were in the book because they were patronized by "unavoidable straights"—meaning that, like Automats, they were queered by chance more than by design. Among the more interesting gay restaurant options, there were the Ham and Egger on Broadway and 71st Street ("Absolutely overflowing with anything") and the downstairs of the Laundry Chute

Coffee Shop on 74th Street, east of Amsterdam Avenue ("Puerto Rican Drags; transsexuals, etc."). For high heel lovers, there was the Russian Tea Room, where foot fetishists would "find Bunion Heaven in the dark back Guard Room in the UN Plaza Restaurant." When I first read that, I thought: Gay men are amazing at getting dick with, and at, dinner.

In the 1960s, Los Angeles queens who really wanted in on the action knew to go to Arthur J's after two a.m. Opened in 1955, the twenty-four-hour diner at the corner of Santa Monica and Highland came alive in the postmidnight hours, because anyone who didn't get picked up at the bars knew that at Arthur J's, the cruising would continue. In fact, there was so much gay sex happening in the Arthur J's bathroom that the waitresses were instructed to clean the floor with ammonia *every hour* to keep horny gays out so that gays who actually had to use the bathroom as a bathroom could do so. The restaurant closed in 1982.

Gay restaurant newspaper advertisements in post-Stonewall America didn't skimp when it came to using the promise of sex to fill seats. In the 1960s, the Stud, one of three of the biggest leather-western gay bars in Los Angeles, opened a restaurant called Wayne's Meat Rack. For lunch and dinner, there was comfort food, such as the Levi Gu, a Polish hot dog with sauerkraut on grilled sourdough, and the Warlock, grilled meatloaf also on sourdough. A print ad for the Stud shows two hot leathermen sharing a meal: One is bald and has a thick mustache, and before him lies a plate of spaghetti. The other, wearing a leather hat and vest, is holding a forkful of mashed potatoes. They look hungry and happy, and a little horny.

I've always loved these kinds of sex-forward ads, and I've got two favorites from this era. One is for Trinity Place, a San Francisco restaurant owned by Chuck Holmes, who in 1971 founded the legendary gay porn studio Falcon. The poster features an elegant black-and-white illustration of a handsome man with a stoic sugar-daddy expression to go with his dark three-piece suit and wide, striped tie. Behind him, a trim man in a T-shirt, perhaps a boyfriend or boy toy, has his hands on the man's shoulders. Below is the tagline "If he's hungry, take him to lunch." And how's *this* for copy:

> And what a menu our chef has prepared to satisfy those healthy appetites—everything from delectable Mushroom St. Thomas to savory Filet of Sole Florentine to our hearty, build your own Trinity Burger. It won't cost you an arm and a leg, either. If he's still hungry after all this, it's out of our hands.

The other ad I would frame and hang on my wall is for Church Street Station, a San Francisco diner open twenty-four hours. Dated December 1977, the ad announces that the restaurant serves "something for every body!" But the owners clearly had one *particular* type of body on their minds. Taking up almost the entire space is a trim man's hairless nude torso, with the name of the restaurant strategically placed above his visible, massive black thatch. In his right hand, he holds a coffeepot, from which he pours a thick stream of coffee into the white diner coffee cup that hides his penis. The servers at Church Street Station didn't work in the nude, of course. But the fantasy that you would be served by and could flirt with a man with *that* kind of body, or that people with that kind of body might be there for dinner, was enough to get butts in seats.

The smarter restaurant owners know that if you want to attract a hungry clientele, you could do far worse than open across the street from a bar or nightclub where gay men get horny. I saw that firsthand when David and I visited Atlanta in 2023 and ate at a gay restaurant in one of the unlikeliest of places. For a gay guy who has spent his entire adult life in New York, Chicago, and Washington, D.C., it was jarring for me to go to a gay bar in a shopping plaza.

David and I had been at the Atlanta Eagle for about two hours, during which we spent time at the second-story dance floor and at an outdoor area that included a darkly lit sex patio hidden behind tall wooden fencing. Upstairs, I nursed a $6 Rum Runner and watched as small groups of mostly elderly men sat in folding chairs around banquet hall–style round tables to watch *Mr. Charlie Brown's XXX Rated Cougars*, a drag show, named after one of Atlanta's most famous drag queens. As the show ended, I made my way past a bear in an "I Love Cum" T-shirt and an otter in a sash that said "Atlanta Eagle Rubber."

As we left the Eagle, David took me across its crowded parking lot to Su's, a Chinese restaurant that he had discovered online. Small and unassuming, Su's was located in the same strip mall as other gay bars, including one that catered to Black men. We watched, in awe, as for two hours Su's got queered in real time. It was almost empty when we arrived, but quickly it filled with hungry LGBTQ+ people, mostly Black and Latino men, flirting with strangers at adjacent tables while picking at glossy orange chicken or pointing their egg rolls at one another for emphasis. Two guys looked as if they had just met and were splitting pepper beef on what I hoped was their first date. Two men sat together in silence as their fried rice got cold and their Grindr inboxes got hot.

As we split a vegetarian stir-fry, David and I talked with two very friendly men: Fluffy and his roommate, Austin. Fluffy said he lived in Atlanta but was originally from Puerto Rico, where he said the food was better. Austin showed us a video on his phone of his considerable dick-sucking skills. Both men engaged with me as fellow gays, effortlessly and frankly in a manner that might have been considered out of bounds if the dining room hadn't been so gay. I'm not certain that Fluffy or Austin would have struck up a conversation with me at the Eagle—nor I with them—because saying hello would have come with the expectation of a come-on. Saying hello at a gay restaurant might too. But often it just means one thing: Hello.

There are three important takeaways from Su's. First, nobody goes there before eleven p.m., but because of its proximity to gay bars, it has adapted its entire business model, which means staying open much later than other Chinese restaurants might.

Second, the bars in the shopping plaza, at least on the night that we went, seemed to be separated by race and social class. But people from every bar went to Su's for food. It turned gay easily.

Finally, of all the Atlanta restaurants that people said we should check out, nobody said we should go to Su's. Yet every single person eating there at one a.m. was gay, making it one of the gayest restaurants I ate at in Atlanta. Queering had worked its magic.

———

I was on the phone for maybe a minute with James Foster, the general manager of Flex, a bathhouse in Cleveland, when I asked him why Flex served meals on holidays.

"For us, it's important," he said, "because a lot of people don't have family to actually—"

James went quiet. I thought we got disconnected. There were a few seconds of silence before he started talking again.

"I'm sorry," his voice trembled. "We're both getting emotional here."

James was with Rocky Joseph McCombs, his assistant manager. The line was quiet again for a few seconds longer.

"I don't speak with my actual family," James continued, his voice still unsteady. "Most of my family is my made family. For us to provide food during the holidays is extremely important to me because that's how I was raised. You spend it with your family. Not having a family anymore, my patrons have become my family."

"We've both been in the community for quite some time," added Rocky. "We know what it's like to be alone for a holiday meal."

You wouldn't know Flex is the world's largest gay bathhouse if you drove past it down a quiet stretch of Hamilton Avenue in an industrial neighborhood east of downtown Cleveland. The building—all 50,000 square feet of it—is a beautiful example of Midwestern architectural reclamation: It was once a Greyhound bus garage and maintenance center where buses got their oil changed before heading back on the road. When Cleveland native Charles R. Fleck bought the space and opened Flex in 2006, he made the smart decision to keep most of the building's Streamline Moderne architectural flourishes, such as rounded corners and glass block walls. The marble staircase and chandelier are both original. It takes a lot of work to clean a venue this big, where water areas and sexual playrooms blend into one another.

"I feel it in my feet and back every day," James laughed.

I've been to Flex many times and trust me: the place is massive. Once inside, after picking up a towel and a key for a $15 locker (best for quickies) or a $24 cabana (for the gentleman with time to kill), you could easily get lost on your way from the hotel to the orgy rooms, or from the gym to the high-ceiling play space and back to the swimming pool and Jacuzzi. Unlike other American bathhouses that can feel full on a busy Saturday night, Flex is so big, it's almost impossible for it to feel packed.

The closest I came to seeing it so was during CLAW, Cleveland's annual leather and kink weekend. It's one of the biggest such events in the country, and it brings in people from around the world for a weekend of workshops (my favorite was the foreskin restoration session), dances, sex, and playtime with whips, harnesses, and other sexual accoutrements. Throughout CLAW weekend, there's usually a line out the door at Flex. Even then, with every sling occupied and the gloryholes and sex benches all accounted for, Flex feels like it could easily still accommodate a hundred more people.

It's got nothing to do with food, but my favorite Flex memory was when I took a group of New York gay friends there during a gay boys' weekend in Cleveland. We stood together in a circle, all of us in towels, inside one of Flex's bigger rooms. The main attraction was the hairy muscle-boy porn star Teddy Torres, who was in town for a special appearance at Flex. Teddy came up to me and, perhaps sensing something I did not, slapped me in the face, twice. The Cleveland convention and visitors bureau should put Flex on its list of must-do visitor experiences.

Back to food. For many gay men, especially those who are single or older, eating a meal at a bathhouse can be a social lifeline. It may be the only time they dine out or dine with other people or eat, period. That can especially be the case during the winter holidays. When Flex puts out an online ad that says "Be part of our family for Christmas," it's acknowledging that for many gay men, family is chosen and holidays can be a bitch.

"With the holidays, we get a lot of people that are very transient, and they will stop in on a whim and the next thing you know, they'll grab a plate," said James. "'You're serving food on a holiday?' they'll ask. You'd be surprised by how many people have been touched by that small sentiment."

For St. Patrick's Day, there are corned beef sandwiches and pierogi. On Easter, there's ham, and on Thanksgiving, there's turkey and all the trimmings. One Memorial Day, Flex served two hundred hamburgers. I had to ask an indelicate but necessary question that any bottom reading this is thinking: If one of the goals of going to a gay bathhouse is to have sex, what's the best food to serve?

"We love the chili," Rocky answered. "The staff hates the laundry."

Bathhouses with food aren't gay restaurants, but they serve the same purpose: To connect gay men over food in a sit-down setting. Is the food any good? Sometimes. Does it matter? Not really, because for many gay people, dining out doesn't have to be about good food. I don't mean that as a culinary insult, but rather as a way of saying that queer dining and placemaking have considerations that go beyond flavor.

Most American bathhouses operating today no longer offer restaurant service, sticking instead to vending machines with pre-packaged snacks and drinks, as they do at Steamworks in Chicago. But that wasn't the case in the 1970s and '80s, when bathhouses and sex clubs offered men the chance to socialize over food and fucking.

New York's Continental Baths, at 74th Street near Broadway, had an "absolutely first rate restaurant" that served "cheap and good breakfasts," *Philadelphia Gay News* recalled in 1976.[7] (The writer didn't care for the rest of the place: "Full of addicts, utterly filthy, stay at your own risk," he wrote.) In Chicago, the Man's Country bathhouse had a restaurant called the Meet Rack, where you and the man you just blew could grab a bite before checking out the Truck Stop, a fantasy area with a full-size cab of a semitrailer. In Los Angeles, the North Hollywood Spa offered a twenty-four-hour full-service café with food to eat there or to go; the Mark IV bathhouse, a competitor, advertised brunch and Bloody Marys every Sunday afternoon. Cleveland's Depo Baths went fancy pants with wine-and-spaghetti afternoons. (I'm guessing the easiest way to spot a top was to see who was eating the meat sauce?) Barbecue was the draw at the competing Club Cleveland. Miami's Locker Room served roast beef dinners at night and, starting at three a.m. on weekends, breakfasts with a ham-and-cheese omelet, bagel and cream cheese, and screwdrivers.

Most bathhouses have offered some kind of small bites, since a stay there can be a few hours or even overnight. The St. Mark's

Baths in New York's East Village had a snack bar counter, where gay historian and writer Vito Russo worked while he wrote *The Celluloid Closet*, his landmark book about the history of queer cinema. The counter had an odd elegance that contrasted with the raffishness of the place; it was done up in chrome and black geometric colors, "the coin of the realm for late '70s gay designs," as activist Jay Blotcher poetically told me. Blotcher, who worked there with Russo, had a good view of the counter: It was across from the cage where Blotcher checked in horny patrons. The counter, he said, was "really a mini restaurant."

Bathhouses were usually open twenty-four hours, and during the daytime, owners went out of their way to help men get off and get back to work on a full stomach. In the early 1980s, Philadelphia's Bank Street Baths sold a daily businessman's lunch with "real deli sandwiches and real desserts" that were "tasty and reasonably priced."[8] Bank Street Baths was the only bathhouse in Philly, one observer noted, that offers "actual meals on the premises, as opposed to the vending-machine junk food at the Barracks and rubber microwave hamburgers at the Club Baths."

Historically, bathhouses have mostly served gay men. But in 1996, at its former downtown Cleveland location, Flex hosted a "Womyn's Nite" potluck. The bathhouse provided table service and "beverages"—the quotes in the newspaper ad stump me—and women were asked to bring snacks, salads, entrées, or a dessert to share. This was not some daytime picnic; doors opened at four thirty p.m. and the party continued until seven thirty a.m. I've been to plenty of bathhouses, but I've never been to one with a potluck (or with women). Alas, I couldn't find any reviews or coverage of the event afterward, but I bet they had a blast.

A few weeks after I spoke with James and Rocky, David and I met them and Flex's resident chef, Ric Scardino, on a cold

Sunday afternoon in January. The walled-off parking lot was full, perhaps because customers knew that a semi-homemade hot meal and a warm Jacuzzi would be the ideal antidote to the frigid temperatures outside. I counted maybe twenty men there, mostly baby boomer age, but a few who looked to be Millennials or older Gen Xers, walking around in towels and occasionally smiling. James ushered David and me past the check-in window and gave us a tour of the first floor. (Most of the sexual spaces at Flex are on the second.) We walked down darkened, labyrinthine hallways to the hotel suites that come with queen- and king-size beds and, in one room, a personal fuck bench. We took a peek at the rectangular pool outside, which, on a hot summer afternoon, would be hopping. We passed the empty indoor pool with room to fit twenty-five bodies of all shapes, and peeked into the booth where, on special occasions, an in-the-flesh DJ spins live, as DJs have done at gay bathhouses for decades. I've been to bathhouses where I was sure I'd get crotch rot or an STI just by looking at the floor. Walking through Flex, by comparison, I felt as if I was visiting Martha Stewart's freshly house-kept mansion. For a place built for sex, Flex smells faintly of bleach, not sweat.

When Flex first opened, it had a small restaurant space and a full working kitchen that cranked out easy-to-fry concessions, such as catfish and fries. That service has since stopped, although James, who has been the general manager since 2020, told me he'd like to open it again. Meals are also served at Flex's other locations in Los Angeles, Phoenix, and Atlanta, but not weekly. The managers are all on a text chain in which they show off their buffets in an attempt to one-up one another.

I met Chef Ric in Flex's modest kitchen, where he multitasked in preparation for his guests. His red sauce simmered on the stovetop, awaiting the homemade meatballs he'd brought with him in a big Tupperware container. On one burner he was melting butter to brush on soft dinner rolls that he was warming in the oven.

Retired and single and "as gay as they come," Ric looked younger than sixty-eight, maybe because of the spark he gets in his brown eyes when he talks about cooking for strangers. He grew up in a Sicilian household in Buffalo, watching his grandmother make meatballs from scratch, and started flipping burgers as a teenager at a Howard Johnson's that, unlike the one Stu frequented, was not a home to a rotation of gay erotic dancers. He has worked in the food industry ever since, with detours in bar management and hair and makeup. Lean in body, with short brown hair and an olive complexion, Ric had lived in Cleveland for almost forty years, most recently in Old Brooklyn, a working-class neighborhood.

Ric's gig as Flex's resident chef started Memorial Day 2021. Flex had already reopened a few months earlier because Ohio's coronavirus restrictions had not been as restrictive as in other states. (Other Flex locations and other bathhouses around the country, especially those in bluer states than Ohio, were shuttered far longer.) It helped that Flex had a hotel license, which allowed it to open sooner than other businesses, including gyms.

James and Ric had been friends by then for some twenty years, having met at a local gay bar where Ric bartended. Ric remembered the day he started making food for Flex, when James called on a Sunday afternoon with a favor to ask: "Can you come here and grill for us?"

"I got cleaned up and came down here and stopped at the store and picked up buns and hot dogs and burgers and salad and pickles and mustard and relish and all that," Ric recalled.

On a typical Sunday, Ric will serve up to twenty men in a lounge area right outside the kitchen's pass-through window. Sometimes, people strike up conversations with strangers they just fucked, will soon fuck, or may never fuck. Some men eat alone. Ric starts prepping for Sunday's meal on the previous Thursday. He always makes sure to offer a vegetarian option, and never makes the same meal two weeks in a row. During CLAW, there can be as many as 150 mouths to feed; meals during that busy weekend are the only ones he charges for, at the bargain price of $5 for a plate of pulled chicken or a sloppy joe.

Ric gets paid—he didn't tell me how much—and tips are welcome, if not always forthcoming. "How many guys walk around with money in their ass crack?" he asked. "A lot of the guys come up to me and give me $20 or $10 and say this is for all the times I couldn't tip you."

And what about eating at a bathhouse before or after a visit's other entertainments? Ric didn't bat an eye as he explained that cheese is binding, "so make sure there's cheese involved."

"Sloppy jocs is better than chili because chili has beans," he explained. "When I'm doing a menu, I'm thinking about what I would want to eat before I . . ." His voice trailed off.

Ric told me about an "old Italian guy" named Alfred who had recently died. Alfred was in his eighties, and was a Flex regular on Sundays and holidays.

"The first Thanksgiving, I was cooking and he was like, 'I can't believe this, I can't believe it,'" Ric said in a whisper, his voice full of gratitude. "There are certain guys you do extra for."

James jumped in with a story about another elderly regular, a man in his nineties.

"He walked out of his room and I said 'Merry Christmas' to him and he looked at me and had tears rolling down his eyes," James recalled. "He said, 'It's not like it used to be.' I said, 'Don't forget, we still have Christmas dinner coming up at four.' He's like, 'I'll stay here for that.' I went ahead and renewed him and gave him a year membership and said, 'Now there's no reason you have to spend the holidays alone.'"

My lunch at Flex that afternoon was a tasty combination of a warm roll and cheese ravioli covered in Ric's glistening red sauce, served by Ric himself on a paper plate with a poinsettia-print napkin and a plastic fork. As I ate, I chatted with a towel-clad man named Dan who was sixty-five, had thick brown hair streaked with some gray, and a smooth chest. Dan lived alone in Canton, a small city about an hour's drive from Cleveland that's best known as the home of the Pro Football Hall of Fame. Dan was a regular at Flex, usually for a few hours on Sunday, especially on sunny summer days to lounge at the outdoor pool. He's a fan of Ric, and of Ric's food.

"I don't have to go home and cook tonight," he said, with a gentle laugh. "The food is always good."

After I finished my ravioli, Ric told me that he will continue turning Flex into a weekly pop-up bistro as long as there are gay men hungry for companionship and a friendly hello. Why? Because at Flex, Ric said with a laugh, "you get someone that gives a shit cooking for you. And I know not to serve you chili."

8

It Was Never About the Food

Drag, Brunch, Drag Brunch

The word "brunch" likely appeared for the first time in an 1895 issue of the publication *Hunter's Weekly*. British author Guy Beringer, in an essay called "Brunch: A Plea," defines brunch as "a corruption of breakfast and lunch"—a meal that "combines the tea or coffee, marmalade and kindred features of the former institution with the more solid attributes of the latter." Brunch begins, he continues, "between twelve and half-past and consists in the main of fish and one or two meat courses."[1]

In defending his concept, Beringer sounds like some of the messy queens I know who *live* for Sunday afternoon unlimited screwdrivers and made-to-order eggs: "In the first place it renders early rising not only unnecessary but ridiculous. You get up when the world is warm, or at least, when it is not so cold. You are, therefore, able to prolong your Saturday nights, heedless of that moral 'last train'—the fear of the next morning's reaction."

Brunch as a common activity likely dates back to at least the 1930s, when American hotels started to champion a late-morning meal. Sunday brunch, specifically, started to become popular after World War II as church attendance in the United States began to decline. Gays started to make brunch their own, adding drag queens and music, starting most likely in the late 1960s.

The marriage of a meal with a drag show has roots that were planted much earlier.

———————

The Torch Club was located about 20 miles south of Akron, Ohio, in an unincorporated zone of rural Stark County. It was one of countless small American nightclubs that brought in touring acts made famous on the Orpheum Circuit, a chain of vaudeville theaters that started opening in the late 1800s. The Torch Club didn't book big-name acts that played massive theater palaces, such as Playhouse Square, 50 miles away in Cleveland. Instead, it hosted lesser-known performers now lost to history, such as Eileen McCauley ("Dynamic Trucker and Shim Sham Artist") and Romona, known for her bubble dance, an erotic frolic popular in the '30s that involved strategically placed balloons or balls over a female dancer's naked body. The Torch Club showcased novelty performers, such as knife throwers and mind readers, but also racist minstrel acts in blackface and redskin that perversely tickled white audiences at the time. The club was open nightly from nine p.m. to two thirty a.m. for dining and dancing with no minimum or cover.

In 1936, the Torch Club hosted a one-week engagement with a group of female impersonators imported from Cleveland's

Ambassador Club, who performed as the Hollywood Playboy Revue. Fanny Brice mimic George Hayes and Mae West impersonator Val Turek were among the performers who took the stage for three shows each night. Print ads left little doubt that the Hollywood Playboy Revue featured men dressed as women. The opening night ad explicitly said "Swish—Swish," which was slang then, and still is, for gay men. Another ad promised that patrons could expect to see a "feminine style show by all the lads." Eighty years before Beyoncé boasted "I slay," another ad claimed: "They will positively slay you." The engagement was such a hit, it was held over through early March, when the owners started charging an extra 25 cents to get in the door. To go with the shows, the Torch Club served a modest menu of "Italian spaghetti" with meatballs for 50 cents, and a goose liver sandwich for 20 cents (about $12 and $4.50, respectively, today); toasting that sandwich, however, set you back an extra five cents. The cocktail menu offered an Angel's Tit, a layered drink of maraschino liqueur and heavy cream, for just 40 cents.

It's important to point out here that there's a difference between female impersonation, with its roots in vaudeville, and drag, which can be traced to private spaces and bar culture. As scholar Lucas Hilderbrand describes it, female impersonation worked "by testing the credulity of the straight audience with a skillful masquerade of gender verisimilitude," whereas drag "has by and large foregrounded the incongruity of a man in a dress—which makes it camp." "Drag" now refers to any man or woman who dresses up to perform as "the opposite sex," regardless of their sexual orientation or gender identity. Female impersonators, gender illusionists, drag queens: They're cut from the same cloth, but have served different purposes for different kinds of queer expression depending on era, audience, and intent.

It's hard to say how gay drag-and-dinner shows like the ones at the Torch Club were behind the scenes. The female impersonators might have been gay and may even have been out to their co-performers. Straight club managers and bookers often looked the other way at homosexuality, as long as their talent kept the coffers full. I have no doubt that gay people had dinner at the Torch Club, drawn by the same fascination with gender and performance that keeps gay bars packed during episodes of *RuPaul's Drag Race*. The Torch Club's heyday was during the era of the Pansy Craze, and even in this corner of Ohio, pansies were part of the cultural landscape. There would have been nothing suspect about men together enjoying a night of swish entertainment, especially if those men were accompanied by women.

The Torch Club had its troubles. On June 4, 1936, it was bombed by what police suspected was dynamite thrown through a rear window. It was back in business the next day as if the bombing had never happened, announcing in a newspaper ad, "And Yet, the Show Goes On."[2] (It's unclear who was responsible for the bombing.) That year it also hosted such acts as Billy Byrle, "the celebrated male Jean Harlow"; the "Boys Will Be Boys Revue" with emcee Danny Brown, a well-known impresario; and the "First a Boy Then a Girl Revue," featuring the female impersonator Pepper Cortez and a performer named Giggles. The club closed down sometime in the late 1930s or early '40s as vaudeville started to become old hat.

Drag hasn't been the only art form that restaurants called on to attract gay customers. For many gay theater artists in the '60s, the place to be was the Caffe Cino, on Cornelia Street near Bleecker in the West Village. Run by Joe Cino, a New York native and a gay man, the unconventional coffee shop and theater space is credited with starting the Off-Off Broadway theater scene. Cino opened performances by announcing with a flourish, "Welcome, ladies and gentlemen, it's magic time!" Shows took place on a 12-foot stage but also spilled into an area with seating for about fifty. Open from 1958 to 1968, Caffe Cino was a hub for theater makers who explored gay themes, in such works as

Lanford Wilson's *The Madness of Lady Bright*, a monologue by an aging drag queen, and Robert Heide's existentialist *The Bed*, about two gay men who can't get out of bed after indulging in drugs and alcohol. A teenage Bernadette Peters got her big break at Caffe Cino in the hit production of *Dames at Sea*, a takeoff of musicals from the '30s.

Caffe Cino audiences dined on sandwiches, soda, and hot drinks made on a large espresso machine with beans from the oversize coffee grinder that hulked near the doorway, forcing people to squeeze their way inside. One of the specialties was "Hot Eggs à la Cino": sweet peppers and eggs scrambled in the espresso machine for just 95 cents. There was also hot cider, rum milk, and hot lemonade to go with the cheap bologna and salami sandwiches; at $1.20, the ham and cheese was the splurge. The imported cheese plate featured standards, such as provolone and Cheddar, but for 90 cents, you could add Bel Paese, a semisoft Italian cheese. Although his plays were never mounted there, Edward Albee said of Caffe Cino: "It was so exciting and so necessary and fed so many people."[3]

Before he died in 2023, prolific playwright Robert Patrick told me that nobody went hungry at Caffe Cino.

"We were working as office workers and typists, and very poor and very skinny," said Patrick, who first hung out at Caffe Cino when he arrived in New York City in 1961. "I don't think people came for the food. They came because there was never even a minimum. You didn't have to buy anything."

It was at Caffe Cino that Patrick made a splash with his 1964 play *The Haunted Host*, a foundational work of early American gay theater. Caffe Cino is also where Patrick met his lover John P. Dodd, a well-known lighting designer who died of AIDS in 1991. Cino, himself, died by suicide in 1967 at age thirty-six, following the accidental electrocution death of his then-lover, John Torrey, Cino's electrician.

A year later, the café closed. The site, 31 Cornelia Street, was listed on the New York State Register of Historic Places and the National Register of Historic Places in 2017. Two years afterward, it was designated as a New York City Landmark by the NYC Landmarks Preservation Commission. As of this writing, the space is Bombay Bistro, an Indian restaurant.

The Torch Club is an early example of how dining and drag became bedfellows. But gays have been marrying the two *for* the gay community since at least the 1960s.

In 1968, brunch at the Los Angeles gay bar The Clown was from noon to three p.m. and cost just a quarter.[4] Lost & Found, an Italian restaurant, served a Sunday Champagne and orange juice brunch for $1.25 (about $12 today). Coffee wasn't just for gay brunch, either: Such bars as the Black Night and the Tropics regularly made fresh pots after hours, from about two to four a.m., the better to keep the parties going. (Gay bars: Do this.)

In New York in 1968, the Big D Bar & Grill, popular with gay motorcycle clubs, charged 99 cents for Sunday brunch that came with a Bloody Mary. A quick detour into gay motorcycle clubs: They've been around in the United States since the 1950s, with names like the Satyrs and the Border Riders that reflect their members' renegade interests in riding. Such clubs were where gay people into leather gear and kink lifestyles found safety, camaraderie, and sex. Their cross-country gatherings almost always included stops at restaurants. In 1972, the Spartans Motorcycle Club Leather Angels (SMCLA) were treated to "a lavish assortment of cold cuts and trimmings" during registration at the D.C. Eagle, as Richard Kjelland reported in *Wheels*, the newsletter of the Cycle Motor Club. Dinner was served at a restaurant called Pier Nine, where the "cold, thin-sliced roast beef was accompanied by two hot vegetables, fruit cup and salad." Sunday brunch was at the

Plus One ("the best scrambled eggs ever encountered on a run or event!"), and the Eagle served up an early buffet ("The Beef Stroganoff was delightful.") Motorcycle gays could *eat*.

Gay brunch became even more common starting in the '70s at restaurants but also at bars and clubs where gay men expected there to be food. On Sunday afternoons at Philadelphia's Nugget Saloon, a piano bar, three dollars would get you two eggs, home fries, bacon, ham or sausage, a fruit cup and toast and coffee. (A bucket of Bloody Marys was $1 extra.) On Sunday afternoons, the Philadelphia nightclub Equus served scallops with peppers and onions, or sausage and tomato sauce omelets. A favorite cocktail was the Colorado Bull Dog, which consisted of vodka, white cacao, Kahlúa, Coke, and cream.

"Eggs benedict may be fine in Topeka," the owner told *New Gay Life*, a Philadelphia newspaper, in 1977. "But here at Equus, we make *brunch extraordinaire*."

It makes sense that gays made brunch their own. Fewer gay people than straight people have kids, which means that weekend mornings are less likely to be centered around kids and their needs, and much more likely to be a continuation of gay socialization from the night before. Gay brunch usually starts later on a weekend morning, as late as two p.m. at some restaurants, which is enough time to wake up from whatever festivities happened the night before and look good enough to leave the house. There's a communal feeling to brunch that's similar to a night out with friends at a gay bar, but brunch is quicker and brighter.

Philadelphia was among the cities where gay brunch started to blossom as the see-and-be-seen meal of the week. In 1981, *Philadelphia Gay News* ran a gay brunch roundup in a column by writer Lee Robbins called "Brunch Munching" (subheadline: "Enjoying a gay institution that's spreading faster than gossip"); Robbins said Sunday brunch had become so popular among Philadelphia's gay community that he had dozens of places he could have reviewed.

His picks were elan in the Warwick Hotel ("the steam-table scrambled eggs are best left untouched and undescribed"); Twentieth Street Café ("understated elegance," "broiled swordfish fresh as a breaking ocean"); and his favorite, Woody's (the boneless chicken quiche "was the best I have had in Philadelphia").

Robbins eloquently explained how brunch, a meal that used to be reserved for the home, had started to help meet a "newly realized need." He went so far as to credit gay people with brunch itself, claiming that if one of the early goals of gay liberation "was to re-create the family for gay people," what better way to do that than to gather for a meal like what Mom used to make? Even better if it happened on a Sunday, which for many gays was "the gloomiest day of the week, if you didn't have a lover and hadn't found a Saturday-night friend who was still friendly in the harsher light of morning."

Brunch, he wrote, was a gay achievement: "High camp, S&M and long, leisurely Sunday brunches are three of our less profound but more pleasurable contributions to America upon post-Stonewall departure from the closet."

Drag historian Joe E. Jeffreys has an interesting theory about why a drag variation on gay brunch might have started, and it has to do with how straight people responded to AIDS.

"I often talk about drag as the indigenous queer performance form, in that it is by the people, of the people and for the people," Jeffreys once said. "But drag brunch was largely about making queer performance accessible to straight audiences."[5]

It makes sense. During the AIDS crisis years, benefit drag shows provided straight people who wouldn't set foot in a gay bar or restaurant an opportunity to support their gay friends who were sick or dying. Such shows were sometimes held during brunch hours, making it easier to attend for parents with kids and people—straight and gay—who didn't feel like hanging out with younger, wilder gays. Drag brunch made it easier for people who were HIV positive or had AIDS to attend and not worry about being home at a reasonable hour. Combine the hour and tribal relevance of gay brunch with the entertainment value and cross-sexuality appeal of dinner-and-a-female impersonator show and what do you get? Drag brunch.

One of my earliest exposures to drag brunch came from a gay advice book from 1994: *The Unofficial Gay Manual: Living the Lifestyle (or at Least Appearing To)*, written by Kevin Dilallo and Jack Krumholtz. On the cover is a cute white guy wearing a look that every gay man in my circle wore in some variation that decade: a blousy denim shirt, tan khakis, and a haircut that was short on the sides and long and floppy on top. I remember *devouring* the book, thinking I had finally found everything I needed to know to make sure I was living my best gay life. (To be clear, the book offers a decidedly white version of what it meant to be gay.) I bought almost every record on the list of "16 CDs Every Gay Man Should Own." (I already had Bronski Beat's *Age of Consent*, but had never heard of Liza Minnelli's *Liza With a "Z."*) I watched *All About Eve* and the seventeen other "Films Every Gay Man Should See" thanks to my expertly curated Dupont Circle video store. Ask any Gen X gay man and there's a good chance he read this book, wishes he still owned this book, and credits the book's advice for impressing a date enough to get laid.

In the back of the book, there is a guide that lists popular gay restaurants in several big cities. In Washington, D.C., in addition to Annie's Paramount Steak House, there is a listing for drag brunch at Perry's, a gay-friendly restaurant in the Adams Morgan neighborhood. "Great show, good food and pretty crowd," the entry reads.

Perry's is still serving drag brunch, as it has since 1991. But I had never been there. That's why, on a crisp November morning in 2023, I sat by myself at the tightly packed bar. It was the only seat left; drag brunch at Perry's is often sold out at least a week in advance. Just as I returned back to my seat from the buffet with a plateful of scrambled eggs, grits, and mac and cheese, Jimmy James's anthem "Fashionista" came on the speakers with the exclamation: "No one ugly allowed!" Screams erupted from the crowd of about sixty people seated at tables that were bathed in bright sunlight. They were mostly white women of all ages, but there was also a smattering of white gay men and one large table of Black people celebrating a woman's thirty-second birthday.

Out came the drag emcee India Larelle Houston, who introduced her roster of vivacious queens, including Jalah Nicole, who lip-synched a mean "Proud Mary," looking like Tina Turner's twin. As at most drag shows these days, Houston—who looked regal in a floral floor-length gown, heavy eyelashes and a towering, coiled black wig—invited audience members to join her and be recognized for birthdays and "if you're pregnant and happy about it." Among the revelers were a thirteen-year-old white girl named Eden and an eighty-three-year-old Black mother and military wife named Shirley. Houston got loud as she towered over Shirley and thanked her—a "queen," Houston called her—for coming to drag brunch.

"Thank you for Thanksgivings and Christmases and all of those things, even though you may sometimes have not known where the money was going to come from but you made a motherfuckin' way," Houston said. Everyone cheered, including me. Houston was my kind of drag hostess: She wasn't afraid to make fun of people, but she wasn't too ruthless in her sense of humor either. And she made the singles rain.

A few months before I visited Perry's, I got on the phone with the restaurant's sixty-four-year-old owner, Saied Azali. Right away, he explained to me why he loved his gay clientele.

"Gay men are stylish and good looking and I love what they wear," he said, talking a mile a minute. "And they like art and dancing and avant-garde music. They are open to things."

Saied moved to the United States from his native Iran before the revolution there in 1978. He came to D.C. for graduate school in chemical engineering, and worked in the restaurant business to make money, including at Perry's, where he started out as a waiter. In the '80s, he regularly visited New York, where he went to nightclubs, such as Pyramid Club and Area, where drag queens reigned.

"In Iran, we had drag queens, but it wasn't as open as here," he added. "It opened my eyes." (May there one day be many books and movies about Iranian drag queens.)

Saied is not gay but he partied with his gay friends in the '80s. "Gay clubs are fun," he said matter-of-factly. "They have better music. There are better-looking women there. Women like good music and good-looking guys."

Saied became the owner of Perry's in 1985. When drag brunch started there in 1991, a few years before I moved to Washington, Adams Morgan had a reputation as a pretty gay-welcoming neighborhood. In its early years, most of the Perry's clientele was "gay men and some lesbians and some transgender people," Saied recalled. "It wasn't a big crowd, but it became big."

When Azali started talking about the ways in which parents have supported the queer people who have eaten at and worked at Perry's, including drag queens, he became emotional.

"The parents, for some of the performers, support their kids, and the customers bring their kids because they want to be drag queens," he said as his voice broke. "It's nice that a mom can say to their kid that they are accepted." I witnessed that at play during brunch. As the show wrapped up, the drag queen Whitney Gucci-Goo, who worked the crowd to Katy Perry's "I Kissed a Girl," thanked her mother—who was in the audience to celebrate her own birthday—for helping her become "the woman I am today."

My friend Patrick Kwan, who is gay and Asian, once explained to me that gay people taking their straight friends to drag brunch is like Asian people taking their friends to Panda Express. "Nothing," he said, "is too spicy."

Patrick's observation swam in my ears one Sunday afternoon in 2023 as I looked around the New York City drag restaurant Lips, a pioneer in drag and dining. When Lips opened in 1996 at Two Bank Street in the West Village, it attracted the drag luminaries Charles Busch and Laritza Dumont, who cavorted under umbrellas that hung "riotously from the ceiling as if to protect patrons from the purple rain of light streaming down from the whirling disco ball," as *Ladylike* magazine described it.[6] Entrées were named after famous drag performers, including the Lypsinka (Maine lump crab cakes with sweet pepper corn salsa) and Cashetta (herb-crusted salmon with mashed potatoes).

As for Lips, it, too, expanded to several cities across the country, including San Diego in 1999, where memorabilia from Boy George and RuPaul lined the walls and a video monitor showed the campiest excerpts from *Dynasty*. Fast-forward to 2010, when rent hikes forced the original Lips to move to Midtown East, which had a heyday as a gay neighborhood in the 1960s and '70s but today is mostly a gay wasteland except for the East Side Club, a gay bathhouse.

In 2023, I made a reservation at Lips for Broadway Brunch, one of its more popular weekend shows. My friend Dan and I got seated snugly next to strangers at long banquet tables before a small stage. The crowd was mostly Gen Z and Millennial women of sexual orientations that were hard to discern, plus a few tables of Gen Xers who I assume were mostly gay men and their straight women friends. The room was evenly divided among white, Black, and Latina women, with a few boyfriends patiently along for the ride. Sadly, the menu copy was a creative fail: Instead of being punny or clever, each entrée had a bland Broadway-themed name like *Rent* Grilled Chicken or *Cats* Ham and Cheese. (Nobody thought of Thoroughly Modern Chili?) I ordered the *Mamma Mia!* Mozzarella Omelet that came with a small helping of potatoes. The ninety minutes of unlimited mimosas cost extra. I passed.

The show was a not-that-daring drag revue that parodied *Wicked* and *Annie* and the Broadway queens who know every lyric by heart. Right before the show ended, some twenty people who had paid $15 extra were called to the stage and lined up pageant-style to celebrate birthdays, engagements, and other occasions. With the precision of an industrial-strength conveyor belt, the drag emcee Ginger Snap grilled each person as they sat on a throne, before they got their photo taken with other queens wearing plastered-on smiles. As efficient as the Lips crew was at this money-making pause in the show, it took what felt like five hours to get through every person's story and selfie. If it weren't for Ginger Snap's scalding reads of the crowd—"I smell Long Island Railroad!" she screamed at one point—it would have been a slog of a brunch.

If it sounds like I'm being harsh on Lips, I only somewhat mean to be. It's deeply satisfying to see how a Lips-style drag brunch has become so popular. As a teenager, I would have loved to have gone with friends to watch a drag queen in a sequined bat-sleeve bolero jacket high-kick her way past chafing dishes of hash browns as the speakers blast Laura Branigan's latest hit. How my life would have been different if I could have taken my mom to drag brunch for her fiftieth birthday and have a queen in sky-high boots gently lower a tiara onto her head and place a Party City plastic scepter in her hand as the crowd blew kisses. Just think of how much more money the drag performers I remember in Cleveland back in the 1980s and '90s—Melissa Ross, Mona Desmond, Twiggy—would have made if they could have played sold-out, two-matinee afternoons at restaurants packed with people who paid $60 or more a pop. Queens who are just starting out or who have been in the business for decades can make good money doing brunch shows now. Long may drag brunch live.

But the popularity and ubiquitousness of drag brunch also feels disappointing, and not just for the mediocre food. I like my queens to be potty-mouthed and insulting in the Don Rickles and Joan Rivers traditions of offensive reads for maximum impact. It's not a successful drag show without at least one walkout by disgruntled audience members. (Bianca Del Rio is a master at this style of comedy drag, but she's too famous and comes with too high a price tag to do weekly drag brunch anymore.) Sadly, the audiences at drag brunches today generally aren't into getting insulted. I've rarely heard a drag queen be more cutting than asking if anyone in the audience is from New Jersey. I get it: What manager wants an angry mom asking for her money back on a reservation made *months* before because a drag queen was mean to her bachelorette daughter? It makes me sad that drag brunch is as subversive these days as a dinner at Red Lobster. Yet drag brunch is more popular than ever. That's what happens when gay cultural traditions get co-opted by straight eyes. Brunch at Lips got me thinking: If its customers are mostly straight women, are they still eating at a gay restaurant? Or has the popularity of drag brunch birthed something terrifying: a gay-themed restaurant? How did drag brunch go from being rebellious to milquetoast?

What happened to Hamburger Mary's offers some answers.

In the fall of 2021, I was on assignment for *The New York Times* in West Hollywood, where I interviewed Colton Underwood, the charming former *Bachelor* contestant who was documenting his coming out in a new Netflix reality series. It was late on a Monday, and as I walked down Santa Monica Boulevard, I saw that Hamburger Mary's was open. It wasn't crowded, which was a draw. I had never been to a Hamburger Mary's, another point in its favor. There were only a few people there, including a large group of women at a big table near the stage, where a drag queen whose name I didn't write down made risqué remarks about hot dogs. The woman in a tiara, with a sash over her shoulders, obviously was the birthday girl or bride-to-be. I asked to sit as far away from them as I could. I finished my perfectly fine Beyond Burger, paid my check and thanked my gay waiter, and walked home and went to bed.

But I remember thinking: *That's it?* That was Hamburger Mary's, what I thought would be the gayest restaurant in the country? Granted, I was there on a chilly-for-L.A. Monday night. Maybe if I had been there on a Saturday evening or for Sunday brunch, I would have seen more people, including gay men, the main customer base I assumed Hamburger Mary's attracted in way-gay West Hollywood.

I was disappointed that my first Hamburger Mary's experience was worlds away from the Hamburger Mary's that Jerry "Trixie" Jones and some friends opened in 1977 at 12th and Folsom in San Francisco's iffy South of Market neighborhood. According to the company's website, the original restaurant was a place where "the mismatched flatware & dishes, kooky artwork and antiques added to the kitsch and charm of the place—an 'open-air bar and grille for open-minded people' (a motto we still use today), where everyone was welcome." It was the kind of place where you would see tables of drag queens, long-haired waiters, and maybe pre-senatorial Dianne Feinstein, a regular there when she was the mayor of San Francisco. Rose Christensen, who ran the original Hamburger Mary's location for decades, said it was like working at a "gay-friendly truck stop," where cream for coffee was served from baby bottles with the nipples cut off.[7]

Two of my favorite gay restaurant menus are from the Hamburger Mary's early days, perhaps the late '70s. The cover features the restaurant's name in bold black type below a piece of sheet music for the 1911 song "Have You a Little Fairy in Your Home?" A long-haired little girl at the center holds her face in her hands. Another Hamburger Mary's menu features an illustration of a man and a woman—there are echoes of William Powell and Myrna Loy in *The Thin Man* murder-mystery film series of the 1930s— facing each other and holding hands. It's the kind of image that gay men who knew the difference between Rita Hayworth and Susan Hayward would have adored.

In its first years, Hamburger Mary's was open twenty-four hours a day. Michael D. Craig worked the two a.m. to ten a.m. shift, when the restaurant attracted gay men from local gay bars and bathhouses, but also truckers who started coming in for breakfast around four a.m. The restaurant stopped being open all night as the neighborhood's drug scene changed—"The people who got into speed and cocaine, they were harder to deal with," he remembered.[8]

Like me for the Melrose, memories of long nights at the original Hamburger Mary's are as fresh as yesterday for many of the people who worked there. At seventy-one, writer Mark Abramson still fondly remembered his favorite waiter: The man with long, silky straight hair like Jackson Browne, who wore skin-tight jeans and baggy tank tops that showed off his naturally lean torso. The server had a scar that wrapped around his body in a spiral, as if somebody had knifed him. He was the quiet type. Mark didn't remember his name.

"I suppose, these days, the health department wouldn't let waiters wear things that showed their armpits," Mark lamented. "But Hamburger Mary's got away with anything."

As with many gay restaurants in the decades since, location was key to the success of Hamburger Mary's. The Cauldron and the Cornhole, two gay sex clubs, were nearby. The neighborhood wasn't pretty or touristy, as it was when I visited San Francisco in 2023. But for many gay men who frequented the area for sex or cruising, Hamburger Mary's was a welcome retreat. In 1981, Michael O'Connor took a sabbatical from working as a medical librarian at Harvard and moved to the Folsom Street Hotel at 7th and Folsom in San Francisco. His neighbors were Filipino immigrants, repair shop guys, and straight retired merchant marines who lived in single-room occupancy buildings for low-income tenants. O'Connor ate there almost every day, drawn by the comfort fare and unlimited coffee refills.

"The first time a hamburger was served to me there, there was a mountain of sprouts," Michael told me. "I had no idea what it was, but I acquired a taste for it."

Longtime manager Rose explained that in the late '70s, Hamburger Mary's started being discovered by "elites from Nob Hill," who would walk in the door with their I. Magnin bags and think, "it was so cute to be eating at this weird place, so they could go home and tell all their friends." AIDS changed the fabric of the restaurant and its customers and employees. Rose said the restaurant kept employees who couldn't work on the payroll, so they wouldn't lose health insurance.

"A lot of people had their last meal in public there," she continued. "I think to this day how much PTSD I still have. Seeing regulars come in as they got thinner and sicker on oxygen and then just never came back."

In the '80s, other Hamburger Mary's locations opened across the country, first in Hawaii, then in Portland. Some locations were opened by the original owners and others through licensing agreements. (The company today prefers "family of locally owned independent restaurants" instead of "chain.") The drag shows that dominate there now were not the restaurant's main bread and butter back then, although men often *served* in drag. The original San Francisco location was sold in 2001 after decades of "lawsuits and lovers and license disputes, deaths and taxes," as the *SFGate* reported. During the dot-com boom of the late '90s, many employees left to study for and work in the tech industry.

After years of delays, a new Hamburger Mary's location opened in the Castro in 2018, but the novelty of a drag restaurant had worn off for many people, including Eric Pratt, a critic for the *San Francisco Weekly* who gave the restaurant the kiss of gay death when he called it "as much of a chain as Applebee's." Under the brilliant headline "Mary: You in Danger, Gurl," he argued that the restaurant gives the impression "of parading dated, predictable tropes of gayness around for tourists." The restaurant closed not long after.

Hamburger Mary's is still in business around the country. Its origins as a quirky bistro are long gone, replaced with by-the-book drag brunches and cocktail menus. In 2023, there were fourteen Hamburger Mary's locations across the country, including in Denver, Las Vegas, Milwaukee, and Toledo, Ohio. I reached out several times to Hamburger Mary's headquarters via their website to see whether anyone wanted to talk, but I never heard back.

Drag brunch is not just straighter than ever. It's now as corporate as it gets. In 2022, *The New York Times* sent me to Chicago to report on Taco Bell's drag brunches at select Taco Bell Cantina locations in five cities across the country, hosted by the Mexican American drag queen Kay Sedia. The events were, unsurprisingly, sold-out hits—and so much fun. On a sunny Sunday morning, David and I waited in line outside the Taco Bell Cantina down the street from Wrigley Field with gay men, straight women, and a number of straight-guy Taco Bell fanatics, including one young father who drove three hours from Dubuque, Iowa, to be first in line. Inside, the narrow restaurant was decked out in shimmering backdrop walls draped in multicolored sequins and boas. On every table were Taco Bell–branded handheld fans. To eat, we were each served our own boxes with our choice of Grande Toasted Breakfast Burritos plus hash browns and donut holes. (Booze was extra.) Kay Sedia started the show by introducing local drag king Tenderoni, who made me blush with his risqué swagger and close-up crotch thrusting. The drag queen Miss Toto wowed with high kicks and precision splits. But David and I really giggled like crazed schoolgirls when the drag performer Aunty Chan lip-synched to a mash-up of "She Works Hard for the Money" and "9 to 5" while pretending to be an under-the-gun fast-food worker taking orders over her headset. It was one of the funniest drag bits I've ever seen. My breakfast burrito wasn't bad either.

Drag purists and people who complain about the corporatization of queer culture probably aren't fans of Taco Bell Drag Brunch. Like Burger King's Pride wrapper–wrapped Whoppers and Shake Shack's Pride Month milkshakes, Taco Bell's foray into drag must seem to them to be an even more crass way to appropriate, commercialize, and monetize what was once a subversive queer art form. I get it, but I had a blast, and the drag performers got paychecks and press coverage. It was a win for Taco Bell, too, which got word out on social media and in the press that it's not afraid to push envelopes. Robert Fisher, a senior production designer at Taco Bell and the founder of Live Más Pride, Taco Bell's LGBTQ employee resource group, told me the company made a point to ask its queer employees for input on the brunches so they would feel like organically gay experiences, "not as if Taco Bell was appropriating drag for the sake of tacos."[9] It worked.

But that level of acceptance is driving the right wing nuts, which is why just a year later, drag brunch once again became embroiled in the culture wars. In August 2023, a group of far-right Catholics prayed the rosary outside of Crazy Aunt Helen's, a restaurant in downtown D.C., just blocks from the US Capitol. The target of their protest was "Shi-Queeta-Lee's Drag Gospel Brunch!" One protester claimed it was "offensive and blasphemous" because the menu featured mimosas called "Bottomless Jesus Juice" and "Blood on the Cross," otherwise known as a Bloody Mary.[10] One of the organizations behind the protest, a far-right group called The Public Advocate of the United States, said in a statement: "The event had drinks that mocked Christians, a preying not praying joke, and tipping of the 'gospel' singers. Overall, a clear mockery of God and Christians nationwide." Based on photos of the event, customers disagreed.

Also in 2023, the owners of the Hamburger Mary's location in downtown Orlando filed a federal lawsuit against a bill signed by Governor Ron DeSantis that targeted permits and liquor licenses if venues hosted "adult live performances" and allowed children inside—language that opponents said was meant to target drag shows and the First Amendment. The suit argued that the law did not define such terms as "lewd" and "child," leaving the restaurant to figure out which performances and audience members it covered. The owners of the restaurant said bookings fell 20 percent once they told customers that children would no longer be permitted at any of its drag shows.

"The language used in the statute is meant to be and is primarily vague and indistinct. It does not mention 'drag' by name but it is so broad as to include this art form in the state's interpretation under the newly created or amended laws in question," the lawsuit said.[11]

A judge temporarily blocked enforcement of the law, prompting Florida to ask the US Supreme Court to narrow the injunction to apply only to Hamburger Mary's. The Supreme Court denied the request, and to date the law is blocked. Citing an increase in remote working and a slowdown in foot traffic in downtown Orlando, the restaurant moved to Kissimmee in the summer of 2024.

It's no wonder that gay brunch has become a politicized flashpoint. For many queer people, drag brunch is harmless fun, and the idea of a youngster dancing with a drag queen is heart-warming, not creepy. Drag is a means of artistic self-expression, a gender expansive declaration of queer joy, whether it's from a teenager devoted to *RuPaul's Drag Race* or from an elder who soaked up drag style at smoky dive bars in the '60s. But to others, especially those emboldened by the second Trump administration's hard-right pivot, a family-friendly drag brunch is an oxymoron, proof that queer culture has infiltrated American culture and is threatening to make kids gay or trans or Satanists. That's ridiculous, of course. But as long as there are drag queens who need work and diners who want to wake up late on a Sunday and get wasted over sad waffles and greasy bacon strips, the battle between drag as a force for good versus drag as the devil's bidding will rage, as it has for decades, at restaurants everywhere. Maybe right-wing opposition to drag brunch shows that it's still important for gays, even if it's not mostly gays who are going anymore. I'm betting on the queens.

9

The Hustler Brasserie

Gallus, Atlanta

If I could time travel to have just one meal at a restaurant featured in this book, it would be to 1980s Atlanta and Gallus. Not because the food was extraordinary; it was known for being good enough to impress a date. The reason I'd want to visit is that Gallus was like a gay restaurant department store. On one floor was a fine-dining, white-tablecloth restaurant. Above it was a piano bar, and in the basement, hustlers and their customers sealed deals. You could eat there and be home in time for the evening news (with your partner, or wife) or you could hang out for hours until you scored, for free or for a fee. Gallus was a cruise bar as much as a restaurant, a sex emporium as much as a cabaret.

They don't make gay restaurants like Gallus anymore, and they may never again. Buckle up.

––––––––––––––

My friend Christina lived and worked in Atlanta in the '80s, around the time that RuPaul started to make a name for herself in the Atlanta drag scene. Christina said that *the* person to talk to about Atlanta's gay restaurants was Ashley Nicole Dawson. Ashley and Christina were friends from back in the day when they and other "ye olden showgirls," as Christina put it, worked at Gallus.

To Christina, Ashley was more than just a keeper of the keys to Atlanta's gay dining past; she was a lifesaver. As two of the few transgender women who worked at Gallus in the '80s, Christina said that she and Ashley "were often treated as court jesters by some of the white privileged gays."

Christina said Ashley gave her hope that a trans woman "could work a 'normal' job, even if that was as a waitress at a gay restaurant," Christina wrote to me. Christina remembered taking her mother and stepfather to Gallus when she was early in her transition, because she wanted them to meet Ashley, "a normal trans woman."

With this in mind, in August 2023, on a hot-as-hell Friday night in Atlanta, I pulled up a metal stool at Woofs, a popular gay sports bar, and sat across from Christina's dear friend. Ashley had just gotten off her shift as the Woofs head chef. We sat on the quiet dartboard side of Woofs, apart from the raucous noise of bears, cubs, daddies, and a sprinkling of twinks who were munching on hot wings and knocking back cold glasses of SweetWater Summer Lager. Ashley would soon turn sixty-five, but she had the glow and energy of a woman forty-five years younger, even in her black chef's uniform. I barely got a chance to ask her a question before she made me blush.

"I've lived in Atlanta since 1977 and I'm being interviewed by this very handsome man," she said directly into my recorder, laughing.

Ashley had moved to Atlanta from a small town in Alabama, a pivot that left her shell-shocked. She had never seen so many LGBTQ+ people or gay businesses the likes of places like Hollywood Hots, a drag and disco venue, and the Locker Room, a popular bathhouse.

"Even though it was the South, it was a step above where I was from, the dancing, kissing, and restaurants," she told me. "I'm like, 'Where the fuck am I?'"

Leaning on her passion for restaurants and hospitality, Ashley got a job at Gallus, where she washed dishes and eventually worked her way up to waitress and bartender. She told me that as Gallus's first transgender employee, she got asked a lot of questions about her identity from gay employees who "had never seen a transsexual."

Gallus's well-appointed formal dining room was on the second of three floors. There were candles and formally folded napkins on the thirty-odd tables, along with wineglasses and place settings. The leather-bound menus offered a diverse but standard selection of seafood, meats and pastas, and also more elevated entrées, such as filet mignon with twice-baked potatoes. (The house dressing was and will remain a well-hidden secret, Ashley insisted.) What kept many customers coming back was Gallus's signature dish, Chicken Elizabeth: a double-breasted chicken with ham, cheese, cream sauce, tomatoes, and brandy.

A meal at Gallus was likely to be a flamboyant affair. That's the way Art Smith, who runs the invaluable Gay Barchives Facebook group, remembered it. For Sunday brunch, "you went in there *dressed*," he told me. "You wore at least a button-down shirt. You tried to look nice."

Gallus took reservations, which surprised many first-timers. "When you'd say you need reservations, they'd go: 'I'm going to a high-class place!'" Ashley remembered.

On the third level was a sophisticated piano bar where "Mac the Knife" was a standard. The windows were covered in pink chiffon, and there were small tables scattered throughout where you could have after-dinner drinks and dessert. Gallus showcased local drag queens, such as Brittany Fairchild, known for her Cher impersonation, and Three Tons O'Fun, whose rotating cast of zaftig queens included Black Rose, Morticia Deville, Chocolate Thunder, and Tallulah Banks. Gallus was a big supporter of local gay causes, especially during the worst years of the AIDS crisis. Straight people ate there, too, but its primary customer base was gay men.

But it was on the bottom floor, the cruise bar, where Gallus drew its hungriest crowd.

Gallus Restaurant and Bar opened in 1973 as a restaurant-nightclub at Sixth and Cypress on the outskirts of the city of Atlanta in a building that had originally been a private home back in 1893. In the 1930s, it was a rooming house, and during World War II, it was home to women working in war efforts. Gallus's heyday was in the '70s and early '80s, when Atlanta's gay nightlife scene was thriving, at places like Sweet Gum Head, a high-glam drag bar where performers like Rachel Wells and LaVita Allen drew gay and nongay crowds alike.

Dining was a big part of the Atlanta gay scene in the 1970s. When it opened in 1975, the nightclub Backstreet offered around-the-clock fun, including an upstairs café called The Fat Cat, where hungry gays could satisfy their disco munchies with "The King," a hamburger steak marinated in teriyaki sauce and crowned with pineapple. Around the same time, at Jim's Grill, a twenty-four-hour diner, gays who worked as professional entertainers, including drag queens, were often served complimentary dinners. ("All Gay People Welcome," proclaimed one ad.) The Krystal Burger, around the corner from Gallus, was the place to eat after a night of dancing and flirting at the Armory or Weekend's. For many folks the place to really soak up the grease was a restaurant on Cheshire Bridge Road that advertised itself as "A Dining Destination Fit for a Queen." It was called the Dunk 'n Dine, but regulars had another name for it: the "Gag 'n Heave."

"The food wasn't great but everybody was drunk and high," Ashley remembered. "I never went there sober."

But Gallus was in its own class. Gallus was *the* anchor on the Cyprus Street cruising corridor, a once sketchy area where, since at least the 1920s, male hustlers did a brisk business, as did adult bookstores and other gay venues, including the sister bars Plumb Butch and Plumb Nelly. Hustlers—or "yard dogs," as they were called at Gallus—worked out of Gallus's basement, offering their services to men—gays, straight-but-curious trade, closeted and married guys—who knew that Gallus was the place to score a quickie for a fee.

"Gallus was a central location for chicken boys or runaways," Ashley told me. "They would meet up for older men. It was a known thing. It wouldn't be acceptable in hybrid society. But it was what gay people did."

Before taking a hustler home or to a nearby motel, a man might first take him to the second floor for dinner or the third floor for dessert and conversation. A gentleman would offer dinner to his younger, poorer companion without having to be asked; a brute wouldn't invite him to dinner at all, or would do so only after the young man asked for food. Gallus didn't take a cut of the hustlers' profits because it wasn't a brothel and there were no pimps; management looked the other way because having hustlers hustle there was a win-win-win: for horny customers, for hustlers looking for money, and for a restaurant eager to profit off of booze and steak dinners. Discretion was assumed.

"You wouldn't be shamed or outed because it was a gay restaurant," Art said. "It's not like your boss would see you."

Wayne McDaniel was a regular at Gallus from 1979 to 1983. When we talked in 2023, he was sixty-six and lived in Chattanooga, Tennessee, and he remembered Gallus as if he'd been there the night before. He animatedly talked about an obese friend of his who used to pick up hustlers at Gallus "because the only way he was going to get a date was to pay for it." He and his friend were pals with the bartenders and the staff, who always alerted regulars to the shadier hustlers. Wayne's friend was also a size queen.

"We were at the bar one afternoon, and he had gotten to the point where he had been lied to one too many times about size," Wayne remembered, in a Southern drawl that made his naughty stories sound even dirtier. "So, he would make them prove if they had a big one. We're sitting there, and the next thing I know, this voice says, 'Oh my god, Wayne, you gotta see this one!'"

A photo from Gallus that I can't get out of my head was one that I found in the archives of the University of Georgia. It features a packed dining room of mostly young men in T-shirts and jeans or shorts, seated at round tables next to tall windows through which bright sun shines. It looks like any other Sunday brunch except for the guy with dirty blond hair captured midstride wearing nothing but tiny black underwear, his gaze aimed right at the camera. You know you're at a gay restaurant when there's a guy in his underpants in the dining room.

It was a pleasant dining room too. At least that's how it looked in a video that aired in the summer of 1984 on *Impulse Video Digest*, a gay cable access show that covered Atlanta's gay scene. (I'm going to describe it for you, but do yourself a favor and go to YouTube and search for "Gallus Restaurant Spotlight.") Titled

"Atlanta Cuisine" and set to Petula Clark's "I Know a Place," the segment starts with a montage of Gallus's extravagantly '80s interior decor. Tall, Tiffany-esque stained-glass windows let in light that washes over fresh-cut flower arrangements. Chandeliers and small lamps illuminate the cloth napkins and glassware that had been precisely placed on every table. A hot waiter in a white shirt and dark pants—with a thick '80s mustache, the kind that still makes me melt—clears glasses from the bar, with a smile.

The video cuts to the exterior, and the camera slowly backs away to reveal the white three-story building with balconies on every side. The camera then follows the same mustached waiter as he walks downstairs to meet another hot bartender with the same mustache, only this man's wearing a blousy white muscle shirt. And then, what do you know: There's Ashley, looking gorgeous in a white blouse and red lipstick.

David Hart, the manager, wears a crisp white shirt as he addresses the camera. Standing next to a vase filled with pink carnations, he talks about Esperanto, the gay club that operated in the building before Gallus, where "in our current dining room, it featured go-go boys." The camera then cuts to diners enjoying their meals as David explains that the average price of a meal is $7.95 to $9.95, but for $16.95 you can splurge for rack of lamb. (In 2024 prices, we're talking about $24 to $50 for a dinner.) Most of the food is fresh, David adds, before the camera cuts to a man butchering meat—the only Black person to appear on camera other than Ashley.

Gallus's wine list at the time was undergoing some updates, David continues, since his regular customers "like the variety, they like the idea of change" because it "adds something" to the dining experience. "This goes back into the idea of making small things count—fresh linen, fresh flowers, good wines," he says.

David ends the interview by inviting viewers to dine there for their next special night out. "We don't have a dress code," he explains. "We just ask that you be comfortable. After all, it's your night out and we want to make it as nice as we can for you." Intrigued to learn more, I tried to track down David, or to find out what happened to him, to no success.

———————

Luckily, however, I was able to get in contact with someone whose memories of Gallus were razor sharp. James McRae told me he considered Gallus "a piece of decadent hell." He didn't sound disgusted. He sounded thrilled.

"If somebody said they had dinner at the Gallus, you know they ended up down in that basement," said James, who was fifty-nine and living in Brunswick, Georgia, when I spoke with him in 2023. "It wasn't just [that] you went and got something to eat. You made a night of it. You were out for more than steak."

Gallus attracted men of many ages, but the typical diner was a middle-aged man with money—maybe not the most attractive person in the world, but if he had money to pay for drinks, he could get a blow job in the basement. Or, James added, he could "sit up next to somebody and have them ride around in the car with you and give them head."

James knew this because he tended bar in the Gallus basement, where the jukebox never stopped, nor did the cocaine.

"We'd go to each other in the middle of our shift and say 'Where is she?' which was our code for coke," he recalled. "'I got her,' somebody would say. You'd go to the bathroom and do a bump and we'd all just get it when we could get it. It's how we go through those long nights." It wasn't uncommon for fights to break out inside Gallus and outside on the street, which is why Gallus had a security detail that was heavy on "bull dykes that you didn't want to mess with," James added.

"You'd get drug out by those girls and you did not want to tangle with them because they did not play," James remembered. "We had walkie-talkies behind the bar, and if somebody started causing a riff, they'd be there in two seconds. The feeling of decadence and seediness was there, but it was safe. You didn't have to worry about physical harm."

Most of the time, anyway. In 1991, Robert Lee Bennett Jr., a forty-four-year-old former Atlanta lawyer from a wealthy Pennsylvania family, was charged with being what Gallus regulars called the "Handcuff Man," known for picking up male hustlers, spiking their drinks with drugs, handcuffing and beating them, and, in some cases, setting fire to their genitals. In 1983, Bennett was banned from Gallus after a hustler complained to the police that Bennett was known to be violent. In 1992, Bennett was sentenced to seventeen years in prison; he died there on April 1, 1998.

Gallus closed in 1993, the victim, among other reasons, of a gentrified Atlanta, and of a gay community that had divorced itself from the notion that fine dining and sex could go hand in hand at a restaurant. Ashley lamented that there might never be another restaurant like it again.

"I don't know how it would go over in this day and age," she said. "A lot of people have other outlets besides gay bars now, which is pretty sad considering that gay bars were the bedrock of safe places."

A restaurant like Gallus today would be a novelty, she explained, "that you would want to try only once or twice, instead of something that you were religiously at every weekend."

As we finished our conversation, I thanked Ashley for her time. She thanked me for a trip down memory lane, something she said few people in her day-to-day life wanted to do anymore. "I always think there's something from the past that needs to be remembered," she smiled.

10

Convenient Joy

The Gay Restaurant Golden Age

ots of things I love have golden ages: Television, Broadway, horror movies, gay porn. Gay restaurants too.

Starting in the 1960s, gay restaurants engaged in gay placemaking in unprecedented ways as newly visible and politically engaged queer communities came out like never before. At these restaurants, opaque windows and vague signage were out. Street-facing glass and gay-is-good branding were in. To be gay and dine out during this golden age meant eating in dining rooms filled with only gay men or lesbians, many of whom probably lived in the neighborhood, a gay one. A 1973 issue of the *Hollywood Press*, a self-described "sexual freedom publication," included a list of several exclusively gay if short-lived restaurants in Los Angeles. Among them were David's, "a luxury dining club for gay guys only," and Valli Haus, which "caters to men exclusively." In this era, there was nothing unusual about eating in such sexually segregated spaces, and many gay restaurant owners and patrons wanted it that way. The *Hollywood Press* listing for House of Ivy, a gay bar, couldn't have been clearer: "ALL MALE PLEASE."

In that era, gay newspapers regularly covered a city's gay restaurant scene; Philadelphia even had an annual Lambda Award for Best Restaurant that catered to the gay community. Dining out meant being cooked for by gay chefs, waited on by gay servers, greeted by gay owners, and entertained by gay performers, sometimes around the clock. These restaurants were meeting a basic human need: A 1982 survey by the *Philadelphia Gay News* found that 66 percent of the gay market dined out for at least a third of their meals, probably for the same reasons we do today: convenience, lack of cooking skills, the desire for social interaction with other gay people.

As a deeply closeted teenager in Cleveland in the '80s, I wasn't aware that the city had this kind of a gay dining scene, but it did. On the city's working-class West Side there was Beauregard's, billed in ads as "Cleveland's Only Totally Gay Dining Experience." The dining room was done in exposed brick walls and original tin ceilings. It accommodated around thirty people, and most of the time those were gay men who wanted a good burger to go with the nightly sing-alongs centered on the house piano. Off-duty Cleveland police officers worked security. In 1999, I remember reading about Lake Effect, a short-lived restaurant that was opened by Buck Harris, a Cleveland LGBTQ+ activist and the host of *The Gay Nineties*, the country's first gay and lesbian radio talk show. Lake Effect was in a renovated hundred-year-old former meat cutters union hall, down the street from Club Cleveland, part of a national chain of gay bathhouses. The building had sweeping views of Lake Erie, and inside, the dining room was dominated by artwork depicting what one critic described as "a backstage troupe of transvestites preparing for a show."[1] The kitchen turned out gazpacho, maple-glazed salmon, and other standard bistro fare.

I wasn't aware of it, but I ate at a gay restaurant all the time in high school. The place was My Friends, a twenty-four-hour diner in Lakewood, a suburb on Cleveland's West Side that was known at the time as Cleveland's main gay enclave. My friends and I would eat at My Friends almost every Friday night after seeing a movie at the Cedar-Lee Theater across town in Cleveland Heights, or in the early morning hours on our way home from an all-ages Skinny Puppy or Ministry concert at the nearby Phantasy Nightclub. I could always count on there being boys in dramatic new wave trench coats and unsubtle eyeliner eating there. (I remember wondering: Are they gay? Am I one of them? I think I am.) My friends and I also ate at Truffles, a dessert café where we shared towering slices of chocolate mousse cake and a cappuccino, thinking we were fancy as shit. I don't remember there being Pride flags or anything that marked Truffles as gay, but I remember thinking that any place in the Cleveland area that served desserts this elegant and had a sidewalk garden just had to be homosexual. After nearly twenty-five years in business, Truffles closed in 2007. (I was unable to track down owner Dan Sheppard.) But My Friends is still open and still makes a top-notch spinach and feta cheese omelet with toast that comes already buttered, as it should.

I didn't get a real taste of the gay restaurant golden age until I came out and started eating in New York in my early twenties. One of my favorites was Big Cup. The Day-Glo-colored café opened in Chelsea in 1994 and served a mostly gay male clientele who sat for hours on plush couches colored coral and gray. The walls were painted Pepto-Bismol pink and accented with oversize flowers in a lemony yellow. A rack of zines and stacks of gay night-life rags were on hand for customers who wanted to catch up on gay happenings around town.

I lived in Washington, D.C., when Big Cup opened but I visited New York often, and I'd spend entire afternoons there, refilling my mug with meh coffee. I always got the Rice Krispie Treats, Big Cup's signature sweet that became a must-have after it was featured in gay guidebooks. In the days before Big Cup closed in 2005, it took on an air of "eulogistic pensiveness," according to *The New York Times*. Among the many handwritten remembrances that customers affixed to a wall was one that said: "Closing will significantly affect my sex life."

The '90s were good for lesbian restaurants too. In 1993, Minnie Rivera and Stacy Pison opened Orbit in the West Village, one of a small group of lesbian-friendly restaurants that opened in Manhattan.[2] Others included Henrietta's Feed & Grain Company, KISS, Harvest, and Universal Grill, which the local gay guide *Homo Xtra* called "the gayest restaurant in the entire world."

Rivera explained her reason for opening Orbit this way: "Le Cirque is a great restaurant, but I can't go there and hold my girlfriend's hand. The people would go crazy and so would the maître d'."

This dining out golden age was not a delight for everyone in the gay community, especially people of color. A 1974 guide to Detroit gay bars and restaurants, for instance, noted not just the venue's addresses and the clientele's age range but also patrons' racial makeup. Dean's Restaurant and Bar was "mostly white males and females"; Foster's Lounge was "mostly black males." I imagine the descriptions were used by some patrons as a guide for where to go, but for others, it was an easy way to tell which places to avoid.

Still, queer people of color carved out their own dining spaces during this golden age. In San Francisco, the Mexican restaurant La Rondalla was known as a gathering place for LGBTQ+

Latinos starting in the 1960s, not long after Carlos and Esper-anza Barrios opened it in 1951. Christmas decorations adorned the 2,500-square-foot restaurant year-round. The late Alberta Nevarez, a transgender mariachi and ranchera singer who went by the stage name Teresita la Campesina ("Teresita the Farmgirl"), regularly performed there dressed in a traditional Mexican *zarape* (a blanketlike cloak) and a dark blue sequined dress with a mag-nolia flower in her dark brown hair. La Rondalla closed in 2016, for unknown reasons. A sign on the door simply said: "We are closing—God Bless you. P.S. We Love you all."

Alston Green, who was seventy-one when we got on the phone in 2023, said he and other Black gays and lesbians who lived in New York in the '70s were fans of the Pink Tea Cup.

Opened by Mary Raye in 1954 at 42 Grove Street near Bleecker, the restaurant served Southern favorites like chicken and waffles, catfish, and mac and cheese. The restaurant's original location sat only about a dozen people.

"They were one of the first soul food–style restaurants that opened downtown, and it attracted a lot of people of color," he told me. "It was a hole in the wall, and they had good food. It was one of the first that got a gay reputation downtown."

Originally owned by Mary Raye and her family, the Pink Tea Cup remained a gay favorite as it changed hands over the course of its life. In 2007, the lesbian magazine GO recommended it as "one of the many restaurants in the Village where you can dyke-watch for hours."[3] The restaurant closed in 2010; a new owner re-created the space in Brooklyn, but that closed, too, in 2019.

In the '70s, there was also Horn of Plenty, a restaurant that served upscale Southern cuisine, located at Charles and Bleecker Streets in the West Village. Specializing in "Traditional Down Home Southern Cooking," as one ad called it, the restaurant was popular with Black gays and lesbians, including Alston, who remembered taking his mother there at least once for dinner. (She loved it.) In 1976, *The New York Times* gave it a terrific small review, praising its baked Virginia ham with raisin sauce and "knockout desserts," including a black walnut pie.

A year later, *Routes: A Guide to African-American Culture* made dinner at Horn of Plenty sound fit for a king: "The hostess greets you as if she's been waiting just for you. After she's taken your name, seated you comfortably in the candle-lit waiting area, & you've had your drinks served, the good vibrations begin to take hold. You're soothed & relaxed for the adventure that awaits your palate." The writer singles out such selections as the Louisiana Shrimp Creole and the Broiled Red Snapper, and gives shout-outs to the owner, David Williams, and the head chef, Vinson Rolland ("a man of warmth, charm, and a love for his profession"). Horn of Plenty moved at least once and stayed in business until at least 1985.

In Atlanta, the Colonnade has been drawing gays of many races since at least the 1970s. (Locals know it as Atlanta's place for "gays and grays.")[4] Jack Clark opened the Colonnade in 1927 in a white-columned house at the corner of Lindbergh and Piedmont. In 1962, it moved to its current location on Cheshire Bridge Road. In 1979, Paul Jones bought it, and Jones's daughter Jodi and her husband, David, ran it until September 2024, when business partners Paul Donahue and Lewis Jeffries, both longtime patrons of the restaurant, took over.

The menu hasn't changed much, offering such old-fashioned Southern favorites as pot roast, fried catfish, Southern pork schnitzel, and the Cheshire Chicken: a grilled boneless chicken breast with BBQ sauce and sliced ham topped with melted Cheddar. (Vegetarians can put together macaroni and cheese, deviled eggs, fried green tomatoes and yeast rolls with butter.) For dessert, I pigged out on peanut butter and coconut pie, a flavor combination I'd never had before but would have again in a heartbeat. (The only misfire was the small dish of canned pears topped with shredded

Cheddar cheese and a side of mayonnaise—flavors I never want to taste together again.) The prices were reasonable, and the food came quickly. Our meal there reminded me of the Melrose: The gays were unpretentious, the food was reasonably priced, and the room was almost, to a person, entirely gay. Unlike the Melrose, the Colonnade was racially mixed.

In the early '90s, Atlanta's Black community forged a home at Waterworks. A 1992 newsletter for a gay multiracial organization called Black and White Men Together included a small item that describes how a record twenty members enjoyed a meal at Waterworks, "a relaxed Southern style dinner at Atlanta's only black owned gay restaurant." This little article, written about a dinner that happened over thirty years ago, may not seem like a big deal. It was probably written quickly as nothing more than a recap for a small readership. But for the men who gathered that night, dinner was special. These small paragraphs were powerful reminders of how hard it was, and yet how absolutely necessary it was, for queer people of color to carve out restaurants of their own. For gay people of color, eating out was often an everyday thing and a revolutionary act all the same.

It was a Saturday night and Casita del Campo was packed. David and I estimated that the dining room at this beloved Mexican restaurant, located in the tony Silver Lake neighborhood of Los Angeles, was at least half gay. We watched as two elders, one in a black T-shirt who brought a cane, and the other in a black jacket with a napkin tied around his neck like a bib, slurped down *albondigas* soup, a classic Mexican dish made with plump little meatballs and giant slices of zucchini. At another table, two older men and a tall younger one in short shorts air kissed before sitting down and quickly digging into their chips and salsa. Small Pride flags adorned almost every wall and door. Our server wore

a rainbow button on the apron that barely held back the muscles
that were trying to escape his white Oxford shirt.

Casita del Campo's menu feels like a throwback to 1962,
when Rudy del Campo, a former dancer and entertainer, served
old-school combinations of tacos or enchiladas with beans and
rice and, to start, a salad. (The fact that I ordered blue cheese
dressing for my salad told me that the spirit of 1962 is alive and
well at Casita del Campo.) For dinner, I stuck with my go-to
Mexican order: cheese enchiladas with a spicy green sauce, but
here I switched it up and added a side of deliciously caramelized
fried plantains. Casita's more adventurous and carnivorous diners could order the *cochinita pibil*, a pork tenderloin marinated
with achiote chile and spices; or the *camarones a la diabla*, a
spicy shrimp sauté. Like Annie's, Casita has established itself as a
gay legacy restaurant by sticking with the familiar.

A few days after our dinner, I returned to Casita to chat with
Rudy's son, Robert del Campo, who now runs the restaurant.
Robert looks like a slightly graying version of the boxer Oscar de
la Hoya, and speaks softly but with the bright energy of a California surfer dad. I didn't get a chance to ask a question before
Robert started telling me that his restaurant is actually a series of
homes—*casita* is Spanish for a small house—joined together by a
central driveway that was built in the 1970s. The booths are original, and some of the chairs bear the names of longtime patrons.
The rubber tree that arcs across the dining room is the same one
that was on the land before the restaurant opened.

Robert's Colombian mother, Nina, started working as a waitress at Casita in 1965 when she met Rudy. Nina was in the garment
industry, but found a job at Casita after someone suggested to her
that she could make more money in a restaurant, even though she
didn't know much English. She looked in the Yellow Pages and
when she came to the letter "C," Casita del Campo stood out as
a cute name. She was still in training when Rudy walked through

the door one day and she was struck by his thick beard. The two later married. Robert was born in 1967.

Rudy was born in Los Angeles but grew up in Mexico, where he developed a love of Fred Astaire films, a passion that fueled his dream of becoming a professional dancer. At eighteen, Rudy was drafted into the Korean War and served two years in the army; he was trained in field artillery, but was also a projectionist whose responsibility it was to show venereal disease prevention films to servicemen. After the war, he studied dance and became a professional, appearing as one of the Sharks in *West Side Story* and in an uncredited dancer role with Judy Garland in *A Star Is Born*. After his dance career, he opened Casita del Campo, where photos of him in those and other big-budget Hollywood musicals adorn the walls.

Robert said that Casita has welcomed gay people, including dancers who knew Rudy from show business, since "day one." Casita, he said, "became a very natural expression and safe place for two men to come have dinner together and not be stared at, ostracized, looked down upon." The restaurant's philosophy, he added, has always been that "we are going to love everybody." The restaurant's signature bright pink exterior—pink was Rudy's favorite color—has become a calling card.

Rock Hudson was a habitué. One day when the actor was sitting in booth #3, Nina introduced herself despite Rudy's urging to leave the actor alone. Her Colombian accent was so thick that Hudson asked one of the waitresses to interpret because he didn't speak Spanish. "My mom *was* speaking English," Robert told me with a laugh.

As with Caffe Cino and other restaurants where entertainment and gay dining went hand in hand, Casita del Campo has a black box–size theater in the basement, where the unwritten rule is that if you want to perform there, you need to have at least one drag performer. Among the shows that have played there are *Chico's*

Angels, a parody of the TV show *Charlie's Angels*, and sets by the comedy queens Dina Martina and Jackie Beat. I reached out to Jackie Beat to see whether she'd share her thoughts about Casita del Campo, and she emailed back almost immediately.

"The feeling of family and community there is undeniable," she wrote. "It has been a haven for LGBTQ+ folks since long before those letters even existed. I think most marginalized people can immediately recognize when they are being welcomed with open arms as opposed to being merely tolerated."

Robert said that when his son Jeremy was thirteen, he came into Casita del Campo one day and sat in a booth by the bar and told his parents that he wasn't into girls. "'I like boys, I'm gay, I think I'm gay,'" Robert recalled him saying. As Robert listened to Jeremy, he burst into tears before giving his son a hug and reminding him how proud he was to be his father. As Robert relayed this memory, his eyes, and mine, began to fill too.

"'I will always be in your corner, no matter what,'" he remembered saying to Jeremy, speaking to me in almost a whisper as a single tear slowly rolled down his cheek. Jeremy now frequents Casita del Campo for both the margaritas *and* the cute bartenders. "He's here in his element," Robert added.

As our conversation ended, Robert wanted me to make the point that Casita welcomed not just the gay community but "everything under the sun," an urgent message because "prejudice and racism haven't disappeared in Los Angeles." He was hopeful that at least one of his sons would take over when he decides it's time to step aside and let a new generation of del Campos welcome a new generation of queer customers.

"The day I die," he said, "I want Casita to still be here."

Why has Casita del Campo outlasted its competitors from the gay restaurant golden age, when Los Angeles has so many other options for Mexican food at all culinary levels, from mom-and-pop taco stands to high-end restaurants? One reason is that Robert owns the building, which means he's immune to rent hikes. But it's more than that. Eating at Casita is like eating at an old-school Italian red-sauce restaurant in any city's Little Italy, but with chips and salsa and way more gays. For many Casita del Campo fans, eating enchiladas from a kitchen that hasn't changed its recipes a whole lot in decades, with people who probably haven't changed their ways much either, makes it a glorious place to be.

That's what the gay dining golden age was all about: eating with other gay people even if the kitchen wasn't aiming for a Michelin star and the check might be higher than a comparable meal at a straight restaurant. The same calculus is happening at a Mexican restaurant not far from where I live in Hell's Kitchen. It's called Arriba Arriba, and almost every time I pass by it, the dining room is filled with gays and their gal pals. I've been there a few times, and trust me, these gays are not looking for deconstructed tacos and tiny $30 margaritas but, rather, a place to have fun and hang out with friends and eat food they know and knock back cocktails that won't break the bank. To be honest, I'm not a fan of Arriba Arriba; there's a reason some people call it "Diarrhea Diarrhea." But on most days, especially Mondays when Broadway is dark and actors gather there before their workweek starts, Arriba Arriba is the gayest restaurant in New York City.

I miss this golden age. I have always chosen to live in gay neighborhoods because I love being surrounded by other gay men who want the same things I do: romance, friendship, sex, good food. When I left Cleveland in 1989 to live in New York City, it blew my mind that I could patronize gay bars, restaurants, and shops where I almost never had to run into straight people. I still search out gay restaurants when I travel because I want to eat out with gay men, not to avoid having to eat with people who aren't like me but because eating with my people is just fucking *fun*.

It's hard for younger queer people to imagine today, but there was a thrill to picking up a gay guide at the local bookstore or bar and learning where to go to eat with only other gay folks. In 1969, the N.Y.C. *Gay Scene Guide*, a thirty-two-page guidebook from the Apollo Book Club, listed over 175 places for gay men to drink, party, be entertained, have sex, and eat in the city. It recommended twenty restaurants in Manhattan, many of them in the West Village. Among them were Fraser's Restaurant (Waverly at Sixth Avenue), "where the gay kids go before the bar tour," and Finale Bar (Barrow at Seventh Avenue), "one of the oldest gay restaurants where the atmosphere is friendly and casual," and where the Shrimp Victoria—a dish of shrimp, sour cream, and mushrooms—is "great and reasonably priced."

The longest entry was for the Post and Coach Inn (Eighth Avenue and 41st Street), which was praised not just for its good food and reasonable prices but also for its location at the Port Authority Bus Terminal. "If you'll take a table at the rear," the guide says, "you'll be able to also enjoy (through the glass windows that open directly into the Port Authority main ticket floor) such delightful delicasies [*sic*] as 'sea-food' and lively young spring chickens as they pass by your view."

In the 1980s, a great way to learn about gay restaurants was on cable access television. In 1984, the public-access *Gay Morning America* ran restaurant commercials that were read live by George Sardi and Johnny Savoy, two of the show's camp hosts. There was "the hamburger you'll never forget" at the Centre Pub on St. Mark's Place in the East Village. The Big Dish in the West Village was known for its honey-dipped chicken, and the gay-owned and -operated Big Wok was "the only Chinese restaurant on Restaurant Row." The hundred-seat Kaspar's in Chelsea, across from the Fashion Institute of Technology, served lunch and dinner with "nothing but nothing frozen—from food, foul, meat, fish and whatevah," George said.

Someone else I know would like to hop in a time machine and visit every gay restaurant in a local gay guide: Ted Allen. I first met the longtime host of the Food Network cooking competition *Chopped* through Chicago's gay journalist circles back in the '90s. Ted loved the Melrose as much as I did. He remembers it as a place with "all these insane gays with their weird clothes and frosted tips and whatever fashion crimes we were committing in that era."

I reunited with Ted one October afternoon in 2023. We had lunch at Cafeteria, which we agreed was barely a gay restaurant anymore; most of the tables were occupied by opposite-sex couples and by large groups of what looked like office coworkers of various genders on lunch breaks. We lamented that it was no longer the Cafeteria we remembered from two a.m. in the late '90s, when the dining room was abuzz with the sounds of muscle boys talking to drag queens and pommes frites flying out of the kitchen faster than you can say "Crystal Waters."

Ted said he and the other hosts of the original *Queer Eye for the Straight Guy*, the gay reality show that ran on Bravo in the early 2000s, used Elmo, another gay restaurant up the street, as a kind of clubhouse.

"It had really comfortable big booths where a big group could fit into," he recalled. "I remember the food being good, not earth shattering but definitely good. That place, to me, was overwhelmingly gay in a great way."

Ted and I also reminisced about long-gone gay bookstores with restaurants tucked away in the back, like the small café inside A Different Light, the now-closed LGBTQ+ bookstore in Chelsea. I can't tell you how many times friends and I ate quesadillas or slices of pie (and sometimes bought a book) at Kramerbooks & Afterwords, now called just Kramers, a beloved and gay-friendly bookstore in Dupont Circle. On weekends, it was open twenty-four hours and, as at Annie's, there was often a waiting list for a seat around three a.m.

But Ted and I got really animated as we talked about Food Bar. Joe Fontecchio, whose résumé included Cafe Luxembourg and Chanterelle, and several partners opened the restaurant in Chelsea on Eighth Avenue near West 17th Street in 1992. Food Bar quickly became *the* hot spot for young and pretty muscle gays, club kids, socialites, and wannabes.

In 2023, I spoke with Tom Johnson, who designed ads and interiors for Food Bar. Among his signature designs were handmade lampshades with thematic scenes—gay marriage, gay love—which changed regularly. (He said he also helped convince the owners to name the restaurant Food Bar, not Prince Fatso's, as they had once considered.) At the height of weekend dinner service, Tom remembered Food Bar abuzz with gay conversations about who was there and who wasn't, or who was spinning at the Roxy that night, or which club kids and drag queens would be hosting next week's parties at Danceteria or Barracuda.

"Food Bar was supposed to be affordable and open and overtly gay," he said, sixty-three when we spoke. "It became that right away."

Food Bar was one of the restaurants that cemented Chelsea as a gay dining destination, more for the scrumptious men and the often scandalous scene than for the food. It's hard to overstate the extent to which Food Bar was an intensely sexual environment. Blogger Kenneth M. Walsh once described it as a place where "more men have ~~had sex in the bathroom~~ been on dates than probably any other restaurant in the world."

As fun as Food Bar was, Lord help you if you were not conventionally attractive; Chelsea in the '90s could be a nasty place for anyone who wasn't white, fit, and didn't look like a *Homo Xtra* cover boy. I was never thrown shade at Food Bar. But I remember sitting there for dinner one Friday night, thinking I was too chubby to be eating with so many hot gay men barely eating from their plates. It would have been illegal for Food Bar to turn people away, even though megaclubs like the Limelight did it all the time. (I remember walking up to Disco 2000, one of my favorite weekday parties at the Limelight, around one a.m. and being whisked through the front door while people who weren't wearing shaggy wigs and carrying lunchboxes failed to get inside. That's just how it was.) Every time I approached the host or hostess at Food Bar, I was sure *this* would be the night that they would say I wouldn't be allowed in. They never did.

Even actual models felt intimidated eating there. Mark Allen, a go-go dancer whose boyishly handsome face and tight-as-hell body were plastered on nightclub flyers and posters across New York City, remembered eating at Food Bar on occasion. (He preferred low-rent, gay-welcoming restaurants in the East Village, such as Veselka and the Odessa Diner.) Eating at Food Bar, he confided in me, felt weird "because nobody was there to enjoy the food."

"It was the male version of going to a restaurant with skinny, beautiful girls," he clarified. "They're not going to eat the food."

Food Bar's menu was American bistro fare but gilded with a '90s edge. For starters, you could share calamari with a spiced rice wine vinegar sauce. An entrée might be a saffron risotto with shrimp and peas, or roasted chicken with matchstick potatoes. If you were a muscle boy and needed to protein up, you could start with a bowl of lentils topped with arugula and Parmesan, and for your main course have sliced steak salad and beefsteak tomatoes. Chocolate soufflé cake was popular for dessert.

Pepe Villegas, an artist who worked at Food Bar as a waiter, bartender, and host, remembered serving many celebrities who orbited '90s New York. Among them were makeup artist Kevin Aucoin, gay porn director Michael Lucas, and club kids Candis Cayne and Girlina.

"It was incredibly flirty," Pepe, fifty-nine, told me when we spoke in 2023. "Food Bar became almost like a fun shelter. It was a magnet."

Pepe remembered Sunday brunch attracted the rowdiest diners, mostly because people's Saturday night highs were still subsiding. "When you couldn't party anymore, you would go to Food Bar and get your carbs and come down," he added.

Food Bar's popularity eventually slowed, becoming less of an attraction as it started to show its age. (I feel you, girl.) In 1996, the Food Bar space got a facelift and a new name, Che 2020. Three years later, the old name came back, but in 2008, Food Bar closed for good.

In 1999, the gay men's magazine *Genre* noted how much America's gay restaurant scene was blossoming. On the cover, under a close-up of a wet man's come-hither smile, the headline beamed: "Eat, Drink & Be Mary." Inside, the introductory questions were all too familiar: "What is a gay restaurant or café? A great pickup place? Buff waiters in white T-shirts? Passable food but great glamour?"[5]

The answer, according to the authors, was that gay restaurants shared a common style: "Comfortable yet hip, they are amazing places to dine and gather, where the fellowship flows like lite beer." The pull quote? "Offer a bite of your bleu cheese burger to the guy sitting next to you and watch what happens."

Among the restaurants described were places I remembered as part of my dining out experiences: Buddies in Chicago for the "butch brunch," and Food Bar in New York, unsuitably described as "Ralph Lauren gone food." There was a sidebar of gay cafés, too: Xando in Washington, D.C., Ooh La La in Chicago, and my beloved Big Cup, "gay ground zero in Chelsea."

Most of these restaurants are gone. But I consider that a dearth, not a death. That's because there remains a thriving remnant of the gay dining golden age, the kind of place where you can linger with mostly gays over a lumberjack breakfast or a plate of potato skins at noon or three a.m. I'm talking about the diner—America's buttery, bountiful, dependably gay, twenty-four-hour gift.

Because the Night

Diners

By midnight, the crowd at the counter had mostly thinned to just me and the queen to my right. Tucked into a nearby booth were two older men with brightly colored wispy hair—one, blue; the other, neon yellow—who sat in silence as they took dainty bites of their cheeseburgers and, with lifted pinkies, dipped their fries into itty-bitty ponds of ketchup. The three-quarters booth in the front window under the OPEN 24 HOURS sign had turned over, replacing five gay leathermen with five new, slightly older gay leathermen, including one who wore a leather vest over his bare chest and a blue kerchief around his neck (a signal, in the visual language of the gay hanky code, that anal sex is his thing). The clientele wasn't all men: A woman in a faux fur coat and pendant necklace pouted as she talked softly to a male companion sitting across from her.

A few minutes later, my waiter picked up two plates at the pass-through window and placed them before me. On one, two Frisbee-size pancakes sat smothered in a pat of butter the size of a billiard ball. The other plate propositioned me with a thick omelet stuffed with sautéed fresh spinach and small cubes of sharply salty feta cheese. As my waiter walked away, I noticed that his chestnut brown hair and furrowed brow were slick with sweat from hustling between the counter and the cramped dining room.

"Where's *my* food?" demanded the queen a few chairs down. He was older than I was, and wore a black T-shirt, black shorts, and black-framed eyeglasses. A minute before, he had been speed-surfing Grindr. "I was here first," he barked.

He was not. I was, and my waiter knew it. With orders piling up and empty cups of coffee to refill, the server was not having this queen's tantrum.

"Your food will be ready when it's ready," he scolded Snippy Queen. "Don't rush my cook. He's busy."

Snippy Queen got quiet. About ten minutes later, after he had finished his cheeseburger, he seemed calmer. The waiter noticed.

"Are you better now?" the waiter asked.

"I am," Snippy Queen replied softly, smiling briefly. "Thank you."

After Snippy Queen left, the waiter quickly cleaned up his plates.

"*She* was angry," I observed.

"She probably couldn't find any dick," the waiter said unsmiling, without skipping a beat. "She was *hungry*."

This is how it goes every day of the year at Orphan Andy's. Open since 1977 in San Francisco's Castro neighborhood, the diner is a legacy gay restaurant. I was there on a Sunday night in September 2023 around eleven p.m., to see just how gay Orphan Andy's would be during the Folsom Street Fair, the annual sex-and-leather event that brings kinksters of all sexual orientations and genders from around the world to San Francisco for a weekend of frisky camaraderie. I'd had fun strolling through the street fair earlier that day. Now it was time to eat.

Dennis Ziebell and Bill Pung, partners and owners of Orphan Andy's, have maintained the colorful and kooky restaurant since it opened. I'm a fan of diner chic, and Orphan Andy's didn't disappoint. Around fifteen people—mostly gay men, to my eyes—sat at the counter and at small booths decorated in red vinyl upholstery, or at tables in green Formica with chrome edges that glistened. Large plastic dividers separated the booths in an attempt to mitigate the spread of COVID-19. On the walls hung framed images of Marilyn Monroe, dolphins, and a poster for a stage production of *Women Behind Bars* starring Divine. Butterfly kites and sparking colorful lights hung from the ceiling. Stained-glass lamps, like the ones I used to see at the Friendly's my family went to in the '80s, dotted the dining room. From my seat at the counter, I couldn't see the grill, but there was plenty more to spy in the kitchen: gleaming pans and ladles hanging over the sink, loaves of round-top bread, an industrial-size bag of fries. Four Spanish-speaking men were on duty behind the counter. The cook used an old-fashioned bell in the restaurant's pass-through window to signal when orders were ready. The front door was cracked open so the late-night air could cool us down.

I went back to Orphan Andy's the next afternoon, thinking it would be empty and quiet, the better to talk to regulars. Instead, there was a handful of gays and some straight tourist families with kids in line outside the door. I grabbed a seat at the counter and waved hello to the cook, Jonathan Pace, whom I'd met the night before and told I was there to work on a book about gay restaurants. Jonathan had been working at Orphan Andy's for twenty years, and like on most days, he was busy at the sizzling grill making French toast, steaks, and eggs. He popped his head out of the kitchen and introduced me to Mikey Sanchez, one of the servers.

"He told me about you," Mikey said, smiling. "We've been calling you Barbara Hutton."

Barbara Hutton, Barbara Hutton. I couldn't place the name.

Sensing my confusion, Mikey clarified, giggling: "The reporter from *Mommie Dearest*."

I laughed and bowed my head in gay shame.

(Mikey almost got it right: Barbara Bennett is the *Redbook* magazine reporter in *Mommie Dearest* who interviews Joan Crawford, played by Faye Dunaway. Jocelyn Brando, Marlon's sister, played her.)

Mikey was originally from Brooklyn, but lived in Chelsea for a while and worked at the gay bar Barracuda. Before his shift there started, he usually went to Big Cup, where the gay staff gave him the Rice Krispie Treats they didn't sell that day. He said San Francisco doesn't have that kind of gay coffee shop anymore. He misses it.

"The Castro could use it," he sighed.

I also met D. J. Brown, who lived eight blocks from Orphan Andy's. He was disabled, which made it hard for him to stand and cook for himself, which is why he ate sometimes more than once a day at Orphan Andy's. He kept coming back for several reasons: the friendly service, the old Woolworth's diner feel, the large portions. "I usually can't finish a meal," he admitted. His go-to? The mashed potatoes, especially when Jonathan made them with chunks of skin-on spuds and lots of butter.

In 1999, D. J. owned a small gay greasy spoon called La Café in Wichita, Kansas, where he's from. "Glitter and be gay at La Café" was the tagline. It was only open for about six months, but in that time, he said it was one very small way that Wichita's gay community felt supported.

"There was a time when we needed safety in numbers," he explained. "Today, kids are coming out at twelve years old. It's such a different world. They don't know the struggles you and I had."

Orphan Andy's is a restaurant unlike any other restaurant in the Castro, a neighborhood where there's not much of a gay *there* there anymore, not like it was the 1970s. Orphan Andy's is a San Francisco survivor. And the reason is simple. It's a diner.

If there is one revelation I have after several years of thinking about, writing about, and dining out at gay restaurants, it's this: Diners are gay. *Gayed*, to be more accurate: Restaurants in the American greasy spoon tradition have, for decades, been places where gay people of all shapes, orientations, and colors have made gay turf, often out of necessity when our loud gay asses had nowhere to eat after the clubs.

It makes sense. Most can accommodate people eating alone or large parties. They offer food for any taste or diet, made from scratch and to order. They generally welcome customers regardless of who they are, as long as they behave and don't dine and dash. Diners are often the only place in any town that are open late or around the clock—good news for queer party people.

Diners also tend to be more socio-economically inclusive, the kinds of restaurants where a good meal can still be affordable. Eating at a diner can be a leisurely pursuit, where you can sit with a plate of fries and a Coke and not get a side-eye from the owners, unless the place is busy and you're dawdling. To be clear: When I talk about diners, I don't mean the annoying class of ridiculously overpriced, huckleberry-buckwheat pancake–serving neo-diners that have popped up in America's tonier towns in the last decade or so, the kinds of restaurants that are designed to mirror the look and menu but not the affordability of old-school diners.

Other than cruising otters at the Melrose and getting to know David at the Skylight, my other big gay diner memory happened in the late '80s at My Friends, that twenty-four-hour Cleveland diner where I spent countless hours eating pancakes and mozzarella sticks with my high school friends. This formative event took place very late one night after an industrial-music dance party that my Goth-punk friend Diane and I had just left. We finished our meal, exhausted from dancing to Nitzer Ebb and Cabaret Voltaire, and she excused herself to go to the bathroom. I was at the table alone for a while, wondering what was taking her so long. I went to check and before I could knock on the door, she came rushing out, screaming, "My baby, my baby!" She didn't have a baby, but what she did have was a sick sense of humor: Smeared across the toilet, the sink, and the floor was at least a cup's worth of chunky, tomatoey, oily meat sauce that she had somehow smuggled into the bathroom.

Still screaming, Diane booked it out the front door, and taking her cue, I did too. We managed to get to the parking lot and into my car and sped off without anyone stopping us. (We had already paid.) Maybe it's because we both had on Gothwear and black wigs—mine a pageboy that covered my eyes—but the next time we went to My Friends, probably six weeks later, they didn't recognize us. I haven't seen Diane in decades, but we're friends on Facebook, connected by this memory of a fake miscarriage, and the fact that she was one of the first people I came out to. ("I know," she told me then. "So what?") Thank *god* we didn't have smartphones in the '80s.

Gay filmmaker Todd Stephens remembers similar drama between young gay men and their female partners-in-crime as a regular at the Country Kitchen in Sandusky, Ohio, where he grew up and where he made his glorious gay coming-of-age film *Edge of Seventeen*.

The Los Angeles–based Cooper Do-nuts chain once had thirty-three locations in California. *Courtesy of the Evans family and www.cooperdonuts.com. Used with permission.*

Inside Gene Compton's Cafeteria in San Francisco's Tenderloin neighborhood, circa 1966. © *Henri Leleu, Heri Leleu Papers (1997–13), GLBT Historical Society*

Jonny Orsini, left, and Nathan Lane played characters who meet at a Manhattan Automat in the 1930s in the play *The Nance*, which ran on Broadway in 2013. © *Sara Krulwich/The New York Times/Redux*

An undated photo of Annie Katinas, the gregarious namesake of Annie's Paramount Steak House in Washington, D.C. *Courtesy of Georgia Katinas*

The Mexican restaurant Casita del Campo has been serving Los Angeles since 1962.
© *Erik Piepenburg*

Orphan Andy's, a twenty-four-hour diner, opened in San Francisco's Castro neighborhood in 1977. © *Erik Piepenburg*

Noel Furie, left, and Selma Miriam at Bloodroot, their feminist and meat-free restaurant in Bridgeport, Connecticut. Selma died in 2025. © *Annie Laurie Medonis*

In 1984, the Atlanta drag queen Diamond Lil released an album that included an ode to the Silver Grill, a diner popular with gay men. *Courtesy of Author's Collection*

A selection of foods served at Flex, a bathhouse in Cleveland. *Courtesy of Flex Hotel Gym and Spa Cleveland*

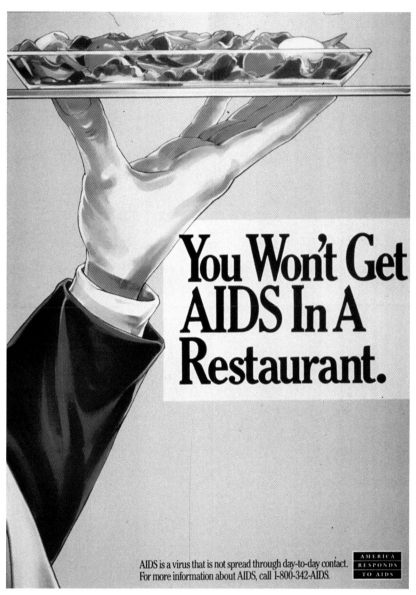

In 1987, the America Responds to AIDS campaign included a public service announcement explaining that AIDS was not transmittable via food service. *Centers for Disease Control, 1987, Public Domain*

In 2004 at Florent, an around-the-clock restaurant in New York's Meatpacking District, the artist Spencer Tunick photographed a group of naked people living with HIV. The image appeared on the cover of *POZ* magazine. *POZ May 2004. Reprinted with permission.* © *2004 CDM Publishing, LLC*

These 80 HIV-free spirits bared their beautiful HIV-infected bodies for artist Spencer Tunick, March 13, 2004, to mark *POZ*'s 10th anniversary.

Before it closed in 2017, the Melrose was a popular twenty-four-hour diner in Chicago's gay Boystown neighborhood. © *Erik Piepenburg*

Food Bar was a hotspot in New York City's Chelsea neighborhood in the 1990s. © *Tom Johnson*

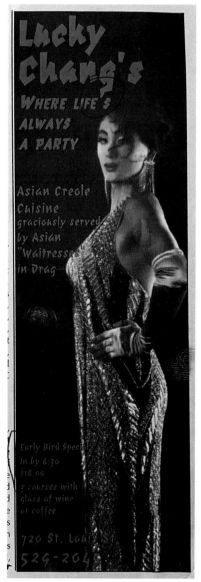

An undated advertisement for Lucky Cheng's, an Asian restaurant that opened in 1993 in New York's East Village.
Courtesy of Josephine Jason

Arnold "Butch" Pendergast and Martha Marvel outside the Napalese Lounge & Grille in Green Bay, Wisconsin. *Courtesy of Martha Marvel*

A Pride mural by the artist Loschue (Chue) Lo greets visitors at Napalese Lounge & Grille. © *Erik Piepenburg*

Derek Kitchen, left, and Moudi Sbeity at their restaurant Laziz Kitchen in Salt Lake City in 2016. *Courtesy of Moudi Sbeity*

Telly Justice, left, and Camille Lindsley, the founders of HAGS, a fine-dining restaurant in New York City. © *Seth Caplan*

An oversized rainbow sculpture greets visitors at the Hamburger Mary's location in West Hollywood. © *Erik Piepenburg*

Portraits of Alice B. Toklas and Gertrude Stein by the artist Jo Hay hang in the dining room of Alice B. in Palm Springs. © *Erik Piepenburg*

In 2023, giant mushrooms and supersized butterflies were among the seasonal decor inside the atrium of insideOUT, a restaurant in San Diego. © Erik Piepenburg

Country Kitchen had a "Big Boy's vibe," he told me, referring to the chain of country-style diners that were popular in the Midwest, and was the place to go if you were a weirdo teenager in the '80s. In the '90s, it's where he and other gays ate after the Universal Fruit and Nut Company gay club emptied out after last call.

"I remember being sweaty and smelling like cigarette smoke— I didn't smoke, but you know how it was going out back then— and half-drunk or stoned and eating scrambled eggs after the clubs," he recalled. "It seemed like it was all gay at that hour. I feel like half the dining room was filled with queens."

Stephens said the Country Kitchen dining room could be flirty, but there was never any action in the restaurant itself. ("I think there could have been some last Hail Mary passes," he added.) The restaurant wasn't exactly hostile to its gay customers, but it wasn't welcoming either.

"I don't remember bad vibes," Todd said of Country Kitchen. "But it was a bunch of teenagers working a graveyard shift, who didn't give a shit."

For closeted teenagers who were just figuring out their queerness, eating at the Country Kitchen could be a split-personality experience.

"Sometimes, you'd go there with your family during the day, and it was like a different place," Stephens said. "I wasn't out to my family then, so if we went there after church for breakfast, it was sort of like, 'If they only knew that I was here at three a.m.'"

For pre-Stonewall New Yorkers who were on a budget but hungry for sunny-side-up eggs and crisp bacon, it was hard to beat the Silver Dollar, a twenty-four-hour hole-in-the-wall diner near Christopher and Washington Streets, a stone's throw from Manhattan's West Side piers. Throughout the '60 s and '70s, during the morning breakfast rush the Silver Dollar was chockablock with truck drivers starting their days, and police officers and ambulance drivers on the overnight shift ending theirs.

But after midnight, especially during the hot summer months, the real truckers and cops were replaced by "truckers" and "cops" and other butch-looking male homosexuals in a range of ages and races, as the Silver Dollar got wild, and sleazy, thanks to hustlers, drag queens, macho clones in construction worker drag, and transgender women and sex workers who gathered there to nurse cups of coffee and share plates of fries as they gossiped about who just got blown at Peter Rabbit or Badlands, nearby gay bars. When a tipsy queen played Diana Ross on the jukebox, there was no stopping drunker queens from getting on the tables for some group ass shaking, at least until the Silver Dollar's owners told them to knock it off. Someone usually had poppers in their pocket to keep everyone's head rushes a-rushing.

As a young gay man, gay rights activist Martin Boyce was a regular at the Silver Dollar, perhaps because his father, who knew that Martin was gay, warned him to stay away from the hustlers who hung out at the Riker's diner near 43rd Street and Second Avenue, not far from where Martin's family lived. Martin told me that the owners of the Silver Dollar were indifferent to anything gay happening past the counter or the kitchen, "so it turned into a place where all these queens would go."

"Gays were very loud and pronounced at the time," he said. "Our conversations could be heard from the outside."

Marsha P. Johnson was at the Silver Dollar the night that a friend of hers, a little gay named Joey, was at the counter sobbing because he owed a guy $50 and was scared shitless that he'd get beat up for not having the money.[1] The guy got tired of waiting for Joey outside, so he burst into the Silver Dollar and, in front of everyone, threatened to kick Joey's ass if he didn't pay up.

"No, you ain't gonna kick anybody's ass," Johnson warned the guy.

"You know," he replied, "I can have a carload of guys down here in twenty minutes."

"Yeah?" Johnson said. "Well, I can have *two* carloads down here in *ten* minutes."

The guy left, confused but concerned that Johnson wasn't bluffing. Johnson paid for Joey's coffee—adding on a hamburger deluxe and a malt—and left the Silver Dollar, returning twenty minutes later, having paid back Joey's $50 to the angry guy outside.

"Didja eat?" Johnson asked Joey.

"Thank you, Marsha," Joey replied, through tears. He took a bite of his burger, and peace was restored to the Silver Dollar.

New York had the Silver Dollar but Atlanta had the Silver Grill, a diner so gay, a drag queen wrote a song about it.

The Silver Grill was open from 1940 to 2006. Its tiny parking lot was a hassle for visitors who drove, but no big deal for the gay men who turned Midtown Atlanta into a gay neighborhood in the 1970s. During the Silver Grill's gay heyday in the 1970s and '80s, it was a place to show yourself off, and to parade about with the man you'd picked up the night before. The Silver Grill was "very frequented by every gay person in the city," recalled James McCrae, a regular there and at Gallus. Lord help the man who didn't look put together.

The dining room was narrow, with just enough room for the mostly female servers to maneuver between the counter, booths, and tables that were squeezed together just so. There was a pass-through kitchen, where in the open window you could watch the cooks at work. Daily specials were written on the chalkboard; one day you might find fried pork chops and the next, meatloaf with collard greens. For dessert, there was banana pudding and strawberry shortcake.

The Silver Grill was a go-to lunch spot for gays who worked nights or the overnight shift at the all-night gay club Backstreet. James said there were always big personalities disagreeing over something or other at the Silver Grill, but it never got violent.

"Maybe a queen slapped another queen," he said over the phone, his soft Southern twang nestled in my ear like a long-loved quilt.

One of the reasons I'm drawn to the Silver Grill is because of a server named Peggy. Before we get to this extraordinary person, it's worth noting that at a lot of Midwestern diners I went to in the '80s and '90s, my server was usually a brash, sailor-mouthed woman who took no bullshit from anyone. She was usually middle-aged or older, usually straight and married, who either by choice or necessity started working in restaurants in her youth and never walked away. Her manner on the job was kindly and welcoming but efficient and no-nonsense, especially if it was busy. Her makeup was probably applied with a heavy hand, or not at all, and her hairdo rarely changed. She wasn't perky, but she wasn't rude, either; part of her charm was that she could be abrasive. If she had a potty mouth, she wasn't afraid to use it, and around troublemakers, her mama bear instincts reared up. In a fight over your drunkenness or your table's nastiness, you would lose. She usually wasn't gay and maybe didn't hang out much in gay bars. But she considered her gay customers her boys, and in return, they had her back.

At the Silver Grill, this woman was Peggy Hubbard. The first things you'd smell when you walked into the diner were the fried chicken and biscuits. But the first thing you'd see—other than that only gay men were eating there—was Peggy's signature look: a tall and stiff black bouffant, thinly painted-on black eyebrows, silvery blue eye shadow, and a ring on almost every finger. She smiled, sometimes, but Peggy would cuss you out if you did anything to make her mess up your order.

"She did not mind letting you have it," Ashley told me. "She didn't take no shit. Miss Peggy, honey. She was a character."

There's a must-see video on YouTube from 1984 that was made for Atlanta's *Impulse Video Digest*. Peggy's in it, hustling food through the dining room in her red waitress uniform and painted-on black eyebrows. She put on a blue uniform for her sit-down interview with Tina Devore, one of Atlanta's most famous drag queens at the time, here dressed out of drag. Peggy's barely-there smile suggests she'd rather be anywhere else, yet she doesn't look annoyed or angry or put out. She just looks like she wants to either get back to work or go home.

Peggy softens as she tells Tina that she's worked at the Silver Grill for twenty-six years, having started in 1958. Tina asks if she served any gay customers in 1958, and that's when Peggy starts naming names: There was Curtis, who worked for Texas Drilling, and his companion, a man she remembered as Bill. "They were both gay," she said.

"That's amazing," replied Tina. She then asks how Peggy deals with her celebrity status among the gays.

"I'm real open minded," Peggy answers nonchalantly. "They treat me nice and I treat them nice." She looks like she's never heard a dumber question in her life.

Peggy finishes by talking about participating in a recent AIDS benefit, where she stayed "until five o'clock in the morning." The interview ends and the segment finishes with more shots of Peggy taking customers' orders and cooks pulling fried chicken hot and dripping from the fryer. The dining room is almost completely filled with mustached men wearing muscle T-shirts and preppy pullovers—an early '80s gay wet dream and evidence that the Silver Grill was a gay restaurant *par excellence*. Peggy died in 2016 and Devore in 2021.

James considers Peggy a heroine, especially because of her no-fear attitude when it came to serving and supporting gay people living with HIV and AIDS during the worst years of the AIDS crisis in Atlanta, a city hit hard by the virus.

"With AIDS, it was a weird vibe that affected every aspect of your life," he said. "To have a place where you could get your mind off of it, something social that didn't involve blood tests and positive diagnoses and scars and Kaposi's sarcoma—any break we got, we were appreciative of."

If there was another face of the Silver Grill, it was Diamond Lil. Born Phil Forrester in Savannah, Georgia, in 1935, the future Diamond Lil moved to Atlanta in 1965 and began her performing career as a drag queen at Mrs. P's, a restaurant in the basement of the Ponce Hotel that at night turned "sort of gay," she later said. She had a few jobs, including writing a nightlife column and running a small antiques business near Peachtree and 11th Streets. In the early '70s, she started performing at the city's famed cabaret-bar Sweet Gum Head, where she played regularly for the next decade. She spoke, as one fan described, in "a harmonious Southern lilt equal parts Minnie Pearl and Dixie Carter."[2] She wasn't a glam queen but more of a tragicomic Southern sexpot, performing ballads and up-tempo numbers while handing out fried chicken from an Easter basket.

Unlike a lot of drag queens who lip-synched the classics, Diamond Lil sang in her own voice and wrote her own songs. She released several albums, but the one that she is most known for is *Silver Grill/Queen of Diamonds*. The full-length collection of all original material came out in 1984, early in a decade when such bands as R.E.M., the Indigo Girls, and the B-52s, and performers including RuPaul and Lady Bunny, put a national spotlight on Atlanta as a gay cultural hot spot.

The album is a chaotic, lo-fi mess of scrappy rock, raw punk, sorta disco, old-school rockabilly, and lonesome country numbers; a proto–*Hedwig and the Angry Inch* sung-spoken by Mae West in heat. Her vocals are no coincidence: Diamond Lil was inspired by West, whose 1928 play *Diamond Lil* was a hit on Broadway. (The difference being that Atlanta's Diamond Lil was punkier and unluckier in love and sex than Mae West ever was.)

I first heard Diamond Lil in the summer of 2023. David and I went to his childhood home in Connecticut for one of our regular visits to see his family. One afternoon, he and I caught everyone off guard when we said that we needed some time alone with a vinyl record. We shut the door to his father's old office and put the album on a record player turntable that David's family had kept. The voice that came through the rickety speakers was breathy, ridiculously so, as if the lovelorn lady singer was having one long orgasm. As she talk-sings the first chorus, you realize that this gal isn't singing the praises of a rapacious lover. She's smitten with fried chicken:

> *Silver Grill chicken, it's gonna make your mouth water*
> *Plenty of coleslaw and French fries come oooooooh with the order*
> *I lost my heart just trying to get my fill*
> *When I ate at this country diner called the Silver Grill*

It's no "Scenes from an Italian Restaurant," but it's also not the work of just any old singer-songwriter. It's the title track off of a 1984 album independently produced by Diamond Lil, who once said that when she sings "Silver Grill" at gay bars, "You can hear a pin drop. Everyone just stops talking. People just have a place in their heart for the Silver Grill." I have the album on vinyl—it was issued only on vinyl—and I consider it a treasure of my collection.

"Silver Grill" is a rarity: a song set at a gay restaurant. Diamond Lil sings about a "handsome daddy" lineman who melts (then breaks) Diamond Lil's heart one day, when he gives her a hug. The relationship is doomed from the start: She's single but her "faded Levi daddy" has a wife and kids. Diamond Lil may not get the date she wanted, but she'll always have fried chicken. The song is a down-in-the-dumps country ballad set at a gay restaurant where differences in sexual orientation and gender identity are no big deal, where a drag queen and a piece of working-class trade could hit it off. It upended my assumptions about what a gay restaurant in Atlanta would look like in the early 1980s.

Diamond Lil's star began to fade in the mid-'80s, as tastes changed. She semiretired, and got a few gigs here and there at local clubs, but nothing like before.

"I used to have two or three queens who'd help me with everything: wigs, makeup, gowns," she said in 2003.[3] "Well, they're dead."

Diamond Lil—"the queen of glamour and grease," as she was called in a public access commercial for her album—died of cancer in 2016 at the age of eighty. An obituary in the *Atlanta-Journal Constitution* said her influence on the city's drag scene was "profound."

As Lady Bunny, now one of New York's legendary club kid–drag queens, told the paper: "She really was magic."

———

A diner in a gay neighborhood sometimes serves as a meeting room, a reading nook, a makeshift theater—more than a restaurant, in other words. In one case, it also served as a waiting room.

In the late 1970s, Will Schwalbe was a regular at the St. Marks Baths, a gay bathhouse in the East Village. It wasn't uncommon for him and lots of other gay men in New York to spend all weekend there socializing and having sex at a time in New York when gay bathhouses were thriving. Will went to the baths alone and mostly went to bars with friends, and he had friends he saw only at the baths or bars. But it was a given that if one of his friends peeled away to chat with or go home with somebody, his circle wouldn't bat an eye.

That wasn't the case at restaurants, where the expectation was that you were with your people for the duration of the meal. Like ordering made-to-order food at a diner, for Will there was one cardinal rule when it came to a bathhouse: For God's sake, don't eat from the buffet. (Don't tell the guys at Flex.)

"Granted, I clearly wasn't worried about getting any illnesses from the people I was sleeping with," he said. "But I knew to stay the hell away from the buffet."

It wasn't just food poisoning that put the fear of god in bathhouse gays. In the late '70s, if you had sex with lots of strangers—or, like today, if you have sex with lots of strangers—there was a good chance you caught giardia, a parasite that causes extended puking, severe burping, and explosive diarrhea.

Like many of your gay friends, if (or when) you caught giardia, you made an appointment with a doctor whose office was on the second floor of a building that overlooked Sheridan Square in the West Village, not far from the Stonewall. When you saw this doctor, he gave you something that caused your body to generate stool that could be tested, but it took an hour for the medication to travel through your system and take root. So, with other gay men from the waiting room, you went downstairs to the Tiffany Diner for coffee and—if you could stomach it—a snack to help speed things along in your system. When you were ready to poo, you bolted back upstairs and handed over your freshly produced sample and waited for the doctor to give you a course of medication to make it all go away so you could go back to the baths and have more sex as soon as possible and do this all again soon.

That's right: Turds queered the Tiffany.

I met Will over breakfast one morning in 2023 at the Bus Stop Cafe, a ten-minute walk from the old Tiffany. The doctor's office "was this hysterical scene of gay men who were not particularly well, because they were seeing him for a reason, having breakfast and then racing upstairs to get back to his office," he told me with a laugh.

The Tiffany opened in the late 1960s in a 1929 art deco building at West 4th Street and Seventh Avenue, near Christopher
Street. Inside, there were pink Formica tabletops, beveled glass,
vinyl booths that had seen better days, and oversized menus in
both size and in reasonably affordable food options. Diner 101:
omelets, grilled chicken breasts, steamed vegetables of the day,
pies. Serving the West Village, the Tiffany was a restaurant where
nobody batted an eye when such downtown theater icons as pioneering drag performer Charles Busch or Charles Ludlam, the
provocateur-founder of the Ridiculous Theatrical Company, sat
down together in a booth after a show. The gay men who waited
tables there had a reputation for blurring the lines between server
and served; writer Jaffe Cohen explained to me that it was the
kind of place where "a gay waiter might sit down and engage you
in conversation even as you're waiting for your appetizer."

At night—early morning, really—the dining room was a popular destination for gay leathermen on their way home from a night
of fisting or piss play at The Saint and the Mineshaft, two gay
clubs. Firebrand artist David Wojnarowicz, who died of AIDS in
1992, was a regular; in his book *In the Shadow of the American Dream*, he describes in his singular stream-of-consciousness
voice the Tiffany as a place where drug addicts, hustlers, and
other down-and-out New Yorkers were as prevalent as cups of hot
coffee.

Considering the upscale playground the West Village has
become today, what he so vividly describes sounds like a restaurant from an alien planet:

> Three no-wave women behind us in the next booth with
> black short razored hair and gold-black circles around
> their eyes and cheap plastic black-and-white bulby ear-
> rings and sleazo clothes, neat lookin' and they left after
> flashin' us some lingering stares; over to the other side

in a booth were two women on quaaludes nodding out over eggs and toast, chewing with eyes closed for minutes at a time.

The Tiffany closed down two years later, in 1994, after a fire—I'm not sure whether the doctor's office was still upstairs—but reopened after a year with new management and a new menu. The vinyl and pink in the 120-seat space were replaced with mahogany and marble paneling, etched mirrors, and a granite-trimmed art deco facade. "It was just a diner with hanging plants and faux wood until they decided to spruce it up, and it became much uglier," Cohen complained.

In 1995, *The New York Times* pooh-poohed the Tiffany's refurbishing, calling it "a dowdy, low budget gathering place for a colorful cross section of Villagers" for thirty years. For the price of a cup of coffee, "playwrights and older New Yorkers bought endless hours in the diner's gaudy pink booths." Mark Blasius, an author who frequented the diner in the 1970s, informed the *Times* that the Tiffany was "one of the first unofficial gay restaurants."

"It was a place where, any time of the day or night, drag queens and club kids could easily mix and cavort with so-called respectable people," he said. "There aren't many places like that left in New York."

For Will and other gay men of his generation, the Tiffany was as much a community center as a restaurant, much as the Silver Dollar was for the Stonewall generation before him. For a fancier evening, there was Rounds at Second Avenue and 53rd Street in what was then known as the Loop, a neighborhood for gay men on the make and for gay hustlers out to make money. Rounds was a prime example of a gay restaurant that appealed to older gay men of means who took pride in eating very traditional fare—pork chops, steaks, nice salads—which was then at least twenty years out of style. Not that these gay men cared much about the culinary vanguard: They wanted nothing more than dinner in a gay setting to eat the kinds of fancier meals they'd had, or yearned for, when they were younger. Rounds joined Regents and the Mayflower as gay restaurants with trends-be-damned vibes.

Like Gallus in Atlanta, Rounds was a hangout for hustlers; "young boys, old profession," as one gay guidebook described it. One side of the venue was a piano bar; the restaurant side functioned as a "marvelous interstitial space," Will said, where for at least an hour or two, "the escorts really were escorts, not sex workers." They were "charming company," he added, offering a kind of social intercourse akin to that of a gay dinner party.

"There were hustler hustlers but also, as a young man who wasn't entirely horrible looking, you could hang out by the bar and talk to some gent who would then buy you dinner," Schwalbe noted. "Instead of someone saying, 'Can I buy you a drink,' they could buy you dinner."

In 1994, however, Rounds found itself in trouble with the law. That year, New York City police barred the doors to close it down, citing twelve arrests in the previous year on charges of alcohol sales to minors and prostitution solicitations. It closed for good about a year later.

Then, there was Company. Eating at the bar-restaurant on Third Avenue, between 26th and 27th Streets, was a qualitatively different experience in the '70s than going to a gay restaurant in the West Village. Company attracted gay men who were worried about being seen going into a gay establishment, either because they were closeted or because they feared the waves of antigay violence that plagued New York's LGBTQ+ community during the Koch era. Inside, Company had a '70s nightclubby feel, with posters of Bette Midler and Judy Garland lining the walls of a darkly lit dining room that sparkled with polished chrome accents. Will said the restaurant was named after the Sondheim musical, not that anything in the restaurant outwardly suggested that as the case. The people who knew, knew.

Company was slightly more upscale than other gay restaurants in New York City in the '70s, which is why it became the place to celebrate an anniversary or birthday. (The almost exclusively gay staff would mark birthdays by running around the restaurant with napkins on their heads like wimples, belting the Singing Nun's "Dominique," a 1963 global hit about St. Dominic, a founder of the Dominican Order.) Company was where you took a date for Sunday night's "Super-Saver" filet mignon dinner ($12.50) or the Wednesday-only lobster fra diavolo (also $12.50). A "midnight brunch" was served until three a.m. on Fridays and Saturdays. The restaurant was as racially mixed as the city's gay bars, which is to say not very—"marginally more integrated," Will clarified.

Perhaps counterintuitively, Will said that he missed the thrill of Company's discreet doorway because it acted as "a dividing line between their world and our world." He talked about walking through the front doors as if he were entering a stage from the wings.

"You step into a really dark place but everyone else has been in the dark place," he said. "While your eyes are adjusting to the light, you can't see them, but they all turn and look at you. You can't see the audience out there, but you're a star. You'd see your people and wait to see who came in next."

More than the discretion, Will lamented the loss of intergenerational gay friendships that he fostered over dinner at places like Company and Rounds.

"You could hear people, you could talk to them," he said. "The evening had a kind of beginning, middle, and end that no other social experience has. Going from drinks to dessert, you could have many different experiences over the course of the night. You could be silly and campy and fun through the appetizers, and when the meal came, you could actually, really connect deeply with people."

Company closed around 1989.

———————

Will's observations about Company and Rounds reminded me of an essay that author David Masello once wrote for *The New York Times*, about eating at Regents and feeling that he'd entered a new phase of his gay dining-out life:

> When I looked at the tables of gay men, most in their 60's and older, people I used to dismiss as "old queens" and "over-the-top poofs," I suddenly thought of them as colleagues rather than as outcasts with whom I didn't want to be associated. This was where men who worked as garment district salesmen, Broadway costume makers, window dressers, owners of gift shops in New Hope and Provincetown, came to be with each other.

The patrons, he wrote, "were in no danger of being rejected by some cute young guy, especially in front of friends."

"They could arrive with a three-pronged cane or a bandaged forehead and not be embarrassed," he said. "This was the gay men's equivalent of an American Legion post."

Masello's words resonate with me now as I live through my early fifties. I don't turn heads when I walk into gay restaurants as I used to at Annie's and the Melrose. I feel that I'm being looked at the way I looked at gay men in their fifties when I was in my twenties; that is to say, not looked at much at all. I need to get over that and I get it: It comes with age. But so do colonoscopies and bigger bellies, and nobody says you should be thrilled with either of those.

I'm doing my best to eat at gay restaurants with no expectations other than good food and company and maybe a lingering look from a table across the way. I no longer feel the need to pretend. I can be real, not the gay bar life of the party I was, or thought I was, in my twenties.

Add being serious to the list of things you can do at a gay restaurant that you probably wouldn't do at a gay bar. Nobody wants to scream over the latest Taylor Swift remix to talk about their chemotherapy or a relative's passing or a job loss. At a gay restaurant, you can.

"You couldn't say 'I'm really depressed; my boyfriend left me' at a straight restaurant," Will said. "Your friend who's going through something difficult, you'd say, 'I'm going to take you to Company.' You'd laugh, and then you'd say: 'Tell me what's going on.'"

Though soon, and suddenly, those conversations took on degrees of gravity and meaning that nobody could have anticipated.

"It Felt Safe"

The AIDS Years

I n the fall of 1985, Peter Staley was living in New York City and working as a bond trader on Wall Street. He was closeted at work but in his personal life, he traversed Manhattan's thriving gay scene of restaurants, bars, and clubs. That year, he was diagnosed with AIDS-related complex, a death sentence at the time. So much was unknown about the new disease—how it was transmitted, who was susceptible, what treatments were hopeful, and which were quackery. Peter was terrified.

Angry and desperate to know about treatment options, Peter joined a support group run by Gay Men's Health Crisis, the organization cofounded in 1982 by Larry Kramer that worked on behalf of people with AIDS. In the group, Peter met Griffin Gold, an activist and a founding member of the People With AIDS Coalition, one of the earliest AIDS advocacy organizations. Peter asked Griffin, who was then in his late twenties, out for coffee, and Gold picked the Tiffany Diner, that same restaurant where gay men waited to be treated for giardia, an infection that was curable.

Like many gay men who frequented downtown Manhattan at the time, Griffin thought the Tiffany was "an institution," as Peter told me one sunny afternoon in August 2023 over lunch at Cafe Cluny, a chic bistro in the West Village. Peter and I were within walking distance of the Stonewall Inn and St. Vincent's, the hospital founded in 1849 by the Sisters of Charity of New York and where many New Yorkers with AIDS spent their last days. In 2011, the nine-building complex was sold and converted into residential housing. Four years later, the NYC AIDS Memorial Park at St. Vincent's Triangle was officially dedicated in a public park adjacent to the former hospital, just steps from a Starbucks Reserve and a Nordstrom, neither of which were around in the '80s.

Peter told me that eating with Griffin at the Tiffany was more than just an introduction to a new friend and a diner.

"It was a very, very scary moment for me, and it was a great place that made you feel comfortable and down to earth," he confided in me. "It was a diner and there were gay men in there talking about hard stuff that would be scary to be overheard pretty much in any other restaurant in America at that time. But we were ground zero for HIV and AIDS on the East Coast. It felt safe."

Griffin died of AIDS in 1989. He was thirty-three.

———

Acquired immunodeficiency syndrome, or AIDS, as it was eventually called, was first identified in 1981, when five cases appeared in gay men living in California. HIV, the virus that caused AIDS, was discovered in 1984, and a blood test became available a year later. A turning point in America's understanding of AIDS came in 1985, when actor Rock Hudson, royalty among Hollywood's leading men, died of AIDS at fifty-nine, just three months after he publicly revealed that he had the disease. His startling announcement and subsequent death helped put AIDS on the radar of people around the world.

As horrible as the mounting death toll was in the first decades of AIDS, people impacted by HIV/AIDS didn't stop going out, and that included to restaurants. On the contrary: Gay restaurants were where the sick and those who loved and cared for them went to have meals, trying, if possible, to eat together and laugh and flirt, for a little while, as if nothing had changed. At gay restaurants, you were as likely to hear someone ask, "Did you hear that so-and-so died?" as you were to debate which of the specials sounded the tastiest, or which of the waiters should get into porn.

To acknowledge that during the AIDS crisis gay men acted like gay men isn't to minimize the pain and fear of those dark days. Rather, as historian Allan H. Spear said about documenting African American life during Jim Crow, it is to understand "how in the face of oppression a people could adapt and survive and create a vigorous and vital culture."

During these years, gay restaurants did what they had always done: act as community centers and places of refuge. In 1989, New York City mayoral hopeful Rudy Giuliani met gay and lesbian leaders at Company to talk about recent antigay remarks he'd made about gay rights, including speaking out against gay marriage.[1] As he walked into the restaurant, he was met by a gauntlet of protesters chanting "shame." Giuliani lost the mayor's race that year to David Dinkins.

Chefs and bakers joined the fight in any way they could. Sean Strub, former editor of *POZ* magazine, remembers calling The

Little Pie Company, a New York City bakery, to see whether they would donate pies for an AIDS charity event he was helping coordinate. The person on the phone thanked him for organizing the event and told him: "Anything you need. Anything."

"He said to me, 'I don't care if it's to sell or to feed volunteers or to throw at targets at a protest,'" Strub told me. "He said that I was to call him and he would have pies available and there would never be a charge. I took advantage of that so many times."

The Little Pie Company is still making delicious Key lime and pumpkin pies at its storefront in Hell's Kitchen not far from my apartment. In 2025, it turned forty.

There was another way that meals provided comfort during the AIDS crisis: food and meal delivery services. For people with HIV/AIDS who were poor, lived alone, or were too sick to work and/or had a hard time even accessing food, a new kind of service organization delivered nutritious and medically tailored meals to people who couldn't leave home. One of the longest-running charities, God's Love We Deliver, was founded in New York City in 1986. The goal of this and other groups, including Open Hand in Chicago and Lifelong in Seattle, was to get as many calories as possible into people's bodies. As HIV eventually became more manageable, the groups' missions expanded beyond serving people with HIV/AIDS, and what they served changed as well. The meals became more focused on being nutritious and less on getting as much food into a body as it could tolerate. (Not that there aren't indulgences: On birthdays, clients of God's Love We Deliver, which is still delivering, get a small decorated cake with their name written in frosting.) Such organizations aren't gay restaurants, but like gay bars and bathhouses that serve food, they provide a vital gay restaurant purpose: to make sure that gay people (and not-gay people, too) feel less alone, thanks to a friendly hello from a visitor and a warm chicken dinner with a slice of frosted cake.

As I traveled across the country to research and conduct interviews for this book, I heard so many stories about restaurants—Annie's, for example—where having Kaposi's sarcoma lesions, needing a cane to walk, and other outward markers of being HIV positive or having AIDS in the '80s didn't stop lovers, family members, and friends from enjoying a meal together in public. Scott Frankel, the Tony Award–nominated composer of the musical *Grey Gardens*, remembers eating at Manatus with men who had just come from the nearby Village Apothecary, a pharmacy founded in 1983 as a place to fill prescriptions for early HIV medications.

"You could pick up your AZT and have a bowl of soup at Manatus," Frankel told me. The Village Apothecary is still in business at a new location.

Dining out felt like a return to normal for Damien Martin and his partner, Dr. Emery Hetrick, who in 1979 founded the Institute for the Protection of Lesbian and Gay Youth, which later became the Hetrick-Martin Institute, a school for LGBTQ+ youth in New York City. Martin remembers Hetrick ordering "a lot of food" one day at a New York City restaurant, even though his partner's appetite wouldn't accommodate such a meal.[2]

"He was so determined to live normally, he ordered food as if he could eat," Martin said in an interview with gay historian Eric Marcus.

Martin also recalled a dinner that he and Hetrick attended, when Hetrick was rail thin and had mostly stopped eating because of AIDS complications.

"He insisted on going out," Martin said. "He would cut a piece of food and put it on his fork, and then he would hold the fork up, but he wouldn't eat it, knowing that he really couldn't digest it. And I said, 'If you don't put that,' excuse my language, 'effin' piece of food in your mouth, I'm gonna take that fork and I'm gonna stab you with it.'" Hetrick and Martin died of AIDS-related complications in the late 1980s.

A watershed year for the AIDS crisis in the United States was 1987. The FDA approved AZT, the medication for AIDS. Larry Kramer helped start the activist group ACT-UP in New York City. Cleve Jones started the AIDS Memorial Quilt in San Francisco, and the quilt was displayed on the National Mall in Washington, D.C. Randy Shilts published *And the Band Played On*, his landmark early accounting of HIV/AIDS in America. Princess Diana made international headlines when she was photographed shaking the hand of an HIV-positive patient in a London hospital. Flamboyant entertainer Liberace and Tony-winning director Michael Bennett were among the celebrities who died of AIDS.

It was also the year that President Reagan, having been accused of ignoring AIDS, made a statement in April calling AIDS "public enemy number one."[3] (Reagan didn't mention AIDS until 1985; by the end of that year, about twelve thousand people with AIDS were dead.) At a restaurant on May 31, 1987, Reagan gave his second major speech on AIDS during a sold-out fund-raiser for the American Foundation for AIDS Research (AmFAR) inside a tent at a ritzy restaurant called Potomac, located riverside in Washington Harbor. The guest list included Larry Kramer, and AmFAR gave awards to Dr. C. Everett Koop, then the US surgeon general, and to Dr. Robert Gallo of the National Cancer Institute and Dr. Luc Montagnier of the Pasteur Institute in Paris. Roberta Flack and Marvin Hamlisch were the after-dinner entertainment. Dinner included veal and asparagus and a dessert of "Florentine nests" with vanilla ice cream.

In his speech, President Reagan said that he supported routine testing because "it is time we knew exactly what we are facing."[4] He quoted poet W. H. Auden—"true men of action in our times are not the politicians and statesmen but the scientists"—and insisted that he was "going to continue" talking about AIDS.

"Those of us in government can educate our citizens about the dangers," he went on. "We can encourage safe behavior. We can test to determine how widespread the virus is. We can do any number of things. But only medical science can ever truly defeat AIDS." He didn't use the words *gay* or *homosexual* once, but he did urge Americans to treat people with HIV and AIDS with "understanding, not ignorance."

Reagan's words rang hollow for the three hundred gay rights and AIDS activists who stood vigil outside the restaurant to protest the event. Some in the group were silent, but others chanted loudly enough that guests, who'd paid $250 for a seat and up to $25,000 for a table, could hear. If there was a silver lining, it was that the event raised $500,000, thanks in no small part to the presence of actress and AmFAR chairwoman Elizabeth Taylor, who had the unenviable job of calming anger inside the tent from attendees who booed Reagan, and were in no mood to give him a pass for talking about AIDS so late in the virus's deadly progress.

"I know there are some people who disagree," Taylor, a gay icon, noted after the president spoke. "That was quite clear. But I think what the president said is basically in concurrence with what we all hope and pray for: a cure for AIDS."

Also in 1987, the Centers for Disease Control and Prevention (CDC) kicked off America Responds to AIDS, a public awareness campaign about the virus that reached millions of people over the next decade with the goal of helping Americans talk honestly about AIDS with their children, friends, potential sexual partners, and neighbors.

One of the first America Responds to AIDS campaigns featured posters with portraits of racially and generationally diverse faces accompanied by copy that delivered one of three messages: everyone knows someone with AIDS; everyone may be impacted by someone who has or may get AIDS; and everyone is at risk of getting AIDS. (That last message was a fairly controversial one: Many scientists and AIDS advocates criticized it for suggesting that low-risk populations were at risk when they were not.)

Four years later, America Responds to AIDS launched a targeted campaign to debunk false assumptions about how a person can "catch" AIDS. Each poster featured a colorful illustration accompanied by a variation on the tagline "You Won't Get AIDS From." "You Won't Get AIDS From A Bug Bite" featured an oversized mosquito. "You Won't Get AIDS From Hide 'n' Seek" showed two little kids at play. "You Won't Get AIDS From A Public Pool" had a colorful beach ball glistening in the sun.

A fourth image targeted the restaurant industry and its patrons. The background was pale orange, and on the left was an illustration of a small salad in a glass plate, held aloft by the gloved hand of a white-looking server dressed in a suit jacket. Bold black typography stated: "You Won't Get AIDS In A Restaurant." Smaller print at the bottom explained that "AIDS is a virus that is not spread through day-to-day contact," and offered the toll-free number for America Responds to AIDS.

The point of the poster was to relay the message that HIV could not live outside the body, so there was no danger in using a restaurant's cups, plates, or utensils. By including an arm and hand, the image also told viewers that the virus could not be transmitted by the people making and serving food. The image used a plain-spoken but straightforward tagline to stress that dining out was not a risk—a message that ran contrary to what many Americans thought at the time. In a 1988 survey, more than one out of three American adults said that it was "very likely or somewhat likely" that a person could get AIDS by eating at a restaurant where the cook had AIDS. In one of many such instances in 1987 alone, the owners of a seafood restaurant in Hagerstown, Maryland, closed after just two months in business when rumors started circulating from customers and the restaurant's own employees that a maître d' was gay and therefore was assumed to have AIDS. Business plummeted.

"Basically, we all agreed he was gay, that he might have AIDS, that we didn't want it and he was costing us money because waitresses rely on tips," a waitress told *The Washington Post* at the time. "People don't want to be around people who are homosexual just because of AIDS."[5]

Like a lot of the government's early response to AIDS, the well-intentioned campaign arrived too late, during a terrifying time when fears about AIDS had become a disease in and of itself. Thousands of people in the United States, most of them gay men, were dead; analyses of infection rates show that men born in the 1960s were most impacted by HIV, which means those who were dying in these years were in their twenties and thirties. Misconceptions about AIDS were rampant despite repeated assertions by the scientific community and AIDS activists that HIV was transmitted only through sexual contact, contaminated needles, or other types of contact with the blood of people who already had the virus. In 1986, followers of fringe presidential candidate Lyndon LaRouche called for all people with AIDS to be quarantined, a position that many other Americans considered worthy of discussion.

The mainstream press fueled much of the misconceptions about AIDS and dining out. But it wasn't all scaremongering. A column about AIDS in *The Miami Herald* in 1983, under the headline "Where Will the Killer Disease Strike Next?" asked: "Can I get it from a restaurant waiter or from eating food prepared by a kitchen worker who might have AIDS and cut himself or herself?"[6] Citing the CDC, the magazine said the answer was no. In 1985, *New York Magazine* ran a cover story—headlined "The Final Word on Avoiding AIDS"—that asked several rhetorical questions, including: "What if the cook in your favorite restaurant has AIDS?" The answer? "Research indicates that worries of this sort are basically unwarranted." That year, the trade publication *Restaurant Business* reported that it wasn't able to put a dollar amount on revenue lost to fears over AIDS, because "the situation seems to be measured more in terms of gut feel than actual numbers."

But in many parts of the country, AIDS hysteria was pervasive in the restaurant industry. An executive vice president of the North Carolina Restaurant Association outlined the "typical strategy" for dealing with an employee who had HIV: "Pay his or her full wage in return for a promise to leave town on the next bus."[7] Members of the New Jersey Restaurant Association were advised to keep mum about AIDS rather than "overreact and needlessly plant fear in the customer's mind." The National Restaurant Association took the same approach, reminding members how important it was "that the industry does not focus attention on itself" when it comes to dealing with AIDS.[8]

In 1999, almost near the end of the virus's second decade, researchers at the University of California, Davis, asked how comfortable respondents would feel about drinking out of a washed and sterilized glass at a restaurant if someone with AIDS had drunk out of the same glass a few days earlier. They also asked about the likelihood that respondents would wear a sweater if they learned that the person who had worn it before had AIDS. Neither the sweater nor the drinking glass could possibly transmit HIV, but roughly one-fourth of respondents still said they were less likely to wear the sweater (27.1%) or drink from the glass (27.5%).[9]

The news from this time wasn't all bad: In a groundbreaking ruling in 1996, a US district judge ordered a Tulsa restaurant owner to pay damages under the Americans with Disabilities Act (ADA) for firing a gay worker whose partner had AIDS; the owner had feared that his upscale restaurant would lose business if customers found out about the employee's relationship with a partner who had the virus. The ruling was the first time an employer had been held liable under the provision of the ADA that prohibited discrimination against a qualified individual due to that person's association or relationship with a disabled individual.

Still, discrimination against those with HIV or AIDS continued. (Against those who didn't have HIV or AIDS, too: After Brian Bradley, who died of AIDS in 1995, appeared on Oprah's talk show to discuss being HIV positive, his mother and sister were fired from their jobs as truck stop waitresses.) In 1990, Rep. Jim Chapman (D-TX) introduced an amendment to the ADA that would have permitted restaurant owners and other employers to transfer workers with contagious diseases, including AIDS, to non-food-handling jobs. Despite the lack of medical evidence that AIDS could be transmitted through food handling, supporters argued that the amendment was needed to protect businesses and their employees from the public hysteria over AIDS. In introducing the amendment, Chapman stated: "The reality is that many Americans would refuse to patronize any food establishment if an employee were known to have a communicable disease. Damage to the business can be severe and . . . could cause the loss of all the jobs of the employees that work there."[10] The National Restaurant Association supported the amendment, as did the National Federation of Independent Businesses as well as other business groups representing the food services industry. The amendment passed the House on May 17, 1990.

When the amendment reached the Senate, notorious homophobe Sen. Jesse Helms (R-NC) spoke in favor of it. In his remarks, he said he had taken a "little poll" beforehand, and the answer was unanimous: nobody would eat at a restaurant where people with HIV or AIDS handled the food.[11] Not citing specifics, he noted that a popular restaurant in Milwaukee "lost almost all of its customers" after its former owner, manager, and chef all died of AIDS, and said that another "young man" told him that his parents stopped patronizing a local deli for that same reason.

"Although they do not know whether AIDS is communicable, because of the hysteria whipped up around here, they have been led to believe AIDS is everywhere," Helms continued. "Just suppose a chef in a restaurant who has AIDS or is HIV positive is chopping up a salad and he cuts his finger. Do *you* want to eat that salad?"

In response to the amendment, the disability community mobilized, and over three hundred groups and individuals, including the American Medical Association and Louis W. Sullivan, MD, then the secretary of Health and Human Services, went on the record to oppose it. The Chapman amendment was not part of the Americans with Disabilities Act when President George H. W. Bush signed the ADA into law on July 26, 1990.

By 1987, hundreds of people were packing a room at New York's Lesbian, Gay, Bisexual, and Transgender Community Center to attend ACT-UP's Monday night gatherings. The group needed a place to break bread after the meetings, which sometimes lasted hours and could be as exhausting as they were empowering.

Enter Woody's. Located a few blocks from the community center, this burger-and-fries restaurant was like a second home for ACT-UP members. After the Monday meetings, a dozen or so activists would head over to Woody's and push together tables in the back of a downstairs windowless overflow room. There, they stayed late to debate, bicker, and organize. Among the regulars were outspoken playwright Larry Kramer, who instigated ACT-UP; Maxine Wolfe, an older lesbian and longtime civil rights activist; and Peter Staley.

Both a restaurant and a bar, the gay-welcoming Woody's wasn't that crowded on Monday nights, making it the perfect space for a determined group of people with loud mouths and strong opinions. The ACT-UP folks who usually ate at Woody's—the pasta primavera and cheeseburgers with fries were the go-to dinners—were generally the group's most engaged members, the diehards who couldn't turn off their brains just because the meeting was adjourned.

"We were the ones putting in the extra hours that were willing to go until midnight on a Monday night and didn't have any place to be the next day," Peter Staley explained to me.

Peter said that those group meals at Woody's—where the famously curmudgeonly Kramer was "the happiest I'd ever seen him"—made a big difference in his life.

"Larry Kramer became the father figure, and Maxine, the mother figure, and I got to know both of them at Woody's over beer and bad food, talking gay history and ACT-UP strategy and laughing," he reminisced matter-of-factly.

Sitting across from Peter, I almost started to cry. His work on behalf of people with HIV/AIDS is immeasurable; the fact that he agreed to my lunch invitation is one of the highlights of my career as a journalist. After all, this was the young man who, along with other AIDS activists, famously infiltrated his way to the New York Stock Exchange floor on September 14, 1989, as part of ACT-UP's major protest against high prices for drugs used to treat HIV/AIDS. This was the group who chained themselves to the VIP balcony and dropped phony $100 bills onto the trading floor, disrupting the opening bell for the first time in history.

Looking at Peter's silver-daddy hair, listening to him speak in measured tones about horrible years, made him seem far more distinguished than when I first saw him in 1990 on *Donahue*, the television talk show hosted by Phil Donahue. Back then, he had a headful of brown hair and wore a big ACT-UP button on his suit.

For the entire episode, he came across as a furious and fast-talking young man fighting hard for his life and the lives of friends and strangers. I had never knowingly met someone with HIV, and I vividly remember thinking as I watched that episode that he and the other activists on the panel—Larry Kramer, Mark Harrington, Ann Northrop, and Robert Garcia—were doing something truly courageous, even though I didn't fully understand what or why. I've never met a hero, but I did that afternoon when I met Peter Staley.

Another regular at Woody's was Michelangelo Signorile. Back in the '80s, he was part of the queer club scene, working as a nightclub columnist and a PR representative feeding newspapers tidbits about Hollywood and Broadway. He remembers being at Boy Bar, an East Village gay bar, in 1987 when he got approached and encouraged to attend an ACT-UP meeting by members of the Swim Team, the nickname for a group of hot, muscled ACT-UP members dressed in the East Village gay look of the day (Doc Martens boots were a must). Michelangelo went to ACT-UP's Monday night meetings for years, and remembered them as "raucous and crazy with a lot of fighting and also a lot of celebration over victories and sadness over losses—it was an incredible roller coaster through the night." Afterward, he'd pile the tables at Woody's with press kits ready to be faxed out to the press in advance or handed out to passersby on the day of the protests.

"Restaurants were the only place where we could socialize in a larger setting and really talk about something and map things out," Michelangelo told me.

As ACT-UP's ranks grew, activists went to other restaurants in the West Village besides Woody's. Among them were Benny's Burritos, a popular Mexican spot, and across the street, the Village Den, a neighborhood diner. For ACT-UP members who lived in the East Village, dinner was often corned beef at the legendary

Katz's Deli. On weekends, the East Villagers frequented two spots on St. Mark's Place: Café Orlin for decadent eggs Florentine or, if that was too crowded, Yaffa Café for creamy hummus. Money was tight for many in ACT-UP, but that didn't stop them from pooling funds to pay for shared meals, or covering for those who couldn't pay for themselves. For those who were HIV positive, good nutrition was essential, and there was no way anyone in ACT-UP would watch someone not eat because they couldn't afford it.

Michelangelo lived in the East Village in the '80s, and remembers frequenting Veselka, the twenty-four-hour Ukrainian restaurant established in 1954 by Wolodymyr Darmochwal and his wife, Olha Darmochwal, and famous for its pierogi and borscht. Michaelangelo remembers the scene there as being "so queer," even though the restaurant didn't advertise it as such.

"We would be coexisting with the Ukrainian people and there was absolutely no interaction but no hostility at all," he recalled. "We'd be as gay as you could possibly be, and there would be tons of drag queens there because of the Pyramid Club. And you'd have the Ukrainian couple just sitting there eating their Ukrainian food."

Veselka is still doing boffo business and remains a queer-welcoming restaurant. (I'm partial to their vegetarian plate of mushroom stuffed cabbage and potato pierogi.) It's still serving Ukrainian food, only amid the Russia-Ukraine War, it's in service as a Ukrainian community hub, more so than ever.

Other than Veselka and Katz's, most of the restaurants where ACT-UP members congregated on the regular are no longer around. Benny's Burritos closed in 2022 after thirty-four years in business. In 2018, after thirty-six years, Antoni Porowski, of the Netflix series *Queer Eye*, turned the Village Den into a fast casual concept. It closed three years later. Orlin closed in 2017 after thirty-six years; Yaffa in 2014 after thirty-two.

In February 1990, ActionAIDS, a Philadelphia AIDS charity, had an idea: Ask local restaurants to commit to donate part of their proceeds to the organization on Thursday nights. The organization figured it was a win-win: The restaurants would fill dining rooms on a traditionally slow night and the customers got a dinner with purpose. The first "Dining Out for Life" took place at just a handful of restaurants, including Mom's, London Grill, L2, and Astral Plane. (All have since closed for good.) The event made about $1,500, which ActionAIDS considered a success.

Kevin Burns, who at the time had just started working as a case manager and a Volunteer Buddy at ActionAIDS, recalled that the event "ignited something" in people and at local restaurants.

"I have never met a kitchen staff that doesn't want to feed people—it's a nurturing thing," said Kevin, who retired in 2023 as the executive director of Action Wellness, which is what ActionAIDS is now called. "This was their way of using their skills as chefs and staff to give back and remember people they had lost."

Dining Out for Life eventually expanded beyond Philadelphia. According to the organization, today more than 50 local HIV service organizations partner with over 2,400 restaurants, over 4,000 volunteers, and over 300,000 diners to help raise over $4.5 million for people living with HIV/AIDS in the United States and Canada. Most participating restaurants donate 33 percent of sales, and diners are free to give more. Volunteers are stationed at every restaurant to answer questions and act as a liaison between the restaurant, customers, and the AIDS service organizations that benefit.

COVID-19 did a number on dining out, which forced the event to temporarily scale back. But scores of restaurants still participate every year across the country. In Juneau, Alaska, proceeds went to the Alaskan AIDS Assistance Association, which works with Indigenous populations. Some Southern AIDS organizations work with Dining Out for Life to create public awareness campaigns about combating stigma around AIDS, and to remind communities that HIV is still prevalent. In Tuscaloosa, Alabama, four restaurants participated and raised money for Five Horizons Health Services, which focuses on treatments for specialized populations and Hispanic/Latinx services. For many of these groups in rural areas, a Dining Out for Life event is their primary yearly fund-raiser.

Kevin, who was sixty-eight when I talked to him in 2023, said that, as a case manager in 1989, it wasn't unusual for him to attend two or three funerals a week, and his work back then was focused more on bereavement and making sure people with AIDS died with dignity. He said ActionAIDS changed its name to Action Wellness "to focus on how today people who are HIV positive can achieve wellness, and with good care and support, they can have a normal life expectancy."

"We now focus on access to care and treatment and much less around loss and grief and death and dying issues," he clarified.

Kevin doesn't miss the darkest days of the AIDS crisis, but he does miss being in a gay restaurant. "I worry sometimes that with the loss of gay restaurants, we are losing little bits of our culture," he lamented. "It was lovely to go to a gay restaurant and feel safe and taken care of."

Steve Herman remembers those dark days too. For him, they were forged at Annie's, where he's been eating regularly, as often as three times a week, since 1976. When I talked to Steve in 2021, he was in his seventies, married to his husband and retired from a government job in Washington, D.C. He told me that dining at gay restaurants during the AIDS crisis was an essential part of gay life because the people who showed up at gay restaurants during this time—patrons, cooks, servers, and delivery people—were all in some way affected by the reach of the disease.

"It was important to have a place and to be with people who were going through the same awful things you were going through," he told me. "It was comforting to have a place like Annie's to go to and be able to cry."

To look back on gay dining during the AIDS crisis is to learn about a community that persevered under horrific circumstances. It's a universe away from our Undetectable = Untransmittable era, in which bareback sex for people who take Prep or Biktarvy daily is the norm—a kind of safer sex without condoms. I hope we never again know what it's like to memorialize dead friends and loved ones week after week after week at restaurants where, just months before, we had laughed over a shared plate of steak fries.

———

I did a very stupid thing at a gay restaurant in 1995. I was twenty-four and out of the closet by then, living in Washington and interning at People for the American Way (PFAW), the liberal advocacy group started by the legendary television producer Norman Lear. I had recently gone incognito to a convention of the Christian Coalition, the right-wing organization run by Pat Robertson, to report on what they were up to—standard opposition research stuff.

And yes, I got cruised in the hallways.

Not long afterward, I went to New York to visit my friend Steven, and we had lunch one afternoon at Blue Moon, a charming Mexican café in Chelsea, not far from Big Cup. I had on the Christian Coalition "Road to Victory" T-shirt I'd bought at the convention as a joke—a sartorial choice that I thought in some darkly camp way would make people laugh, considering that the person wearing it was gay as fuck. I mean, who would wear a Christian Coalition T-shirt to an obviously gay restaurant other than a queen who thought it was funny to appropriate evil branding as gay branding? I thought it was Gen X hilarious.

But this was New York in the mid-'90s, and AIDS was killing people. As I researched every day at PFAW, the Christian right was making the lives of gay people like me miserable. I remember a man eating across from us gave me look of pure fury. He never said anything to me directly, so maybe I read too much into it. Even so, I remember thinking, as Steven and I shared chips and salsa, that maybe it hadn't been such a good idea to wear the shirt. It crossed my mind that the gay men eating there might think I was some straight asshole who was actually a member of this hate group, and that I was eating there because I didn't know it was a gay restaurant or, even worse, as a "fuck you" to gay people. To this day, I recall that man's face vividly, and with shame.

This painful memory surfaced as I perused old issues of the weekly gay rag *Homo Xtra* and came across a listing for Blue Moon. It dawned on me, all these years later, that perhaps this angry customer had just come from a funeral or memorial service for his lover, or was, himself, living with HIV or AIDS, and saw in this T-shirt an asswipe who thought gay people and people with HIV and AIDS should be quarantined.

How I wish I could go back in time and wear a different shirt. For Gen Xers like me who came of age during the tapering of the AIDS crisis, a month of mounting obituaries of our peers— gay men we danced with, cried with, ate with, fucked, loved—is unfathomable, yet for a generation of gay men, death was life. For queer people today who have health insurance and the means and resources to afford medication, HIV and AIDS are no longer inevitable death sentences.

It's a universe that I wish Mike Hippler were alive to see. In the 1980s, he wrote a weekly column in San Francisco's *Bay Area Reporter*, chronicling the city's gay politics, nightlife, personalities, and oddities. In a 1986 column called "Scanning the Obituaries," Hippler writes about the twenty-seven obituaries of gay men who died of AIDS that ran in the paper in one month alone. Of the eighteen whose ages were listed, the oldest was fifty-nine, and the youngest, twenty-eight. The men included a restaurant manager, a photographer, a tax accountant, and a pastor. They were from Massachusetts, Ohio, Arkansas, and other faraway states. The obits were written by friends and families in styles that varied from buttoned up to hog wild. A few mentioned when they arrived in San Francisco, "as if this was an event of no small importance in their lives," Hippler notes.

For people who remember the AIDS years, memories of those dark days will never fully go away. Eating at gay restaurants where they once shared meals with friends and lovers can be fraught. In 2023, in the gay newspaper the *Georgia Voice*, the life coach Cliff Bostock wrote about being shocked to walk into Atlanta's Colonnade one night and finding not a place "where all the gay boys went for their mama's homestyle cooking" in the 1970s, but rather "a house of mirrors" full of dead and nearly dead people milling before my eyes.

"There were memories of friends who had died during the AIDS epidemic, memories of a close younger friend who I last saw there during a rare visit just over four years ago," Bostock wrote. "I saw a few men walking through the room I vaguely recognized. We looked at one another, both disoriented by the change that age has brought to our appearance. I felt this gigantic existential, unnamed absence of something that could make sense of this life."

In devoting a chapter just to the AIDS years, I wanted to put into action what Mike Hippler, who died in 1991, once asked for in a column: "I want to be assured that if we—you, me, the people around us—must die, we will not die unnoticed."

"What is said may be incomplete, awkward, or inadequate, but it must be said," he continued. "Even if the official notices of our deaths evoke no more than a relieved sigh from those who did not know us, we must not simply disappear."

13

The Lifeline

Florent, New York City

I met Florent Morellet in 2023 at Café Katja, an Austrian-inspired restaurant on New York's Lower East Side. I had interviewed him before on the phone but, honestly, I wanted to see what this gay restaurant maverick was like in person. I noticed him as soon as I walked in. He wore a gray sweater that handsomely accentuated his silver hair and his blue-gray eyes. He was at a table by himself, with a glass of wine. I waved, and he stood up to give me a big hug, beaming.

A few minutes later, we were joined by Darinka Novitovic Chase, whose husband, Andrew Chase, is the chef-owner at Café

Katja. Darinka worked at Florent as a hostess and in other jobs, for twenty-two years, with breaks in between for grad school and a year in France. Her hair was effortlessly collected in a tidy updo and her eyes shone from behind librarian-chic glasses—a look that still gets her noticed on the street by FOFs: Friends of Florent.

Darinka remembered being in New York for only a year when she first walked into Florent and was hired on the spot. There was only one dress code: no black (too severe). As much as she loved working at Florent, she didn't miss the '90s, as AIDS hit the city hard. She didn't miss the yuppies who started to come into the restaurant once word got out that it was one of *the* downtown restaurants. She missed what it meant back then to party.

"The joy of going out was not knowing who you were going to meet," she shared with me. "You'd get dressed up, hope for the best and look your best and go out and see who's where. You're not texting ten people, saying, 'Who's there?'"

I started to ask Florent about his own memories of his game-changing restaurant that I and many other gay folks considered to be *the* New York City gay restaurant of the 1990s. But I quickly learned that the present, not the past, was where he now lived. Closing the restaurant, he said, was a blessing.

"We went gangbusters for twenty-three years," he reminisced fondly in his still-French-accented English. "But New York already had shifted and transformed. I used to say Florent was the light in the middle of darkness. We had become the darkness in the middle of light."

Mixing French finesse with an American diner sensibility, Florent opened in 1985 at 69 Gansevoort Street along the rocky cobblestones of New York's historic Meatpacking District. It drew a fabulous mix of art scene groupies, queer club kids, leathermen, straight moms, and actual meatpacking workers, back when carcass blood still ran down the gutters. For many gay men, Florent was on the way to and from nearby and notorious sex clubs, such as J's Hangout, where circle jerks were among the draws. During the height of the AIDS crisis, Florent was one of many restaurants that became sanctuary-chapels. It was also just a really lovely bistro, where you could sit at the counter with a glass of merlot, an endive salad, and chicken roulade, and spend an afternoon reading the *New York Observer* and flirting with waiters. In 1986, *The New York Times* dubbed Florent "one of the hottest spots in town."

"It was what New York was supposed to be, but no longer is," fashion designer Isaac Mizrahi, a Florent regular, explained to *New York* in 2008, sounding like me in 2024. "I used to go there in between bars, when I was out with my friends, doing drugs and cruising. Then I'd end up at Florent the next day for a serious lunch meeting and all the same people were there, kind of smiling in secret."[1]

Michelangelo Signorile told me that Florent was an essential restaurant in his universe, too, where gay fashion designers, such as Jean Paul Gaultier, and outrageously dressed party people known as club kids—including Michael Alig, James St. James, and a young RuPaul—reigned over New York City nightlife. Florent was where people gossiped about who was dating or fucking whom—usually over a plate of the restaurant's signature pommes frites.

"If you came from a big party and it was a big scene, you went to Florent because the scene kept going," Michelangelo said.

From its first day, there was no question that Florent was a gay destination restaurant. The clientele at Florent fluctuated, depending on the hour. At lunchtime, the restaurant was generally straight: gallerists, academics, writers, stay-at-home moms. Meatcutters ate steaks there after finishing shifts at the nearby processing plants and butcher shops that traced their roots to the 1800s.

Fashion designer Diane von Fürstenberg, who lived within blocks of Florent for a decade, said the restaurant and its food were "the reason people started coming to the neighborhood."[2] The Bastille Day parties, when Florent would dress like Marie Antoinette, were musts for many gay men.

The restaurant was especially a draw for New Yorkers who lived in Chelsea to the north, or the West Village to the south. In the late afternoon, early birds took advantage of Florent's reasonably priced and delicious—much better than most gay restaurants—French-forward dishes, such as a salty, nutty-sweet onion soup gratinée; garlicky *moules marinières*; and a moist, fatty blood sausage. The food came out of the kitchen fast, served by a queer-heavy staff that included artist-choreographer Richard Move and novelist Vestal McIntyre.[3]

"Lunch was a little bit more boring," Florent said. "The great thing is that it wasn't just one crowd, like most restaurants. It was a changing crowd."

Buzz from favorable press and word of mouth soon turned the restaurant into a celebrity magnet. At almost any time of day, it wouldn't be a shock to encounter Diana Ross, Bette Midler, Calvin Klein, or Amy Winehouse enjoying a meal. Pop artist Roy Lichtenstein ate there every day, always in the same back corner seat and often with a dish of the vegetarian couscous. (Dorothy Lichtenstein, the artist's widow, once said: "We thought, after a while, maybe we don't need a kitchen in our house because Florent served breakfast, lunch, dinner and midnight snacks.")[4] Director Pedro Almodóvar once called up on a Saturday night and asked for and received a reservation for ten people. Clubgoers scarfed down burgers on the way to and from the nearby nightclub Mars, where I used to watch RuPaul work the go-go boxes. Even Carrie Bradshaw, Sarah Jessica Parker's character on *Sex and the City*, dined there—a major step in the turn of the Meatpacking District into a playground for the rich and the first small step that eventually led to the restaurant's closure. The restaurant had become so renowned that in 2015, Showtime announced that it was developing a half-hour dark comedy called *Florent*, starring Alan Cumming, but that never came to pass.

Florent's design director was Tibor Kalman, a Hungarian-born graphic artist whose chic interior touches included blood-red banquettes, a wall of framed maps, and an elongated counter that was often covered in a gingham tablecloth. A neon sign illuminated the word "Florent" in bright pink. Kalman also designed the menu. Its chic typography and clean styling looked as if it were airmailed straight from a Parisian bistro. One of his menus is in the collection of the Museum of Modern Art.

Sex wasn't, strictly speaking, on the Florent menu—but it was there. When it opened in 1985, the Meatpacking District was a gay sexual playground of abandoned industrial spaces among the working butcher shops, which became subterranean sex clubs where casual, anonymous, and eagerly nonvanilla sex was the norm. Traditionally outré sex acts that would make Times Square porn theater patrons blush were available almost every night of the week. Sex workers shared plates piled high with frites between assignations that they secured on the streets outside Florent's front door. Before it was Florent, 69 Gansevoort Street was home to the R & L Restaurant, a diner that opened in 1938 and that patrons of the notorious gay sex clubs the Anvil and Mineshaft, including Morellet himself, frequented until it closed in 1984.

As midnight turned to morning, the crowd at Florent reflected the raunchier corners of gay nightlife. It wasn't uncommon for groups of frisky gay kinksters to enjoy a razor-thin chicken paillard and a glass of velvety house merlot. There were tables filled with leathermen dressed in harnesses and jockstraps, the de rigueur look for entry to the Anvil. As morning approached and the leathermen left, the Florent customer cycle began again.

I went to Florent a few times, most often after dancing my ass off at Mars. I got there around four a.m. one night with my college friend Tatiana, a gorgeous gal with saucer-shaped eyes and curly black hair, who on this night had on tight blue jeans and a crimson red bandeau top, a combination that turned heads when we walked into the restaurant. I had on a blousy disco shirt, burnt-orange bell bottoms, ivory platform heels, and a blond wig worn backward to make it look like a shag. I carried a metal lunchbox—I think it was a Charlie Brown one—which at the time was clubland's must-have accessory. (Mine was empty and purely for show. Others used it for makeup and drugs.) The place was packed and there was a wait, of course. We eventually got a table for two next to a table where sat a pair of gay boys with bleached-blond bobs. One of them had on a leather vest over the hairiest chest that my nineteen-year-old eyes had ever seen. Tatiana and I could barely hear each other over the din of drunk drag queens and preening muscle boys, but we didn't care because we were at Florent. We shared a plate of frites, plus a Diet Coke, to save money. After we paid our bill, I put her in a cab, then I stumbled back to my dorm and slept until noon.

Florent wasn't the only buzzed-about restaurant in the Meatpacking District during this time, but it was the gayest. Keith McNally's Pastis opened in 1999, fourteen years after Florent, and as of this writing, is still in business. While it attracted a cross-section of New York, it didn't have the queer sensibility or the camp joie de vivre that Florent did; its patrons tended to be finance kings, not drag queens.

It also didn't have Florent himself, who was ever-present at his restaurant, seating regulars, smooching celebrities, and welcoming the curious to a playground that was theirs as much as his. Then and still now, he has hospitality in his bones. He looks you in the eye with a smile that says you are the most important person in the world right at this moment. He's quick to laugh and he's eager to ask you questions about your life. Not to sound clichéd about it, but when you're with him, his joie de vivre washes over you.

———

The son of a conceptual artist father and an accomplished cook mother, Florent grew up in a household that encouraged him to explore his artistic interests. He came out as a teenager, and enjoyed the gay scene when he moved to London for college. When he moved to New York City in the late 1970s, his worldly sensibility fit in nicely with New York's underground gay scene. He never came out in New York because there wasn't much of a closet to emerge from.

Florent learned that he was HIV positive in 1987. "Everybody was dying around me, so I became the cheerleader to keep everybody upbeat," he reflected. When he told his mother, who at the time was living in France, she encouraged him to keep his status quiet, even though she knew her son lived his life as an open book. "It could be really damaging to your business," he said she warned him. He called her the next day and told her that it was too important for him to be out about being positive, knowing that many patrons of his restaurant were themselves newly diagnosed and battling opportunistic infections and mental health issues. Some didn't have long to live. Others were afraid to get tested. "So, here I was, somebody who was the most visible queen in the city, who had the guts to just say I was positive," he explained.

His positive diagnosis came during a citywide crackdown on gay sex venues, many of which were just steps away from Florent. When the restaurant opened, the Meatpacking District was a terra incognita, even though it was a close walk from a subway stop at Eighth Avenue and 14th Street. Crime was rampant, drug dealing was pervasive, and the area was widely known as a pickup spot for prostitutes. The crackdown threatened to cut into the foot traffic that Florent relied on during late-night hours, when it was one of the few restaurants with the lights on and serving alcohol-soaking meals.

In 1985, the year Florent opened, New York City shut down the Mineshaft after a lengthy court battle that reached the New York State Supreme Court. From 1976 to 1985, the Mineshaft was a notorious members-only gay sex club at 835 Washington Street in the West Village, where "macho" attire like leather and Levis were required (no preppy stuff) and a bathtub was a sexual appliance. ("I went once and remember that as you walked, the carpet squished," nightlife journalist Michael Musto recalled.)[5]

State authorities issued emergency regulations allowing local officials to close any "homosexual" places where "high-risk sexual activities" such as anal sex took place.[6] The New York Civil Liberties Union argued otherwise, alleging that the governor and mayor "have taken us down a slippery slope that may lead to re-criminalization of private sexual conduct in general."[7] The bathhouses closed, but gay men still met for anonymous sex, including at bars, clubs, private sex parties, and their own homes.

Not long after his diagnosis, Florent surreptitiously did something small but consequential that turned his restaurant into a sanctum for his HIV-positive customers: he started posting his recent T-cell counts, numbers that reflect how many disease-fighting white blood cells there are in the body. He wrote them—a healthy 699 one day, a red-flag 235 on another—at the bottom of repurposed menu boards that faced the dining room. It was required viewing for those in the know.

"I have met many times people who said, 'Florent, you don't know me, but at that time I was positive and in the closet and didn't tell anybody,'" said Florent. "They said, 'When I came to your restaurant where you put your T-cell numbers on the board, I felt everything was okay.'"

In 2004, *POZ*, a free magazine about living with HIV/AIDS, was celebrating its tenth anniversary. Sean Strub, the magazine's editor, wanted to mark the occasion in a special way. He and his staff approached photographer Spencer Tunick. Since the early 1990s, Tunick had made a name for himself in the art world by shooting large groups of naked bodies posed in global public spaces. People stood, squatted, curled up, and almost always stared unsmiling at the camera. The result was a wave of human flesh set against a natural setting or a city landmark; Tunick's locations included a glacier in Switzerland, the Sydney Opera House, Central Park. (Tunick was arrested in 1999 when he tried to take a photo of naked people in Times Square, but the charges were later dropped.)

Strub and his staff reached out to Tunick with an idea: What if he photographed people with HIV and AIDS inside Florent? Was it an organizational nightmare? Probably. But for Strub, it was a risk worth taking.

"I started thinking about how when the magazine first came out, people said: 'What's the face of the epidemic?'" Strub told me. "I thought, 'Okay, why not show the whole body?'"

Strub recalled that Tunick almost immediately agreed to participate, and to waive his fee. *POZ* quickly put out invitations advertising the shoot and asking for people to "Pose nude with *POZ*."

That's how at seven thirty a.m. on Saturday, March 13, 2004, Florent became immortalized in a work of art. About one hundred people lined up outside the restaurant that chilly morning, looking alternately apprehensive and thrilled to be part of such a revealing and public photo.

"It was a lesson in the mechanics of how privilege affects one's ability and comfort in disclosing their HIV status," Strub said. "For people who were self-employed or unemployed and on disability it was easier for them to be public, more so than others who had jobs and were not as public about being positive."

Once people got into the restaurant, they shed their clothes and stood around naked, unclear about where to go or what to do. Other participants were nervous about showing parts of their bodies, including distended bellies and evidence of lipodystrophy, a buildup of body fat that was a side effect of early medications that were used to treat HIV/AIDS. But as Tunick addressed the nudes assembled—including Florent Morellet, himself—any apprehension they may have felt started to wane. During the setup, Tunick asked that those who were not HIV-positive step aside so that only those with the virus were in the picture. He then told people to lie on the floor, lounge on the banquette, or grab a seat at the counter, and snuggle up to complete strangers. He instructed them not to smile. His camera clicked again and again and again as the sea of naked people stared into the lens. About ninety minutes and several poses later, the photo shoot was over, and people started eating scrambled eggs at the same seats where they had just been naked, before dispersing.

The cover that ran was dramatic. It was a gatefold, so it opened up to reveal a spread of naked bodies of different genders, sizes, ages, and colors. Everyone's eyes are trained on the viewer, and nobody is smiling. The photo—flush with bellies and breasts—comes across as defiant and proud but also angry and fearful. There's no mistaking that what you're looking at was photographed inside a diner-style restaurant. Several people are on seats against the long counter, others stand on the banquette, and a few pose behind the counter not far from a coffeemaker.

The *POZ* logo is in the magazine's upper left-hand corner, and right there is Florent's menu board listing that day's specials and, of course, his T-cell count. Strub said there were some distributors who didn't want to put the issue on newsstands "because anything that showed people with HIV could be construed in a sexual context, and we'd get trash for that." But, he said, "most people loved it." For the people in the photo, that day was an act of rebellion and liberation.

"I was nervous, tired, hungry, and worried about how my penis would look in the cold," one man told *POZ*. "Got to Florent, had a cup of coffee, and then I was ready to get naked. The incredible sense of solidarity was overwhelming. Lying in a stranger's arms, naked, made me feel so close to what humanity is all about. Male, female, gay and straight—this was something I'll remember." To see for yourself what that day was like, the events were captured in the documentary short film *Positively Naked*, available on YouTube.

Florent the man has always loved holidays, pomp, shock. In 2006, he was one of the marshals of New York City's Pride Parade. But his rambunctious spirit began to fade under the mayorships of Rudy Giuliani and Michael Bloomberg, as New York City began reconsidering the Meatpacking District as a neighborhood for sweaty gay sex venues and a buzzy French diner. Instead, real estate developers, aided by friends at city hall, wanted to turn the area into a hot spot for monied shoppers, diners, and tourists.

As they did with Times Square, these two administrations—despite fierce opposition from residents, small business owners, and nightlife advocates—decided it was time to clean house downtown. With the help of developers eager to get their hands on prime real estate, the city began in earnest to unsex the Meatpacking District in 2003. That's when the Greenwich Village Society for Historic Preservation and the New York State Parks, Recreation, and Preservation Department helped get the historic Gansevoort Market, a massive open-air farmers' market that had opened in 1884 on the site of the former Fort Gansevoort, listed as a New York City landmark.

Not long afterward, the boarded-up storefronts that Florent patrons once passed became stores again. McQueen, McCartney, and von Fürstenberg were in. Kink and clubs were out.

By 2008, after twenty-three years, Florent closed his restaurant, citing a changing neighborhood, financial concerns, and his own fatigue.

Today, the Meatpacking District is pricey, clean, and soulless, showing almost no signs of the raunchy gay destination it was under Florent's reign. In 2009, the High Line opened as a snaking elevated park above the district's narrow streets, quickly becoming a huge international draw for locals and tourists alike. Six years later, the Whitney Museum christened a new building near the waterfront.

Florent now lives in Bushwick, because he got tired of people from his generation complaining that New York City isn't what it used to be.

"So, I moved to a neighborhood where people were excited to be in New York, like it was when I moved here in 1978," he told me. He loves to go dancing. He misses his husband, Daniel Platten, who died of AIDS in 1994.

For many gay people, the Meatpacking District will never be about pricy clothes or exclusive bars but about something far more important, and eternal: a man named Florent, and how he impacted his community as a plague fell upon his city.

14

The Trendsetter

Lucky Cheng's, New York City

On May 1, 2000, if you were a monied New Yorker with even a whiff of progressive politics, you told your driver to take you to the then-recherché East Village to be dropped off at Lucky Cheng's, the Asian-inspired restaurant that at the time was one of the city's hottest dining destinations. The occasion was Ivana Trump's benefit for LIFEbeat, a music industry–led AIDS charity. The partygoers were the city's gay and gay-friendly elite: Wall Street wives, supermodels, trust fund babies, fashion designers, playgirl social climbers.

Ivana Trump, herself, held court at a banquette covered in crimson red damask that suggested it had been repurposed from an 1890s brothel—the perfect seating for the dining dilettantes who flocked to Lucky Cheng's. She tucked her blond hair into her signature updo, and she had on a string of pearls that coiled tightly around her neck. She wore a 1940s loungewear–inspired strapless bodysuit with a leggy sheer sarong skirt and a bell-sleeved peignoir in a matching white-and-blue print that recalled East Asian ceramics. Designer Marc Bouwer, a favorite of New York society, was the man behind both the outfit she wore and the miniature one on the sixteen-inch Ivana Trump Madame Alexander doll that was ceremoniously unveiled at the party.

Among the stunning photographs taken that night were snapshots of the It models Veronica Webb and May Andersen looking soignée, and a great shot of Ivana Trump smooching Italian aristocrat Roffredo Gaetani d'Aragona, her playboy companion at the time. Trump's then-nineteen-year-old daughter Ivanka was there, too, dressed in a white athletic tank top and matching wide-legged sailor slacks overlaid with a sheer sarong in saffron-colored chiffon, as if she'd just come from the beaches of Goa. Lucky Cheng's saw to it that Ivana Trump was personally attended to by its hostess Miss Understood, a prevailing drag queen–club kid known for her repertoire of colorful and towering beehive wigs. Downtown photographer Patrick McMullen photographed Miss Understood, here in a neon pink wig, sitting with Ivana Trump and d'Aragona and wearing a brightly colored floral print dress that looked as if it came fresh off a video shoot for Deee-Lite, the '60s-inspired band that *everybody* was dancing to in the gay clubs.

Tora Dress was there too. An original employee of Lucky Cheng's when the restaurant opened in 1993, Tora remembered Ivana Trump as being gracious and magnanimous during her visits to the restaurant, everything Ivana's celebrity ex-husband, Donald J. Trump, was not. (I couldn't find evidence that Trump, himself, went to Lucky Cheng's, but I'm doubtful drag queens and transgender servers would have been high on his list of people to meet and be photographed with, then or now.) It turns out that Ivana and her ex-husband did have something in common: A gift for ostentatiousness girded by thrift.

"She would take something off and give it to you," Tora told me. "Of course, we later found out they were costume jewelry from her jewelry collection."

The "we" Tora referred to included her former coworkers at Lucky Cheng's, which when it opened was an unusual, almost radical concept in the restaurant industry, even by New York City standards. It was a California-Asian fusion restaurant with a staff made up almost entirely of Asian drag queens and Asian transgender women who worked in drag contexts. When I met Tora one Sunday afternoon in 2023, she was still working at Lucky Cheng's in managerial roles (scheduling staff, handling customer inquiries) and also acting as the restaurant's unofficial historian. Hair to toe in black, Tora welcomed me warmly and offered me a cocktail that I declined. Throughout our conversation, she spoke to me in a "we're-glad-you're-here" tone that sounded authentic only because Tora had worked for decades in hospitality. (She gave her age as "between twenty-one and death.") That day, I also met Josephine Jason, whose late mother opened the restaurant. Josephine was then twenty-eight and was dressed in a chic black jacket, blue blouse, and black pants, her dark blond hair falling across her face like a silk curtain.

I listened intently as Tora and Josephine told me about the long and wild history of Lucky Cheng's, which joins Annie's and Bloodroot as an American legacy gay restaurant. It officially opened on October 1, 1993, in a building with a noteworthy gay past of its own: A former tenement on First Avenue near 2nd Street, the building operated from 1971 to 1983 as Club Baths, part of a national chain of gay-owned bathhouses. A 1978 ad in

the gay porn magazine *Mandate* plugged the East Village location as the largest gay bathhouse in New York, boasting "seven
levels of pleasure" that included a glass-roofed dome, a labyrinthine maze, and mirrors galore. Like many American bathhouses
in the 1970s (and still), it was open twenty-four hours every day
of the year, and offered patrons, many of whom were regulars,
sex and camaraderie. You could sometimes get a hot meal there,
too: On Christmas, like Flex, it served a Christmas Day buffet
with turkey and trimmings.

Director Christopher Larkin was so taken by the Club Baths
that he filmed a scene there for his groundbreaking 1974 gay
erotic drama *A Very Natural Thing*, about the troubled relationship between David (Robert McLane), a schoolteacher and former monk, and Mark (Curt Gareth), his lover. At one point in the
film, Mark and David break up, and Mark decides to go to a bathhouse. Mark wears a white towel around his trim waist, walking
the halls of the darkened space where men recline in rooms, waiting for an assignation. He then moves to the steam room, where
he does poppers and has group sex, as an eerie score suggests that
he's entered some kind of demented funhouse.

New York City closed its bathhouses in the early years of AIDS,
but the sunken pool and sex-at-every-turn maze that made Club
Baths a go-to fuck den didn't go to waste. In 1986, Wall Street
attorney Hayne Suthon and her old-money family—blue bloods
from Louisiana—bought the building for $2.9 million and turned
it into a Roman-themed restaurant called Cave Canem, Latin for
"beware of the dog." Dubbing the restaurant the "Manhattan
Satyricon," *The Los Angeles Times* reported that its chef, Tom
Gamache, studied Roman cooking and consulted food historian
Rudolf Grewe about what to put on the menu. Diners feasted on
sausages made with lobster and mussels, and a pâté of ground
veal and calves' brains. The *Times* described one dish as more like
a work of performance art than an entrée: "A whole roast lamb

arrives on a huge tray surrounded by candles. When it is cut, a flock of doves comes flying out through the flames."[1]

Cave Canem became a hot spot for yuppie New Yorkers who were enticed by its Latinate menu, buzzy vibe, and architectural oddities, including a koi pond that in the venue's Club Baths days had been a sunken Jacuzzi for gay orgies. Among the photos that Josephine showed me was a snapshot of her mother, topless and wet, cavorting in the Jacuzzi with the notorious club kid Michael Alig. (He served seventeen years in jail for murdering and dismembering fellow club kid Andre "Angel" Melendez before dying of a heroin overdose in 2020 at fifty-four.)

By 1993, it was time for a change, and Suthon—a downtown social butterfly who had become something of a black sheep in her family—went in a different direction when she had the space renovated to make way for Lucky Cheng's. The restaurant opened in New York around the time that Alice Waters, Wolfgang Puck, and other chefs helped introduce California-inspired cuisine—locally sourced, vegetable-focused, ostensibly healthy—as a national dining trend. Lucky Cheng's first executive chef was Chris Genoversa, who cut his teeth as a sous chef at China Grill, a popular and pricy Asian fusion restaurant, located in the CBS Building in Manhattan, which was part of Jeffrey Chodorow's restaurant empire. (It closed down in 2017 after a twenty-nine-year run.) Lucky Cheng's pan-Asian menu was a cheaper variation of the China Grill menu. It reflected California cool; one of its most popular dishes was Ecstasy Shrimp, named, Tora told me, because it came with noodles "that were soft and luscious and sexual on the plate—it was so delicious it made you feel ecstasy." Other beloved dishes included a duck confit, a Japanese-spiced sirloin steak with wasabi mashed potatoes, and the Chinese-spiced chicken salad.

Lucky Cheng's was named after the co-owner Mi Ching Cheng, a New Yorker and Chinese native who worked as a busboy in dozens of restaurants across New York City before Suthon hired him.

(Over Lucky Cheng's front door hung a three-dimensional sign in the shape of a Chinese takeout container, complete with a wire carrying handle.) Cheng's family members eventually also worked at Lucky Cheng's as barbacks, bartenders, and accountants. Mr. Cheng, as Tora referred to him, always wore a three-piece suit to work, and "in his broken English and with a heavy accent," said Tora, asked guests what they were celebrating so the staff could make sure the birthday boy or bachelorette was treated like royalty.

Julie Li, one of Mr. Cheng's four children and a mom of young twins, told me she had many memories as a little girl of walking to Lucky Cheng's from her family's home on the Lower East Side. She used to hang out there while her father worked; the servers treated her like one of their own children.

"I was friends with all the drag queens," she said over the phone from her home in Rochester, New York, her voice flavored with notes of nostalgia and rediscovery. "They would be in the girls' bathroom and I would be a little uncomfortable. But I was in elementary school!"

Julie said the staff encouraged her to "feel grown up," like the time a drag queen handed her a glass of cranberry-and-orange juice and told her it was a Bloody Mary. As much as she enjoyed spending time with drag queens, Julie preferred to hang around Josephine's mother.

"She was really good with kids, more than my dad," Julie explained. "My dad was more strict. If I'd do anything wrong, he'd beat me up. Hayne was the opposite, which is why I liked being with her. She was more carefree. My dad was on the crazy side." Her father died of a heart attack in August 2015 at age sixty-six.

Suthon got the idea to staff her original restaurant entirely with Asian drag queens and trans women after learning that Mei-Ling, the first girl she hired to work there, was—to Suthon's surprise—a trans woman. Mei-Ling was Singaporean and previously worked at the famed Jing Fong, a dim sum restaurant in Chinatown, where she met Cheng. Many of the first and second waves of staff members at Lucky Cheng's originally came from Singapore, but many also came from Malaysia, the Philippines, and Indonesia.

Mei-Ling was tasked with finding staff, and they had to fit a certain look. All the girls who were originally hired at Lucky Cheng's, said Tora, "had to be pretty, and pass muster." To staff a restaurant with Asian transgender women and drag queens was "mind-blowing at the time," recalled Tora, who is Chinese American.

"In Asian culture when you give birth to a son you expect him to get married and have kids, so to be trans was a big mind-fuck," she said. "The owners at the time pounced on that, and let Mei-Ling bring in a staff of Asian drag queens and trans performers with backgrounds in the food industry."

In Lucky Cheng's early days, the women who worked the dining room didn't put on shows or lip-synch to hits of the day—standard entertainment at drag brunch or dinners today. Instead, they focused on service and socialized with guests, asking who was celebrating a special event, or sassily poking fun at the straight men dragged there by their girlfriends. Most of Lucky Cheng's original staff were performers who worked in New York's Asian gay clubs—Star Sapphire, Pegasus, the Web—so, at Lucky Cheng's, they knew how to entertain as well as serve food.

Every section at Lucky Cheng's had its own drag queen server who catered to diners' needs. On nights when straight customers outnumbered gay ones, Lucky Cheng's was queered less by who was eating there than by who was working there.

"People came to see the oddity of it all because Asian drag was so rare, like a unicorn, back then," Tora explained.

In the late '90s, Lucky Cheng's started offering drag numbers as entertainment, and it wasn't the only restaurant in the East

Village that looked to drag to reel in customers. Stingy Lulu's, a 1950s-style luncheonette, had an all-drag wait staff who doubled as performers. After it opened in 1992, it didn't take long for Stingy Lulu's to become a favorite with bachelorette parties—an early sign of how such parties would become standard at restaurant drag shows. For staff at Lucky Cheng's and Stingy Lulu's, these parties could be lucrative, as long as the bachelorettes and their friends tipped well. For customers, such shows were exciting and daring; for straight people, going to one was a sign that you were cool with queer people, a precursor to virtue signaling, I suppose.

But the shows had their downsides. Before marriage equality, having a bachelorette party at a gay venue was to me and many other gay people a sign of disrespect, a way to shove marriage privilege down the throats of a community that didn't have the same right. The increasing embrace of drag at restaurants was also an ominous sign, to some, that drag was becoming less of a gay art form and more of a mainstream commodification of gay entertainment. That said, the formula stuck. Stingy Lulu's lasted more than a decade. Lucky Cheng's is still in business.

Tora said initially she wasn't interested in working at Lucky Cheng's because she already had a good day job as a buyer and designer at a SoHo bead store.

"My family told me, 'You are here in America. You don't want to work in a restaurant. That's what our ancestors did,'" she explained. The restaurant's potential clientele gave her pause too. "There was this connotation of the exotic Asian girl, and who would want to see them but dirty old men. That's the imagery I had."

She wasn't alone. Danielle, a Taiwanese server, told *The New Yorker* in 1994 that as an artist, she was influenced by "Asian sci-fi movies, where the women are goddesses dressed in futuristic fantasy." She added that at Lucky Cheng's, "we're trying to get away from the image of the China Doll. It's so stereotypical."[2]

When the bead store that Tora worked at closed, she decided to take the plunge and start working at Lucky Cheng's. In its first year, most of the clientele were local artists, writers, performers, bohemians, and gay men who could afford the restaurant's higher-than-most-gay-restaurants price point. Volunteers with Gay Men's Health Crisis dropped by with big canisters of condoms that the women gave away as they made their rounds every night.

"Back in the '90s, it was all about ACT-UP, and everyone in the East Village gay scene was dressed up in berets and army fatigues," Tora said.

Word of mouth got louder, and after about a year, Lucky Cheng's started to attract not just locals but celebrities and other wealthy New Yorkers or businessmen with fat expense accounts who wanted to slum downtown for a night before going back home to the Upper East Side. That was also the year that Prince Albert of Monaco asked for two Asian drag queens specifically to serve his table, and the restaurant became an overnight sensation.

In her 1994 review in *New York* magazine, legendary restaurant critic Gael Greene seemed pleasantly surprised by how much fun she was having at Lucky Cheng's. She spotlighted an impromptu game of balloon volleyball that broke out, and gave props to the "wait-waif" staff, including her "gem" of a server, Emerald. Greene had mixed feelings about the food, though. The shrimp wore "tough tempura girdles." The "amazingly luscious beef" was served in "a dark sweet-and-salty puddle with a fiery afterburn."

Over the years, Lucky Cheng's servers brushed elbows with a who's-who of celebrities, including Joan Rivers, Madonna, Mick Jagger, Luther Vandross, Boy George, Lenny Kravitz, and Britney

Spears. (Tora said Grace Jones caused a "big hoo-ha" when she refused to leave a customary tip, declaring: "I'm from Europe. We don't tip.") In 1998, the restaurant's notoriety reached a pop culture climax when Carrie, Samantha, and Charlotte celebrated Miranda's birthday there in the first episode of *Sex and the City*, sort of: The scene was filmed at Lucky Cheng's but the restaurant was not mentioned by name; Miss Understood was among the queens who brought Miranda's cake to the table and sang her "Happy Birthday"—an early example of straight women co-opting a gay restaurant, although the restaurant, and its eager-to-work employees, likely didn't mind. A handful of former Lucky Cheng's employees went on to hit it big, including Laverne Cox and *RuPaul's Drag Race* stars Bob the Drag Queen and Thorgy Thor.

The novelty of a staff comprised entirely of all-Asian drag and transgender servers and entertainers eventually wore off, and by 2000, when Ivana Trump hosted her LIFEbeat benefit, Lucky Cheng's had already started to become less and less of a genuine cutting-edge culinary hot spot. Despite its early fine dining aspirations, Lucky Cheng's eventually became known less for its food and more for its entertainment, including crowd-pleasing "drag boxes," as its lap dances were known.

"You don't come to Lucky Cheng's to eat gourmet food," drag server Dirty said in 2007. "You come to see some bitch in a G-string acting crazy at your table."[3]

Citing dwindling tourist traffic, Suthon left the East Village in 2012 and moved Lucky Cheng's to Midtown Manhattan.

"The phone used to ring off the hook, but as Times Square became a magnet for tourists—we just can't get them down here," Suthon said at the time. "We've tried backflips, standing on our heads; they want to stay up there now."[4]

Its new home at 240 West 52nd Street, next to the Neil Simon Theatre, turned out to be a lucrative move, luring tourists and bachelorette and birthday parties willing to spend money—"our demographic," as Suthon put it.[5]

However, just two years later, the restaurant was dealt a major blow, when Suthon died after a battle with breast cancer. Her ex-husband and Josephine, who was twenty at the time, took over the restaurant. "I was grieving and I needed something to hold on to that was hers," Josephine told me. (Suthon and her ex had divorced in 2000.)

Josephine remembers her mother being inseparable from her businesses, and from her daughter. "I saw her as my mom, but she also belonged to the community." She also noted that her mother, an accomplished pianist, got bored easily, and was always looking for a personal project to work on, a yearning that translated to her embrace of Lucky Cheng's until her death.

"My dad jokes that my mom would make problems just to solve them," she smiled. "She kind of thrived on chaos, and I think that's why I'm so orderly now. I needed a break from it."

Tora remembers Suthon as a rebel. "I met her back in the club scene days when she was more of this wild, crazy—no offense—drunken bitch who was always running around with a bottle of wine or Champagne," she explained. "I was still straitlaced but I liked her because she was unconventional. She and I clicked."

Suthon also had a knack for good PR. "She wouldn't take any drama personally," Josephine told me. "She would just use it to fuel her business. If people were talking about her, if there was a bad review, she would be like, 'Perfect.'"

At no time was that more evident than in 1999, when Suthon agreed to appear on the television reality show *The People's Court*. Lucky Cheng's made headlines early that year when it got into a legal fight with La Maison de Sade, an S&M-themed bar on West 23rd Street near Seventh Avenue opened by the one-and-only Mr. Cheng, the eponymous former Lucky Cheng's cofounder.[6]

"It was one of those restaurants where the customer gets beat up," Julie said. "My parents would never let me be there at night because that's where the action was. When I went into the restaurant, I saw whips and doggie bowls. I thought, *Are they taming an animal?*"

Suthon accused the bar of stealing $2,574 worth of plastic molds that Lucky Cheng's used to make the $39 chocolate high heels in which it served mousse. She also claimed that Cheng "conspired to use one of her kitchen employees to steal the patent-pending shoe mold and then began serving counterfeit shoes in his establishment."[7]

"Mr. Cheng denied everything," the report continued, "saying his staff found the molds for the shoes in a trash pile in the basement of his restaurant."

In an episode titled "Chocolate Heels and Dirty Deals," the case was overseen by former New York City mayor Ed Koch, the show's judge at the time. As Koch deliberated, the courtroom turned into what sounded like a mini–Lucky Cheng's, according to *The New York Times*:

> While he was gone, several of the leather-clad waitresses, managers, and dominatrixes who had joined Ms. Jason at the plaintiff's table began to eat the chocolate shoes. Their fingers were smeared with chocolate and mango-raspberry sauce when the bailiff ordered everyone to rise and listen to the verdict.

Lucky Cheng's lost. Koch ruled that there was no patent for the shoes, and that "Mr. Cheng could use the mold with impunity." Despite losing, Suthon was pleased with the publicity and by the fact that she convinced the producers of the show to bring her many guests—"a scrum of transgender, sado-masochistic funsters," as she called them—to the studio via limousine.

Miss Understood, one of Suthon's witnesses, said the case wasn't over.

"I think we should appeal," Miss Understood insisted. "I appeal to lots of people." But the case was closed.

As the pressures of operating a Times Square restaurant without Suthon grew, Josephine and her father moved Lucky Cheng's back downtown, making it a pop-up brunch spot inside the Lower East Side nightclub The DL. In 2016, they returned to Midtown, opening on the third floor of Stage 48, a venue with a kitchen that catered Cantina Rooftop, a lounge with beautiful outdoor views of Manhattan's far West Side. Many of the same servers who began their careers with Lucky Cheng's in the '90s remained on staff. At one point, it had outposts in Miami, Las Vegas, and New Orleans, but as of this writing, New York is the only location that survives.

An important element to remember about Lucky Cheng's legacy is that, for a generation of Asian drag queens and transgender women, it was the place—perhaps the *only* place—where they could find work without having to leave their identities at home. Ongina, a Filipina American drag performer who appeared on the first season of *RuPaul's Drag Race*, has said that working at Lucky Cheng's was "a rite of passage because they allowed you to be who you are as a queen, they allowed you to be who you are as a person."[8]

"It was work, but it was amazing," she said.

In 2025, Lucky Cheng's was doing great business as a pop-up drag-dinner show in Times Square—worlds away from its downtown roots, but still one of the longest-running drag brunches in America. I saw for myself why Lucky Cheng's had staying power one cold Sunday morning in January 2023, when David and I ate there with our friends Patrick and his husband, Ray. We split a piled-high tray of nachos and laughed our asses off, along with most everyone else in the full restaurant, as Aria Jae, Gioconda, Prima Love, and the rest of the drag queen performers shimmied, twerked, twirled, and lip-synched their way around the restaurant. To my eyes, the tables were evenly split between gay men and straight women. Staffers used big buckets to stealthily scoop up all the dollar bills that had fluttered to the ground. Rihanna and musical theater numbers boomed from the loudspeaker as the queens pulled audience members onstage to celebrate birthdays and engagements.

After almost three hours, the show ended, selfies were taken, and the assembled party people put on their coats and caps and headed back out into the cold Manhattan streets. The sky-high kicks, the ear-blasting Ariana Grande songs, the supersweet frou-frou cocktails: It was a delightful way to spend a Sunday afternoon with friends. Typical drag brunch stuff.

But I couldn't help but think how different that brunch was from Lucky Cheng's first groundbreaking year, when drag queens and transgender women—all of them Asian and gorgeous—served people at a time and in a neighborhood where being out was still a revolutionary act, and when AIDS was making its deathly march through the city. Tora and Josephine both told me they had considered shutting down the business many times.

"I was surprised that it lasted so long," Tora admitted. "I saw the family start to fall apart. It became too many people, and then there were bad seeds. The staff grew too big."

But after three decades, Lucky Cheng's is still drag strong, despite drag queens and dining having become as common as meat and potatoes.

"Now, if you look at what's going on in Hell's Kitchen, every single bar, café, or diner, gay or straight, is doing a drag show," Tora said. "Not the same as us, but everyone's doing almost the same thing with the same girls."

Tora misses the days when dining and drag were their own pleasures and not just an opportunity for Instagram content and social media attention.

"We had our own building, and you could linger and chat up somebody," she told me, referring to Lucky Cheng's earliest years. "Now it's: come in and be entertained and go home."

So, why is Lucky Cheng's still around?

"People," said Tora, "would miss us."

15

Now Serving

The Queer Dining Future

U nlike most gay restaurants over the past one hundred years, where you would open the door and see a sea of mostly men (Food Bar) or women (Brick Hut), today's queer restaurants are far less segregated by sexuality and gender. That's what happens when queerness and awareness of queer people is seemingly every-where, from prestige television to this hour's TikTok trends. Why wouldn't restaurants be equally queer?

But for older generations of gay people, eating out like it's still 1981 isn't hidebound or backwards. It's a rush, and a sanctuary, and good luck to the person who says otherwise.

Come with me to Fort Lauderdale.

"Was that your cock ring?" A queeny voice barked at me as I walked through the dining room one sunny Sunday morning at Union, an American bistro that's the closest thing that Wilton Manors—a gay enclave in Fort Lauderdale, Florida—has to upscale modern dining. I'd dropped my sunglasses, and the metallic *clank* startled the speaker and the five other middle-aged, cocktail-wielding, tipsy queens he was with. As I walked by their table, I dramatically clutched the invisible pearls at my décolletage and let out my best *shocked* gasp. They erupted in laughter. It was eleven a.m. and the restaurant wasn't crowded, but even if it had been, I couldn't imagine anybody pulling a Karen and demanding to speak to the manager because some loud queen asked another queen about his cock ring. This kind of thing just happens at gay restaurants.

David and I were in Fort Lauderdale to see what it was like to eat in one of the gayest communities in the country. I had heard that Fort Lauderdale was a respite from the conservative cesspool that Florida had become, even though the state is home to one of the country's highest percentages of same-sex couples. The 2020 census didn't ask LGBTQ+-related questions, but it did inquire about age, and before I traveled there, I learned that Wilton Manors is a community not of twinks but of twunks: The median age was fifty-three. In a 2018 survey of about 160 senior respondents, the majority (69%) reported that they were gay/lesbian, while 30 percent reported being straight. Three people, the final report noted, "did not appreciate this question being asked."

Wilton Manors elected its first openly gay official, city councilman Gary Resnick, in 1988, and thirty years later joined Palm Springs as the only two places in the United States with all-LGBTQ+ city councils. In 1988, John Fiore was elected to the

Wilton Manors City Council, and in 2000, became its first gay mayor. Two years later he was succeeded by another gay man, Jim Stork. When I visited in 2023, the city was led by Scott Newton, a straight man who generally had a good relationship with the queer community.

The gay epicenter of Wilton Manors is Wilton Drive, lined with dozens of Pride flag-draped inns, clubs, shops, bars, and restaurants. Actually, bar-restaurants is a more accurate term, since most bars in Wilton Manors have the space and zoning freedom to double as restaurants. You go to Rosie's for juicy burgers (beef or Impossible) and a heap of potato tots on the cruisy patio covered in rainbow frills. At Thai Me Up, the crispy bok choy tastes extra good when you're seated at a table under the night sky, especially if you have a (straight, probably) server as charming as Brian, who spent a few minutes telling me about his two tours in Afghanistan. On Sundays, the Vice City Ballers join other gay softball teams to flirt over baked pasta and rice and beans at Georgie's Alibi Monkey Bar. Located in a shuttered bank, it became the town's first major gay bar when Wilton Drive became an official arts and entertainment district in 1997.

David and I were in Wilton Manors with our friend Clark, a fellow Gen Xer whom I've known since the early 2000s when we were roommates in Chelsea. Besides having a Montgomery Clift nose and a cutting sense of humor, Clark is one of the smartest people I know. He's also, to my delight, an expert on models. (Don't get him *started* on the time a well-known fashion magazine tweeted a photo that misidentified Beverly Peele as Naomi Campbell.) When David and I want to watch television over Thai takeout or travel anywhere around the world, we call Clark.

To kick off our Friday night, the three of us had dinner at Tropics Grille on Wilton Drive. On one side was the small dining room that gave me strong gay 1980s vibes: long banquettes with white tablecloths underneath large, generically abstract paintings.

Beyond the dining room I spotted a doorway that led to an intimate cabaret space with a piano. Maybe sixty older gay white men
stood around the large wraparound bar, and floating among them
were a handful of much younger men, most of them Latino and
Asian and dressed in either preppy golf shirts and beige slacks or
peekaboo tops and thigh-baring but not skeezy shorts. I assumed
some of the younger men might have been hustlers looking for
right now. Wilton Manors is known as a town where younger gay
men who are attracted to older men will easily find actual dates
with sugar daddies whom they might love for a few days or a
lifetime.

The menu was neither down-market nor adventurous. Rather,
it featured the kinds of aspirational fine-dining entrées that would
have been at home at Company in the '80s: New York strip,
maple-glazed salmon, liver and onions. One of the few vegetarian
options was the spinach ravioli with pesto cream sauce. I actually
liked it.

Was the restaurant dated? Sure. But to these men, and to me, it
was appealing and sophisticated, and eating there made them feel
visible, not just welcome. Sexual and desired too. It was the kind
of gay restaurant that muscled rich-bitch queens from Miami or
Houston would never be caught *dead* in, and I adored that. I loved
being there with gay men who smiled at me when I walked by and
asked me how I was doing.

Wilton Manors became a village in 1947, when it separated
itself from Fort Lauderdale proper. Its status as an unofficial
gay hub goes back to at least the late '80s, when gay men, mostly,
flocked there in search of housing that was more affordable than
in Fort Lauderdale and other wealthier parts of Florida and the
United States. It was a less costly but also a less sophisticated alternative to South Beach, the region's more famous gay destination.

At the site of the Eagle bar on Wilton Drive, there used to be a
gay restaurant that many longtime locals recall fondly: Chardees.

Anthony De Riggi, a longtime Broward County real estate developer who went by the name Tony Dee, took over its predecessor restaurant, The Palms, and reopened it as Chardees in 1990 with his then life partner, Charlie Mielke. The two offered a concept that's no longer in gay fashion: a supper club with entertainment, such as a pianist and singers, seven nights a week. Eartha Kitt performed there, as did the comedian Judy Tenuta (known for playing an accordion in her act) and the out singer Sam Harris. It was "the place to dine," as one of the restaurant's postcards put it; the all-you-care-to-eat Sunday brunch was especially popular. It also offered a weekly calendar of daily discounts, another element you won't find much of at gay restaurants anymore. On Mondays, all entrées were 25 percent off; on Wednesdays, dinners were two for one; and on Thursdays, the all-you-can-eat pasta dinners came with salad and garlic toast. Dee sold Chardees in 2005 after he and Mielke broke up, although they remained friends and opened another supper club called Tropics. Mielke died in 2013, and Dee died ten years later.

I first heard about Chardees around two thirty a.m. Saturday morning, when the after-hours rush at Courtyard Café on Wilton Drive was starting to kick into high gear. I had taken a seat at the counter, where I scoped out the room. To my right, men sipped coffee alone, and to my left, a drag queen ate a BLT while her companion dipped his sausage links into a tiny pitcher of syrup. At another table, a group of loud queens in sweaty tank tops scarfed down French fries and debated who had the hottest butt at the Eagle that night. Most of the customers were men, a mix of white, Black, and Latino—I heard Spanish spoken at more than one table—dressed not quite to impress but rather to be guy-next-door butch in T-shirts and jeans or shorts. Most of the servers were women, white, and of various ages.

A young man named John stood next to me, rolling cutlery into paper napkins. When I told John—a Black native of Fort

Lauderdale—that I was in town researching gay restaurants, the first thing he said was that there used to be a Piggly Wiggly across the street, where his family and other folks on a limited budget shopped for groceries. There were also trailer parks in the community, and when I told him that someone I met at a bar said that Wilton Manors used to be "crack town," he nodded. (Mayor Newton, who has lived in Fort Lauderdale since 1960, once said that before the town got gay and "more elegant," it was "a middle-class to low-class redneck community.")[1] The Piggly Wiggly was gone. The main attraction there now was Georgie's Alibi Monkey Bar, where Mariah Carey's "Dreamlover" was playing loud enough that the gay guys eating burgers at a table behind me sang along.

What struck me the most over my Wilton Manors weekend was the number of gay elders I saw and met, which I rarely did in my circles in New York. A few of these men made their way through thumping gay bars using canes, walkers, and wheelchairs, which I rarely see in New York either. For the most part, the elders I met were not rich queens who were wintering there from their homes in the Hamptons or the Hollywood Hills. Most seemed to be middle- and working-class people who moved to the area on modest or fixed budgets and are still living that way.

Rick Karlin, a former Chicagoan who used to eat at the Melrose, told me that in his estimation as the food critic for the *South Florida Gay News*, there is no such thing as "fine dining" in Wilton Manors. I agree: Even by my déclassé standards, most of the meals I ate there were satisfying, but nothing to write home about. Karlin told me that what mattered most to local gay diners wasn't artisanal this or heirloom that, but getting a decent and affordable meal with generous portions that could be taken home as leftovers. He was right: When David, Clark, and I ate at the Greek restaurant Ethos, my plate was piled so high with spanakopita, pita triangles, rice, and potatoes that my doggie bag would have fed a hungry senior for a day or two.

When he covered gay Chicago, Karlin said he would rip a gay restaurant apart in print if it wasn't serving good food. Not in Wilton Manors.

"I have to kind of say nicely that the food is not anything special, but the service is so friendly or they could improve their menu a little bit," he admitted. "It's always this 'but,' and put a compliment in. You can be not friendly but you have to be attractive, or you could be friendly but not attractive, but you can't be both. If you're going to be surly you better be good looking."

In his reviews, Karlin makes a note of when the staff is good looking. "My readers want to know that," he told me.

Wilton Manors is gay, but not exclusively so. There were plenty of straight people peeling shrimp and nursing frozen margaritas at every restaurant I went to. When I veered off Wilton Drive and walked along the more residential streets, the dance music stopped, the gay restaurants disappeared, and in their place were modest homes and fast-food restaurants. (And, to my surprise, more American flags than Pride ones.) One morning, I went to a small café called the Alchemist for iced coffee, and even though the outdoor food hall where it was located was only a ten-minute walk from the gay heart of Wilton Drive, the calypso band, the man fondling a snake, screaming children, and tables of opposite-sex couples all told me that I wasn't on gay turf anymore.

———

I first saw Richard Coleman standing in line at Java Boys, a popular gay coffeehouse in Wilton Manors. I'd be lying if I said that I wasn't flirting just a *teeny* bit: He had a trim soccer player's body, short salt-and-pepper hair, and a scruffy beard. I was shocked when he told me he was fifty-nine. He worked remotely as a project manager of some kind, and had moved from Buffalo, New York, to Wilton Manors two months earlier because he wanted, as he said, "to be around a lot of gay people in a gay neighborhood."

"I was tired of being the old one on the dance floor," he said as he flashed me a sly smile. "Some people in the straight world may criticize gay men our age who are still going out clubbing or to a bar, but that's where we go and socialize. That's our outlet."

A self-described loner, Richard admitted that he didn't always fit in, no matter whether he was at a gay bar or a straight one. The gay world, he found, could be "toxic, very vain and very shallow." Yet he felt comfortable living in Wilton Manors, where life was gay 24/7 and being in your fifties or older and dancing the night away was the norm, not the exception.

"I think it's important that we have a place to go and meet other gay people and to socialize with them and have a safe environment to do that," he said.

As I talked with Richard, I was reminded of author Andrew Holleran's 1996 essay for *The New York Times Magazine* called "The Wrinkle Room." It was about Fedora, a gay-welcoming restaurant in the West Village that, if it were still open, would be a legacy gay restaurant. The space opened as a restaurant in 1917, but was eventually taken over by Henry Dorato and his wife, Fedora, in the early 1950s.

One of my first interviews for this book was with Elliot J. Cohen, who remembered eating there—a "not very fancy Italian home cooking place," he called it—in the early '80s with his late husband, the singer Douglas Franklin. Henry ran the bar, Fedora the kitchen.

"They would have some declasse dishes, like turkey tetrazzini with pasta, a little appetizer dish with some lettuce and chopped liver," Elliot recalled. "Douglas swore that Henry made the best vodka sours that he had ever had in his life."

Elliot remembered there being older gay men who sat at the bar to watch *Wheel of Fortune* and wager on what color dress Vanna White would have on. A lot of the clientele was gay but Fedora was "a neighborhood place, an all embracing place," he said, adding: "People who didn't fit in gravitated there."

Elliot said Fedora watched *Wheel of Fortune* in her apartment above the restaurant. When it was over, she'd walk downstairs and enter the font door to applause.

"She would go from table to table greeting everybody, regulars and strangers alike," he said. "She was very gracious."

The restaurateur Gabriel Stulman assumed ownership of Fedora in 2010 after the restaurant had temporarily closed for renovations. In 2020, Stulman announced that the restaurant would not reopen after it had been shut down during the coronavirus pandemic.

Told in gorgeously economic prose, in his essay Holleran recalls eating once, and only once, at Fedora:

> I didn't want to go back because I was newly arrived in Manhattan and, in my 20s, more interested in the bars west of Fedora. I knew previous generations of gay men had trudged these streets—the one that went to Fedora, for instance, or the bar on Tenth Street that friends called a "wrinkle room." But these places had nothing to do with me. It was as if there were a policeman stationed in Sheridan Square, like an archangel separating men into two tributaries—one going to Ty's, the other to the wrinkle room.

Holleran's observations are mournful and wistful and take me back to what it was like to be young and gay and turn heads at the bar when you no longer do. That speaks to me deeply now that I'm in my fifties, and I imagine that for the gay men who are older than me—those who moved to Wilton Manors to keep the gay party from the '70s and '80s going—it does too. The town reminds them of the homogeneously gay neighborhoods they moved to in their twenties, enclaves that were more sexually free, less focused on children, and safer. (And that usually meant more expensive and whiter, too.)

But in Wilton Manors, a wrinkle room restaurant doesn't signify life's end. As Richard reminded me, it was a place where life's last chapters are relished.

I asked Richard whether there were any gay restaurants that he missed. He said he didn't know of any. Then, I asked him the question I asked every gay person who said they didn't know any gay restaurants—"Where did you eat after the clubs?"—and I saw that a lightbulb went on. His answer, as it was with everyone else I asked that question, was a diner.

"People would go to this one restaurant open twenty-four hours, and it would be packed—the Towne," he said, referring to a restaurant in Buffalo. "There would be drag queens coming out from performing and they would be sitting among the people in the restaurant. It was a great scene crowded with people."

Richard was worried that as gay bars and restaurants become less single-sex, gay male culture could lose what made it special. After all, if every gay bar is for straight people and women as much as it is for gay men, then it's just a bar. There's nothing gay about it.

"I remember back in the day in the eighties and nineties, I thought that it would be cool to be acceptable among the straight community and be able to go wherever you want," he continued. "But at the same time, I didn't realize that it was killing our own places."

I can't remember the last time I had such a gay weekend, and I've lived in gay neighborhoods by choice since I was eighteen. On Saturday afternoon, I danced along as Donna Summer and Chic thumped from the outdoor speakers at Hunters, a gay nightclub located in a dull strip mall that was also home to a new cigar bar called Tap That Ash. Despite David's reservations that I wasn't the short-shorts kind of guy—"And where are you going put your wallet and phone?" he asked, making a good but ultimately unsuccessful point—I bought the cutest pair of black shorts that made my thighs look *juicy* from an all-things-rainbow emporium called Pride Factory. (Unfortunately, the clothing store Tops & Bottoms didn't have what I was looking for.) At Wilton Creamery, I got a cup of the He's Not Worth It ice cream, made with toffee bits, Oreos, and caramel, and snapped a photo of a sign advertising the scoop shop's Monthly Topping. The street cruising, the disco hits, the mediocre food, the restaurants with entirely gay dining rooms, the small businesses with suggestive and punny gay names: It was as if the gay restaurant golden age never ended. The gay men of Wilton Manors simply wouldn't have it any other way.

Before we went back to New York, David and I had breakfast at Pub on the Drive on Wilton Drive. The place was empty except for a few employees, including our extra-chipper waitress who, even though the breakfast shift was dead, hustled from the kitchen to the dining room and out to the sidewalk tables, where men nursed morning iced coffees. David and I had eaten there the previous Friday night, when the place was jammed with gay men, most of them over fifty, who were dressed in shorts and T-shirts, knocking back beers and lip-smacking their way through trays of sloppy hot wings. For breakfast, the loudspeakers blasted club music that made it feel as if Friday's party was still in swing, like we were in twenty-four-hour New Orleans or Las Vegas. Under shimmering rainbow ombré netting, I bobbed my head to a thumping club remix of Michael Jackson telling me not to stop until I got enough. As I sang along to Shanice's lilting cover of "Lovin' You," a patron asked the guy behind the bar who sang the original.

"Minnie Ripperton," the bartender replied, before the man could even finish his question.

For gay men who came of age falling in love or making out to Minnie's effortless whistle tones in 1974, there were worse places to be on a Monday morning. For many of those men, being there to enjoy a cup of coffee was a gift that their friends would have loved if only a plague hadn't decided otherwise for them.

People make choices with their feet, and at the restaurants on Wilton Drive, it was apparent that these gay men—mostly white and cis, mostly Gen X and older, mostly men of some financial means—made the decision to live their *Golden Girls* years not in the big cities where many of them came of age, but in the warmth of a gay South Florida enclave. I couldn't help but appreciate how many of these men lived as libertines in the '60s or activists in the '70s or plague-fighters in the '80s, and in some cases, all three. Lesbians live in Wilton Manors, too, but not in the same numbers as gay men.

Wilton Manors may have not been on these men's wish list when they were fisting strangers at the Anvil or huffing poppers on the Equus dance floor. But their lives were now about living in a modest bungalow, with a friend circle of fellow white-haired gays in dad shorts who eat at only gay restaurants and always take home doggie bags. It's a kind of heaven.

———————

There is an alternative vision for gay restaurants in the twenty-first century, though, and it looks nothing like early-bird burgers at Pub on the Drive. To call this new vanguard of restaurants gay is to do them a disservice, since gayness is just a small slice of their identity. The restaurants I'm talking about are intersectional, activist-minded, *maverick*. Meals are plated in queer ways. The chef, servers, and dishwashers are more likely to be transgender and nonbinary than those working at traditional gay restaurants. Restrooms at these restaurants are not gendered, and men aren't assumed to get the check. Posters for social justice movements like Black Lives Matter and refugee resettlement hang next to the Progress Pride flag. These restaurants won't draw you in with an old-school ad in the local gay newspaper, nor do their menus make puns about sizzling meat. At these restaurants, queerness is intentional, joyous, and virtuous, and, as with most restaurants in our queer century, a brand.

―――――――

When David and I sat down for dinner in the cozy dining room at HAGS, a tiny restaurant in New York's East Village, one of the first things we saw on the table was something I'd never seen before at any restaurant: a small clamshell bowl of black buttons with different pronoun options in white type—she/her, they/them, ze/zir—which you could wear so your server knew exactly how to address you. I didn't put one on, but other customers did. I loved that the option was there.

HAGS offered just two seasonal tasting menus, for omnivores and vegans, with either three or five courses and optional alcohol pairings. Before I handed back my menu to our server, I jotted down a list of ingredients I'd never heard of: limequat, vin jaune, tardivo, ash crackers. When it arrived, the food was both delicious and fun to look at, not that I knew what I was eating without asking our server for clarification. Maybe I watch too many horror movies, but almost every dish in my five-course meat-free meal was plated to look like I was eating tiny monsters. A cheese wedge with red pear looked like a fantastical octopus. For dessert, the ganache, banana creme, meringue, and shortbread collectively looked like a snake that had escaped a zoo on Pluto.

Dinner at HAGS is not cheap. Together, our meal cost $400, by far the most expensive meal I had while researching this book, and one of the most expensive dinners I've ever had, period. (David and I have splurged on meals at the French Laundry and Eleven Madison Park, but to be honest, I'd trade both of those meals to go back in time to the Melrose for a bowl of the sweet-and-sour cabbage soup.) There are almost no restaurants in this book where it will cost you an arm and a leg for a meal, because almost no gay restaurants have ever truly been that expensive. There were exceptions. In the 1970s, the waiters wore tuxedos at One if by Land, an "opulent" restaurant in the West Village with "very good food" that "isn't cheap," according to the *New York City Gayellow Pages*. There are many more such restaurants where the price point was high and out of reach for many queer folks. There will be more.

At HAGS, David and I looked to be the only same-sex couple dining there. It wasn't until we'd been there about an hour that the door opened and in walked a tall person with a beautiful thick beard, wearing a slinky floor-length jersey-knit green gown. David and I caught each other's gaze: *Finally, this place got queer.*

HAGS co-owners and life partners Telly Justice, its executive chef, and Camille Lindsley, its beverage director, laughed when I told them this one morning at the restaurant before service started. Telly, who identifies as trans-femme and pansexual, has blond hair that complements her sparkling blue eyes and cheeks that get rosy easily. She had on her HAGS apron over a purple top. Camille's shoulder-length black hair and brown eyes were as dramatic as her all-black outfit, from her blazer to skinny jeans.

Telly reminded me that the restaurant's motto was "by queer people for all people"—dining there, she said, isn't so much about a queer-only experience, but rather "a love letter to dining with queers."

"We do entertain straights," she acknowledged, smiling. "They eat dinner too."

Naming the restaurant HAGS was an attempt to remove any sense of self-seriousness at the kinds of restaurants with four $ signs next to their names in the city guides. Telly and Camille were considering uncommon or unpopular terms around femininity when they agreed on HAGS.

"We both come from the punk DIY scene and we were like, 'Let's name the restaurant like we are naming a band,'" said Camille.

"It feels snotty and bratty," added Telly.

"It doesn't feel like a restaurant name," Camille continued. "It's this reclamation of old witchy women but also this fun salutation of 'have a good summer,' like from a yearbook."

Camille recalled walking out the restaurant's front door before HAGS opened in the summer of 2022 "and some NYU bro was like, 'HAGS? What kind of restaurant names itself HAGS?'"

"Thank *god* guys like that will not eat here—and they don't," she smiled. "It works. It's like a firewall for heteronormativity."

That extends to the cuisine, which Telly said "is uniquely and inherently related to our transness."

"We do a lot of work to show how we feel through various techniques: stuffing things inside of other things, concealing things under other things, feeling like we are protecting or highlighting certain ingredients as a vulnerability share, as a window into how we feel and see ourselves," she explained.

"Like French and Italian cuisines," she added, "there can be queer cuisines."

Telly said that one of the essential considerations in opening HAGS was to make it a safe space for queer expression no matter how and where it happens. Much of the kitchen staff is trans and nonbinary.

"We found that by making it a really safe space for our workers to be as queer, flamboyant, and over the top as they want to be, it encourages comfort in the dining room for folks that want to go beyond that flamboyance," she explained. "That synergy, where everybody in the room on a special night is feeling free and absolutely welcome to the space, is like having a very personal private potluck at home."

We're living at a time when queer chefs, restaurateurs, social media influencers, and cookbook authors are legit celebrities, helping to mainstream LGBTQ+ food culture. No wonder that Telly is consciously and outwardly putting her queerness forward as an identifying marker of who she is and what HAGS stands for. Take a look around the dining room and it may not always seem like HAGS is a queer restaurant in the same way that tables and tables of women made Bloodroot look like a lesbian-feminist restaurant in the '70s. But when a chef names her transness as one of the many things her customers should know about her and about eating at her restaurant, queerness courses through the dining experience.

Telly remembered that, as a young queer cook, she lionized the beloved New York restaurants Buvette in the West Village and Prune in the East Village because they were able to cultivate a meaningful queer space "without sacrificing culinary ambition." James Beard Award–winning chef Jody Williams and her wife, fellow chef Rita Sodi, opened Buvette in 2011, and still run it and other acclaimed New York restaurants, including I Sodi and Via Carota. In 2020, queer chef Gabrielle Hamilton closed Prune after twenty years. Telly said she modeled HAGS on those restaurants, and her hard work paid off. Since it opened, HAGS has been showered with mostly glowing reviews. In 2023, Michelin named Telly its New York Young Chef Award winner.

Interestingly, much like HAGS, Buvette and Prune were operated by queer people but weren't exactly queer restaurants. But that was never their goal. Because demand to go to those restaurants was so high, the owners weren't able to or even interested in choosing their clientele, as gay restaurants did in the past, via advertising and word of mouth, as a way to attract business. As a result, the particular considerations of running a well-reviewed, fine dining, queer-owned restaurant—reservation scarcity, small dining rooms, a reliance on wealthy customers—can make those restaurants less queer. It's the opposite of queering—"straightening," I suppose.

Telly is sensitive to the fact that the restaurant's high price point is a limiting factor for many queer people. That's why her favorite day of the week is Sunday, a.k.a. Pay-What-You-Can day, when she said most of her customers are queer.

"We give the price point of the tasting menu to reflect the ability to have a loss leader day, a day you don't make money," she clarified. "But it pays for Sunday, which is our reason for existence, the heart and core of HAGS, when we get to entertain everybody."

Telly grew up in Philadelphia fearing that she would never be out as a transgender person. She said one of her biggest joys is looking in the HAGS dining room and seeing trans and queer people from small towns "who have come to New York to vacation because there are ways to feel safe and to peacock, things you can't do in whatever town you feel trapped in or love."

As she talked, tears started streaming down her face. She stopped speaking, her cheeks flushed. Camille looked at her kindly. The room went quiet for a few seconds.

"It's really touching," Telly said, her voice barely a whisper. "We get so many people that are like, 'I just wish we had something like this where I was.' The most emotional part of doing this job is seeing people who need it."

Telly told me she wouldn't have opened HAGS if she didn't feel that she needed it herself. "It holds a mirror up to you like, damn, I haven't worked through that baggage."

I asked Telly how she wanted her customers to remember HAGS. She answered quickly. "That we"—meaning LGBTQ+ folks—"have a history and a reason to commune."

———

At first glance, Pub on the Drive and HAGS don't have much in common. At one a.m. on a Saturday night in one of them, you'll find older gay men sharing affordable wings and cheap drinks and flirting over disco on the loudspeakers. At the other, queer-identifying folks who can afford $200 for a meal will go on a culinary adventure of unheard-of ingredients and strange plating with a Cocteau Twins album soothing their ears from the speakers. The two restaurants are opposites of gay dining, but they *are* cut from the same dining cloth in which queerness—or gayness, if "queer" isn't your thing—is baked into the dining room. A Wilton Manors gay might not feel welcome or comfortable in a space that's so radically inclusive as HAGS, and HAGS' queer regulars might not feel that Pub on the Drive is a place where their queerness would be fully understood, let alone embraced. Or maybe I'm wrong. Perhaps both kinds of customers would enjoy exploring the others' space. I consider myself versatile when it comes to what I would do; I'd eat at HAGS and Courtyard Café again in a heartbeat.

Time will tell whether younger queer generations will retire to Wilton Manors and live 24/7 gay lives, working out at gay gyms, getting plastered at gay bars, buying rainbow candles and leather harnesses at gay boutiques, and ordering meatloaf specials at gay restaurants. As many gay people grow up in safer environments almost anywhere, will they still want a queer environment during life's late chapters? The answer in Palm Springs is a resounding "hell, yes."

As someone who prayed for snow days during harsh Cleveland blizzards just so I could stay at home to watch *All My Children*, I could tell right away that my first visit to Palm Springs was going to be a warm alternative to my childhood winters. I mean, the Palm Springs airport has no roof.

Clark and his parents, Tony and Ellen, invited me to vacation with them in Southern California's famously gay city in December 2023. (David had to work so he got our apartment all to himself, the better to be alone and watch Channing Tatum rom-coms.) They rented a house with sweeping vista views of the San Jacinto mountains on one side and Barry Manilow's sprawling estate on the other. They generously offered me my own cozy casita with a pool outside my door. When I left Palm Springs a week later, I went home with a sack of fat lemons picked straight from the tree I could see through my bedroom window.

As in Wilton Manors, it's not an exaggeration to say that every restaurant in Palm Springs is gay, or at least welcoming of gays, made so by the city's generally older gay populations. Then again, in Palm Springs, "young" is a matter of opinion. Some forty-five thousand people live there; about a third are sixty-five and over, and 30 to 50 percent identify as LGBTQ. Most of the residents are white and cis and men on the wealthy side, the kind who can afford to retire there and live in one of the city's signature midcentury modern homes.

Tell a Palm Springs queen that gay life ends at forty and you will get an *earful*. I saw that firsthand while I was in town, as I reported a story for *The New York Times* about KGAY, the only terrestrial gay radio station in the United States. Located in a modest strip mall, it broadcasts a 24/7 mix of dance hits and pop songs from the '70s through this very minute. Chris Shebel, the station's then-sixty-nine-year-old program director, told me that in Palm Springs, older gay men—Stonewallers, boomers, Gen Xers—can live vibrantly, as if their friends and lovers were young again, or had never died in a plague.

"You're not going to be shunned in the bars like you are in our community in a lot of cities," said Shebel, whose husband, Oscar Luis Uvillus, was at the time the reigning Mr. Palm Springs Leather. "You're going to be able to find a job. If you want to keep working past sixty-five, you can do that here. You're not going to be shown the door just because you have gray hair."

I saw hair colors in every shade of gray and silver—I fit in effortlessly—at just about every restaurant in town. Two baby boomer–looking gay muscle men in rainbow-colored tank tops and flimsy shorts got tipsy and loud at Lulu, a bistro where the seats came in rainbow colors and the sweet potato fries were crisp and lanky. On Arenas Road, the city's concentrated gay entertainment strip, Clark and I lunched outdoors at the gay bar Blackbook, where my "Palm Springs Style Nachos" consisted of a quarter sheet of chips served on a small metal tray piled high with cheeses, tomatoes, jalapeños, and a crumbled veggie patty. The only time I ate out in Palm Springs where the patrons were not mostly Gen X or older was at the family-owned Great Shakes, where I tried my first date shake, a sweet, extra-thick, caramel-forward specialty of the Coachella Valley, considered the date capital of the world.

But there was one Palm Springs restaurant that I knew, even before I walked in the front door, would hold yet another vision of what the future of gay dining will look like, something between the contemporary queerness of HAGS and the old-school comfort food vibes at Pub on the Drive. And it has a fin-de-siècle lesbian to thank.

———————

The first thing you notice when you walk into Alice B. is Alice B.—Toklas, that is—and her longtime lover Gertrude Stein, two Americans who met as expats in Paris in 1907 and were partners for almost forty years until Stein died in 1946. Oversize portraits of the two women, made by British-American painter Jo Hay, watch over the ivory-colored chairs, gold globe lamps, and warm wood paneling in the modern California chic dining room.

Renowned chefs Susan Feniger and Mary Sue Milliken opened Alice B. in December 2023 in a complex on nine acres of landscaped grounds of prime real estate just off Tahquitz Canyon Way, a main Palm Springs strip. The city's mayor, Jeffrey Bernstein, and former senator Barbara Boxer gave speeches at the opening, which one publication spiritedly called "the grandest restaurant opening ever." To eat, there was chopped chicken liver on crostini with pickled kumquats and toasted hazelnuts, and vanilla soft serve with crispy sesame seed clusters. The Water Lillies, a male synchronized swimming troupe, entertained in the pool.

It sounds like any opening for any upscale restaurant in Palm Springs. But what makes Alice B. really stand out is where it's located: on the ground floor of Living Out, a fifty-five-and-over apartment community for the LGBTQ+ community and allies. The brainchild of Loren Ostrow and Paul Alanis, Living Out describes itself as "a resort-style apartment community with an unparalleled array of amenities" that include a gym, salon, screening room, and coffee shop where continental breakfast is served daily. Living in Living Out isn't cheap; rents start around $4,000 for one- and two-bedroom apartments. Open to the public, Alice B. is not an included amenity for Living Out residents. But it is a luxurious option.

"It's as convenient as can be," Feniger told me. "If you want to get a drink and let's say you're eighty years old and had to hide all your life, you can come downstairs and have a drink and not feel weird."

One sunny morning, I met up with Feniger in the Alice B. dining room while her team prepped for that night's service. Her small frame was dressed in a blue chambray shirt covered by a white chef's apron. She has a bright smile that almost never disappeared from her face. I had never met Feniger before, but I recognized her from her many appearances on Gordon Ramsay cooking competitions, including *Master Chef* and *Hell's Kitchen*, which I watch devotedly. I knew she was from Toledo, Ohio, and I could hear it in the flat Midwestern *a* that she and I share.

Feniger, who at the time was seventy-one, said Alice B. was four years in the making. She envisioned it as a restaurant that was meant to be gay in name, location, and even in spirit—yet open to everyone.

"Straight, gay—it doesn't really matter," she shrugged. "But there's no question when you walk in, that's the vibe. There's something special and wonderful about that."

Feniger is known for influential, California-inspired Mexican cuisine at her California restaurants, including Border Grill and SOCALO. But at Alice B., she wanted to offer a more global menu, hence the Steak Diane, branzino, a vegan cauliflower wedge, and cornmeal Cheddar drop biscuits. Nothing too spicy, though. Living Out residents and local elders don't do well with spicy.

I had eaten the night before at Alice B. with Clark and his parents. Walking to our table on the patio next to roaring pillar heaters on a cool, sweater-perfect Palm Springs night, I noticed the restaurant was a mix of same and opposite sex couples and small groups, mostly older, almost all white, and practically oozing money. The food was excellent. My vegan risotto was rich and just the right amount of salty, but I went nuts over the thin slice of chocolate cake with Luxardo cherries and whipped crème fraîche.

I asked Feniger whether she had any memories of gay restaurants. She and her wife used to eat at the Los Angeles restaurant Golden Bull, "a dumpy steak house," she called it, with "not great food but great martinis" and a dining room that gay men and women packed during early bird hours. When she first moved to Los Angeles about thirty-five years ago, she also frequented Merrick's, a Mexican restaurant owned by two lesbians in West Hollywood.

"I remember going in there and having this realization of how different it felt to walk into a restaurant that was the LGBT community almost a hundred percent," she recalled. "This was a very different feeling, especially forty years ago."

After our conversation ended, Clark joined me and we took a tour of Living Out. As I walked through suites that were so new the carpeted floors were still covered in plastic, I thought: When I retire, I'd love to live *here*. Where else would everyone at breakfast get my references to Pebbles and Ryan Idol? Where else would we generously tip that cute otter waiter with the lisp because he reminded us of that sexy-ass trick we met one night at Big Chicks or Uncle Charlie's or Badlands?

As Gen Xers and Millennials and yes, Gen Zers, get older, LGBTQ+ retirement communities will be in high demand, and a fine dining restaurant attached to the facility very well could be a model for how these generations will want to eat. After all, foodies who grew up watching *Top Chef* and TikTok tutorials on sheet pan baked feta aren't going to be content with mystery casserole, boiled vegetables and Jell-O. They're going to want adventurous and fresh food made to order. I could see fancier queer retirement communities hiring a *Master Chef* winner or a Michelin-starred chef to run their kitchens.

There is yet another way to think of queer dining in the future, and again, you've got lesbians to thank.

I walked right past Ruby Fruit the first time I tried to find it. I had walked there from the charming casita where David and I were staying, a few blocks away in the fancy-pants Silver Lake neighborhood of Los Angeles. I passed a Baskin-Robbins, then an auto repair shop on the next block, and wondered whether I had scribbled down the wrong number. There was no way a restaurant that's on the vanguard of contemporary queer dining, a restaurant that opened in 2023 and that *The New York Times* had just named one of the twenty-five best in Los Angeles, would be in a strip mall. But then, I remembered what my friend Bill Addison, food critic of *The Los Angeles Times*, told me about dining out in L.A.: Some of the city's best restaurants are in the most unassuming places. I doubled back, and sure enough, tucked between a nail salon and dental clinic was Ruby Fruit.

David met me there for lunch shortly after I arrived. We shared thinly cut, perfectly crisp fries that were smothered in melted raclette that had been sprinkled with tiny pickles and mostarda. In my savory breakfast sandwich, an oozy fried egg and tender wilted greens merged with whipped feta, tomato jam, and a touch of Aleppo chile on buns as soft as soufflé. As we ate, Ruby Fruit's co-owners, Mara Herbkersman, who is also its chef, and Emily Bielagus, its wine director, came over and introduced themselves.

I wasn't surprised that the food was so good. What caught me off guard was who was there on a quiet Wednesday afternoon. Of the fifteen people in the dining room—some eating squash and farro bowls, others sipping iced coffees—David and I were the only men. Everyone else appeared to be younger than thirty-five, to my eye. It was as if we had taken a time machine back to the late '70s, when Bloodroot and other feminist restaurants carved out a space by and for women, only this time, there were laptops on the tables instead of mimeographed newsletters. We didn't feel unwelcome, but we were mindful that we were guests in someone else's house.

Feminine power pulsed through the dining room. As we waited for our seats, the person who turned out to be our server had just finished cutting up flowers that became a spectacular three-dimensional display in the crook of an elbow-shaped counter. One wall featured shelves of cookbooks from Lil' Deb's Oasis and other female and queer-run restaurants, all from Mara and Emily's personal collections or gifts from customers. An opposite wall was covered with a colorful artwork depicting in sophisticated linework what from afar looked like a sex act. ("It's ladies eating ass," Emily confirmed.) The walls were painted a chic shade of mauve—Mara called it "hot bubble gum purple-pink"—that elegantly complemented the three dozen or so tables and counter seats in sturdy wood and marble.

"We wanted to find a color that would fit with the terrazzo that was already here but that felt feminine without being girly, without alienating our trans masc friends—a warm, inviting feminine leaning color," Emily clarified.

And then there was the bathroom. It was nongendered, and a sign on the door read "NO TERFS." Inside, I instantly recognized and sang along to "Closer to Fine," the Indigo Girls' 1989 ode to self-discovery. On the walls hung a few framed Indigo Girls concert posters, plus a bumper sticker on the mirror that shouted: "Keep honking. I'm listening to THE INDIGO GIRLS." The only other time I'd seen a gay restaurant bathroom decorated as a shrine to singers was at the now-closed VYNL in Hell's Kitchen, where Cher and Dolly Parton songs played over little speakers and the divas' likenesses were rendered in eye-popping collage. As someone who came of gay age in the '90s loving the Indigo Girls and other lesbian singers—Ferron, k.d. lang, Cris Williamson, to name just a few—Ruby Fruit's lesbian spin on queer idol worship sent me straight to heaven.

With Mara at work in the kitchen, I took a seat at the counter across from Emily, who was dressed in a brown blouson top that complemented her beech-colored hair that almost grazed her chin. She pointed out that I was there on the day that the restaurant opened itself to the public as a women-in-film co-working space, one of several weekly co-working events that Ruby Fruit hosts with other partners as a way for women in the film and television industry to socialize and brainstorm. Laptops welcome. "It feels like a study hall in here," she murmured softly, glancing around with a smile. She joked that the restaurant had become a real-life version of The Planet, the café from *The L Word*.

"For a long time, lesbians, dykes, people who are nonbinary, genderqueer, and all of our trans friends, there wasn't really a place for us to go," she said. "L.A. has a lot of places centered toward cis gay males. WeHo is an entire town that's theirs. That's amazing, but there was no brick-and-mortar, consistent space specifically dedicated to our community."

Ruby Fruit was named after Rita Mae Brown's 1973 novel *Rubyfruit Jungle*, a landmark in lesbian literature. (The restaurant's Wi-Fi password was the author's name.) Emily and Mara originally imagined it as a wine bar with elevated snacks, but decided to go with a more bistro feel and hours that embraced the sunshine that poured through the front windows.

"The light is really nice, it's calm, and there aren't a lot of places where you can go and get something to eat as well as bring your laptop and do work and come here and have a fancy lunch with wine or bring your kids or your dog and sit outside," Emily explained. "There aren't any places that function in that way, especially for our community where it can be hard to find people who are like you, who have had experiences like yours."

Queerness underscores every aspect of Ruby Fruit, including the kitchen. "There is not a cis dude at the top angrily yelling, which is the trope in restaurants," she said. "That doesn't happen in our kitchen."

There is a little bit of hierarchy: Mara is the head chef and there are sous chefs. Still, employees share stations and are encouraged to suggest items to add to the menu. Emily said that there are no "silly ladder steps" as at most restaurants, where the lowest rung is the dishwasher, followed by cold station and salads, then sauté. The way they pay people is queer too. At the end of the pay period, tips are distributed evenly to everybody. At most restaurants, the back of house makes much less than front of house, and within the back of house, there's usually a hierarchy in which the dishwasher makes less than anyone else.

"Dishwashers tend to be the person on staff who is not white, so there tends to be in restaurants this pay gap," said Emily. "Because the way the cookies crumble, the whiter people are in the front of house, and they're the servers making the most money. As it goes down and folks get browner, their pays are lower. We did not want to do that."

The kitchen staff will come out and polish glassware or run food or bus tables when it's slow in the back and busy in the dining room. Any job that needs to be done gets done because it's everyone's responsibility.

"Every job is really important," Emily continued. "There's no job that we feel is less important and therefore deserves less money than any other job. To me, that's very queer."

As our conversation ended, in walked Sarah Hymanson, a chef-owner of the Los Angeles restaurant Kismet and an old friend of Emily's. David and I had eaten at Kismet a few days earlier and were wowed by Hymanson's marinated feta with roasted fennel and the thinnest-ever slices of Asian pear we'd ever had. I asked Sarah, who was there with her partner, Carmen, what set Ruby Fruit apart from other restaurants in town.

"I eat at all different kinds of restaurants, but I'm always thinking about the way I'm supposed to behave in other spaces," she told me. "In this one, I just feel at ease and I am happy to be in queer spaces. I prefer to be in queer spaces."

———

As gay restaurants have proven for decades, dining out can be a vital way to combat isolation and loneliness in the queer community. It can be lifesaving to eat alongside other queer people, even if you're eating by yourself. It's a relief to know that you're not going to be stared at for your gender presentation or that you could accidentally hit on someone who is deeply homophobic and might instigate a violent scene—feelings that people outside of

queer communities may not fully understand. The pandemic convinced Emily and Mara that gay safe spaces were a matter of queer
survival.

"Coming out of that isolation and on top of what can naturally
be an isolating state—being queer, regardless of where you live,
even in a coastal city—restaurants feel like this natural gathering space," she said. "It doesn't mean if you're queer you have to
be around queer people all the time, although I try to be, to be
honest."

Emily always found it funny to watch a straight couple or a cis
guy walk into the restaurant, having heard about it as a new wine
bar but not having heard the lesbian part.

"It's always this thing where they look around and at the other
people and see the color of the walls and the ephemera and the
books and it all slowly starts to click, and I will say that I don't
notice a lot of those people coming back," she laughed. "I think
they get it. I think they understand."

Emily said the restaurant has done "a good job accidentally of
creating a space that we want to hang out in that feels comfortable
for us and so by extension it's maybe not the most comfortable
space for a straight dude"—which is not to say that straight people
aren't allowed inside.

"It's just how I'm not that comfortable at a sports bar in
Texas, they maybe aren't that comfortable here," she explained.
"And that's okay, because every space isn't for everyone. Queer
people know that very well. We are not welcome everywhere.
Mara and I never wanted to make anyone feel alienated or
uncomfortable. It's just okay for a space to not necessarily be *for*
everyone."

Besides, the restaurant has capacity on its side. "It's small in
here so it fills up with twenty lesbians and then you're in a majority dyke zone, which is great," Emily said. "It's very easily filled
with the people who it's intended for."

That leads to another important queer restaurant question, one that's as old as queer restaurants themselves: Was I among the intended? Were David and I intruding or overstaying our welcome in what was clearly a space for women? Were we actively turning the restaurant into something it wasn't meant to be? Even worse, was I being hypocritical by complaining about the lack of gay male–majority restaurants in New York when David and I were occupying a two-top at a restaurant specifically carved out for queer women? Was I the gay equivalent of those drunk bachelorettes at the Eagle who think they're not drunk bachelorettes at the Eagle, and therefore the Eagle is *their bar*? Was I being a dick?

I'd had a similar experience at Bloodroot, which came as a surprise. Both Ruby Fruit and Bloodroot were queer-welcoming, women-centered restaurants, but they were built decades apart under vastly different circumstances for feminism, queer rights, and, despairingly, reproductive rights. One was foundationally centered on animal rights and meat-free eating; the other served meat with vegan and vegetarian options. One dining room hadn't changed its décor or seating all that much in decades and was proud of it; the other looked *designed*, and was proud of it. Yet both restaurants were in a way sisters, in that their customers are mostly but not entirely women and queer people, and the food is made from scratch by a small staff. Both are run by people with progressive ideals baked into their management styles and labor concerns. If their reviews and loyalists are any indication, neither restaurant is going anywhere soon.

As for our being assholes, there was nothing in anyone's behavior—not Emily or Mara, not our server, not the other customers—that in any way suggested David and I were intruding in a women's space. If anyone gave us side-eye, I didn't see it. But my privilege as a man and as a journalist writing a book on gay restaurants was present, and I knew it. I'm sure Emily and Mara knew it too. I questioned whether I was welcome, in the same way that I might feel if I were in an Asian restaurant filled with only Asian people. I asked myself, do people wish I weren't here, even if they didn't say it? Even if my intention is to celebrate a cuisine or express solidarity with the restaurant and the culture it represents, does my presence transform or alter it? I have to be honest: I was far more relaxed when Emily and Mara came over to introduce themselves. It showed the other patrons that we were their guests, not interlopers.

As with HAGS, and Buvette and Prune before it, once you reach a certain level of popularity, it's hard to curate your audience. You can't control who makes a reservation, and you're not going to turn people away. In the past, nonqueer people might not have gone to your restaurant because they didn't want to be associated with the implication. Now, with greater acceptance, it's cool for nonqueer people to go to a forthrightly queer restaurant. If you want to be a gathering place for queer people, how do you keep it from being overrun by nonqueer people?

The Ruby Fruit may not provide an answer: On January 11, 2025, the restaurant abruptly closed. In a since-deleted Instagram post, Emily and Mara, referencing the Los Angeles wildfires, wrote: "We have come to the heartbreaking decision that at this time, operating the Ruby Fruit is no longer possible due to financial impact from the current natural disaster." A month later, the *Los Angeles Blade*, a queer newspaper, reported that some former staff members alleged that they were mistreated at the restaurant, and alleged that transgender and customers of color were not made to feel welcome. I reached out to Emily and Mara, and Emily wrote back to say they plan to reopen. "We are just finding the path forward," she said. The circumstances surrounding the restaurant's closure may never been fully known. But its loss, like that of many gay restaurants of the past, may long be felt by the people who ate there.

The Olive Garden might brag, "When you're here, you're family." But eat at a gay restaurant and that tagline takes on a far different meaning. When queer people dine out at most restaurants, we are aware of our differences, from our mannerisms to our tablemates to how we interact with other patrons—things that straight people rarely consider because they don't have to. Straight couples who feed each other over a candlelit dinner usually don't get raised eyebrows from the management or from the family at an adjacent table that asks to be moved. At some restaurants, especially in more conservative parts of the country, we know we're being watched. Nobody will do a double take at a group of guys eating chicken wings and drinking beer, but it's a different story if those men are in leather harnesses or in drag. Straight people have never feared being kicked out of a restaurant or arrested because they touched their companion's hand (although interracial couples have certainly experienced this).

Restaurants have been feeding and bringing together gay people for over a hundred years and will be here until there's no more here *here*. They will look like the sausage-and-scrambled-eggs diners of Wilton Manors; the queer, special-occasion fine dining at HAGS; the international bistro vibe at Laziz; and many other restaurants where social justice is as important as that day's special soup. Some gay restaurants have changed in significant ways, as have some gay people. Some restaurants and people have not.

Gay restaurants of the future probably won't look like what James K. Graham thought a gay restaurant should look like. In the September 1979 issue of *Mom Guess What*, a gay newspaper that covered Northern California, Graham, the paper's editor, wrote an open letter to the community under the headline "What Sacramento Needs . . . Is a Good Gay Restaurant." In determined prose, he laid out a case for why Sacramento's "oppressively heterosexual" restaurant landscape needed a gay fine dining establishment.

His recommendations? A small menu with "superb food." Good wines and "a variety of dessert wines, including aged vintage port." The service should be "attentive but not obtrusive," with "sensitivity to the dynamics of gay couples and parties, both men and women." His treatise ends with a proposal:

> Too many gay restaurants have to double as bars, with the concomitant flash and noise, and too many are over-decorated, with a quasi-Wagnerian sense of elegance. This ideal gay restaurant must be rich but subtle, avoiding both cliches and startling originality, and above all avoiding garishness and gimmicks.

You can debate whether or not Graham's dream restaurant sounds sophisticated or stuffy. (I'd go.) From what I can tell, his gay dining dream for Sacramento was never realized. If it had, I bet it would have been a hit.

I wish I could walk out my door right now and sit down at a table with leathermen at the Eagle, or with erotic male dancers at Howard Johnson's. Or, as I need to say one last time, how I wish I could be in my late twenties again and sit alone with a book and a bowl of hot sweet-and-sour cabbage soup at the Melrose, even for one midnight. But those restaurants are gone, and that's okay. There are more and they are everywhere, and there will be many more to come.

And if there isn't one nearby? Remember that 1999 issue of *Genre* magazine, the one that listed America's ten gayest restaurants? It had some brilliant advice.

"If there's no great gay eaterie where you live," it said, "go to the most fabulous place in town and *make* it a gay restaurant."

I'm hungry again.

Let's eat.

Acknowledgments

This book would not have happened if it weren't for the many people who traveled with me, guided me, and generously shared their gay restaurant memories with me over French fries and bottomless cups of coffee. I especially want to thank my partner, David Wise, for answering questions, filling in blanks, stretching my imagination (and expectations), and telling me how the cheeseburgers tasted. Clark Moore, too, for helping me rethink this book's direction. I'm also in debt to people who encouraged me and asked questions that helped make this book sing: Diana Salameh, Marian Wise, Tim Teeman, Jeff Bale, Patrick Healy, Jesse Green, Steven Faerm, Todd Savage, John Birdsall, Christina D'Angelo, Daniel Pfister, Bill Addison, Mekado Murphy, and Dan Urlie.

Thank you to my editors, Carrie Napolitano and Mollie Weisenfeld, for their crackerjack queries, intense curiosity, and willingness to hear me out on the bizarre stuff. I feel the same gratefulness for my agent, Jon Michael Darga, at Aevitas, who held my hand, acted like my questions were not the rantings of a lunatic, and agreed to my demand that he speak to me like a child so I could understand how contracts work. Thanks to senior production editor Cisca Schreefel, copyeditor Iris Bass, and proofreaders Lisa Wigutoff and Andy Lefkowitz for their diligence.

Thank you to the librarians, archivists, and local experts who helped me find what I was looking for or who sent me down the right path to get it: David Landis (San Francisco), Jeff Soref (Los Angeles), Owen Keehen (Chicago), Gary Richards (Cleveland), Morna Gerrard and Lydia Brown at the Georgia State University Library, Hannah Stubblefield at the Atlanta History Center, Ben Smith of the Stonewall National Museum and Archives in Fort Lauderdale, Julia Lalor at the University of Wisconsin–Madison Archives, Ann K. Sindelar at the Cleveland History Center, Olivia Hoge at the Cleveland Public Library, Mandy Altimus Stahl of the Massillon Museum of Ohio, Mel Leverich at the Leather Archives & Museum in Chicago, Erin Bell at the Gerber/Hart LGBTQ+ Library & Archives in Chicago, Isaac Fellman at the GLBT Historical Society in San Francisco, Tony Valenzuela at the One Institute in Los Angeles, Michael C. Oliveira at the ONE Archives in Los Angeles, and the entire staff at the Columbus Branch of the New York Public Library.

Thank you to Brian Schaefer for the monthly book check-ins that were as aspirational as they were inspirational.

Thank you to editor Patrick Farrell at *The New York Times* for taking my pitch that turned into a story that became this book.

The following people gave me early advice on how to pitch and write a book, and without their help, this book might not have happened: Ron Broadhurst, Benoit Denizet-Lewis, Tim Federle, Michael C. Bradbury, Chris Steighner, Jeremy Atherton Lin, and Richie Jackson.

Thank you to Tony and Ellen Moore (Palm Springs), Sharon Wise and Nick Sinnott (Chicago), and Ken Schneck (Cleveland) for housing me on my travels and spending time to talk about what I had learned.

Thank you to Marti Muth, Diana Borri, and all the other women in my life who encouraged me to read everything and write without fear.

I'm grateful to the kitchen staff at the Melrose, my home away from home for many years, for providing me with dishes that warmed my stomach and filled my heart.

Thank you to Brian Eft for being like a brother to me. I will miss you and your sparkling smile always.

Selected Restaurants

California

Alice B., Palm Springs
Black Cat Tavern, Los Angeles
Brick Hut Café, Berkeley
Casita del Campo, Los Angeles
Cooper Do-nuts, Los Angeles
Hamburger Mary's, San Francisco
InsideOUT, San Diego
Orphan Andy's, San Francisco
Papa Choux, Los Angeles
Ruby Fruit, Los Angeles

Connecticut

Bloodroot, Bridgeport

Florida

Courtyard Café, Wilton Manors
Pub on the Drive, Wilton Manors
Tropics Grille, Wilton Manors

Georgia

The Colonnade, Atlanta
Gallus, Atlanta
Silver Grill, Atlanta
Su's, Atlanta

Illinois

Melrose, Chicago

New York

Caffe Cino, New York City
Childs, New York City
Florent, New York City
Food Bar, New York City
HAGS, New York City
Horn & Hardart, New York City
Howard Johnson's, Times Square, New York City
Julius, New York City
Lil' Deb's Oasis, Hudson
Lips, New York City
Lucky Cheng's, New York City
Pfaff's, New York City
Tiffany Diner, New York City
Woody's, New York City

Ohio

Flex, Cleveland
Torch Club, Canton

Utah

Laziz Kitchen, Salt Lake City

Washington, D.C.

Annie's Paramount Steak House

Perry's

Wisconsin

Napalese Lounge and Grille, Green Bay

Notes

Introduction: What's Good Tonight?

1. Allan Bérubé, *Coming Out Under Fire: The History of Gay Men and Women in World War II* (Chapel Hill: University of North Carolina Press, 1990).

2. Ricardo J. Brown, *The Evening Crowd at Kirmser's: A Gay Life in the 1940s* (Minneapolis: University of Minnesota Press, 2001).

3. Hobo's, "The 'All My Children' Lunch Bunch," *Cascade Voice*, June 3, 1983.

4. Erik Piepenburg, "Still Here and Still Queer: The Gay Restaurant Endures," *New York Times*, May 28, 2021, https://www.nytimes.com/2021/05/28/dining/gay-restaurants.html.

5. Greg Morabito, "Bleecker Street Old-Timer Manatus Throws in the Towel," Eater New York, April 7, 2014, https://ny.eater.com/2014/4/7/6247857/bleecker-street-old-timer-manatus-throws-in-the-towel.

6. Meghan McCarron, "'Our Version of Hospitality Can't Exist Right Now': MeMe's Diner on Deciding to Permanently Close," Eater New York, November 16, 2020, https://ny.eater.com/2020/11/16/21570329/memes-diner-closed-interview-libby-willis-bill-clark.

7. International House of Pancakes, "IHOP Supports LGT Pride," advertisement in *Cruise Weekly*, 6, no. 25, 1981.

8. https://www.eater.com/2016/3/24/11300634/tallywackers-dallas-male-hooters; Whitney Filloon, "Lessons Learned from Tallywackers, Dallas's Male Version of Hooters," Eater, March 24, 2016, https://www.eater.com/2016/3/24/11300634/tallywackers-dallas-male-hooters.

9. The Cabana Cafe and Cabaret at the Copa, menu, Miami, Florida.

Chapter 1. The Elder Stateswoman

1. Matt Schudel, "Annie Kaylor Dies; Presided over Landmark D.C. Steak-house," *Washington Post*, August 3, 2013, https://www.washingtonpost

.com/local/obituaries/annie-kaylor-dies-at-85-presided-over-landmark-dc
-steakhouse/2013/08/03/8e920c78-fc56-11e2-9bde-7ddaa186b751_story.html.

2. Tim Carman, "Annie's Paramount Steakhouse, Long a Haven for D.C.'s
Gay Community, Wins a James Beard Classics Award," *Washington Post*, January 31, 2019, https://www.washingtonpost.com/news/food/wp/2019/01/31
/annies-paramount-steakhouse-long-a-haven-for-d-c-s-gay-community-wins
-a-james-beard-classics-award/.

3. David Hagedorn, "Why Annie's Has a Place in My Heart," James Beard
Foundation (blog). January 31, 2019. https://www.jamesbeard.org/blog
/why-annies-has-a-place-in-my-heart.

4. Ling Ma, *Bliss Montage* (New York: Farrar, Straus and Giroux, 2022).

5. "Annie's Paramount Steakhouse Statement of Significance Summary," sec-
tion 8, page 18, National Park Service / National Register of Historic Places
Registration Form, United States Department of the Interior, Washington,
D.C., October 27, 2020, https://planning.dc.gov/sites/default/files/dc/sites/op
/publication/attachments/JRs%20and%20Annie%27s%20Paramount%20
Steakhouse%20Nomination_0.pdf.

6. "Annie's Paramount Steakhouse Statement of Significance Summary."

7. "Annie's Paramount Steakhouse Statement of Significance Summary."

8. Lait, Jack, and Lee Mortimer. *Washington Confidential* (New York:
Crown Publishers, Inc., 1951).

9. 96, Cong. Rec., 4527–4528 (March 29–April 24, 1950).

10. 96, Cong. Rec., 4527–4528 (March 29–April 24, 1950).

11. 96, Cong. Rec, 4527–4528 (March 29–April 24, 1950).

12. Hamburg, Daniel, "Annie's Way Sign Officially Unveiled, Honoring
Longtime DC LGBTQ Advocate," DC News Now, June 10, 2024. https://www
.dcnewsnow.com/news/local-news/washington-dc/annies-way-sign-officially
-unveiled-honoring-longtime-dc-lgbtq-advocate/.

Chapter 2. Tonight's Special

1. "Our History," Delmonico's, https://www.theoriginaldelmonicos.com/our
-history.

2. "Our History," Antoine's, https://antoines.com/about.

3. Paul Sorene, "Walt Whitman Leading Light of America's First Gay Bar:
The New York Bohemians Who Made Good at Pfaff's," *Flashbak*, August 26,
2015. https://flashbak.com/walt-whitman-leading-light-of-americas-first-gay
-bar-the-new-york-bohemians-who-made-good-at-pfaffs-39034/.

4. Charles Hemstreet, *Literary New York: Its Landmarks and Associations*
(New York and London: G. P. Putnam and Sons, 1903), https://www.gutenberg
.org/files/31814/31814-h/31814-h.htm.

5. Henry Voigt, "Pfaff's," *The American Menu* (blog), September 23, 2017.
https://www.theamericanmenu.com/2017/09/pfaffs.html.

6. Stephen Berkman, "Visiting Babylon Boulevard, New York's
19th-Century Bohemian Underworld," *Literary Hub* (blog), December

2, 2020, https://lithub.com/visiting-babylon-boulevard-new-yorks-19th
-century-bohemian-underworld/.

7. Greggor Mattson, *Who Needs Gay Bars? Bar-Hopping Through America's Endangered LGBTQ+ Places* (Redwood City, CA: Redwood Press, 2023).

8. George Chauncey, *Gay New York: Gender, Urban Culture, and the Making of the Gay Male World 1890–1940* (New York: Basic Books/HarperCollins, 1994).

9. Chauncey, *Gay New York.*

10. Tom Miller, "Enrico & Paglieri's—No. 64 West 11th Street," *Daytonian in Manhattan* (blog), November 2, 2013, http://daytoninmanhattan
.blogspot.com/2013/11/enrico-paglieris-no-64-west-11th-street.html#google
_vignette.

11. *The Nance*, script by Douglas Carter Beane, Lyceum Theatre (Broadway), New York, March 21–August 11, 2013.

12. Ben Brantley, review of *The Nance*, by Douglas Carter Beane, *New York Times*, April 16, 2013, https://www.nytimes.com/2013/04/16/theater/reviews
/the-nance-starring-nathan-lane-at-lyceum-theater.html.

13. Richard Bruce Nugent, *Gay Rebel of the Harlem Renaissance: Selections from the Work of Richard Bruce Nugent*, edited and with an introduction by Thomas H. Wirth (Durham and London: Duke University Press, 2002).

14. Colleen Kim, "A Dining Experience to Remember: A Brief History of the Automat," *History Associates* (blog) https://www.historyassociates.com
/automat/.

15. Quinn Hargitai, "After Automats Died in New York, They Flourished in the Netherlands," *Atlas Obscura*, July 15, 2019, https://www.atlasobscura.com
/articles/automat-history.

16. Associated Press, "Automat Won't 'Boogey,'" *Philadelphia Gay News* 1, no. 5, February 1977, https://jstor.org/stable/community.28042747.

17. Associated Press, "Automat Won't 'Boogey.'"

Chapter 3. Bloodroot Revolution

1. Bonnie Carr, "New Feminist Eatery Aims to 'Warm Belly and Mind,'" *The Bridgeport Post*, March 27, 1977, https://www.newspapers.com
/image/60219605/?terms=bloodroot&match=1.

2. Carr, "New Feminist Eatery."

3. Kate Sosin, "Lesbian Feminist Staple Bloodroot Vegetarian Restaurant Is Accused of Transphobia," *INTO*, January 8, 2018, updated on May 28, 2018, https://www.intomore.com/impact/lesbian-feminist-staple-bloodroot
-vegetarian-restaurant-is-accused-of-transphobia/.

4. Bloodroot, "As many of you know, Bloodroot has recently come under attack. . . . ," Facebook, December 31, 2017, https://www.facebook.com/Blood
rootVegetarianRestaurant/posts/as-many-of-you-know-bloodroot-has-recently
-come-under-attack-and-is-currently-be/1522020014501063/.

5. Jen Jack Gieseking, *A Queer New York: Geographies of Lesbians, Dykes, and Queers* (New York: New York University Press, 2020), https://mc.dlib.nyu.edu/files/nyupress/pdfs/9781479891672.pdf.

6. Greggor Mattson, *Who Needs Gay Bars? Bar-Hopping Through America's Endangered LGBTQ+ Places* (Redwood City, CA: Redwood Press, 2023).

7. *Lesbian Connection*, 3, no. 2 (June 1977), https://jstor.org/stable/community.28039174.

Chapter 4. Two Lesbians Walk into Papa Choux, and Other Acts of Resistance

1. Matthew Schneier, "Julius', the Gay-Elder Dive Bar of the Village, Gets Landmarked," *Curbed*, December 9, 2022, https://www.curbed.com/2022/12/julius-gay-elder-dive-bar-greenwich-village-landmarked.html.

2. Edmund White, "The Gay Bar," *New York*, December 13, 2002, https://nymag.com/nymetro/news/classicnewyork/n_8167.

3. F & C Holding Corp. v. State Liquor Authority, 222 F.3d 141, 145 (NY Supreme Court, App. Div., 1966).

4. F & C Holding Corp. v. State Liquor Authority.

5. Veronica Rose, "Landmarks Calendars Julius' Bar for Consideration as an Individual Landmark," *CityLand*, September 29, 2022, https://www.citylandnyc.org/landmarks-calendars-julius-bar-for-consideration-as-an-individual-landmark/.

6. Tony Ortega, "Three Homosexuals In Search of a Drink," *The Village Voice*, December 2, 2009, https://www.villagevoice.com/three-homosexuals-in-search-of-a-drink/.

7. Lucy Komisar, "Three Homosexuals in Search of a Drink." *Village Voice*, May 5, 1966, https://www.thekomisarscoop.com/wp-content/uploads/2022/04/Village-Voice-Three-Homoxexuals-in-Search-of-a-Drink-by-Lucy-Komisar-1.pdf.

8. Komisar, "Three Homosexuals in Search of a Drink."

9. Scott Simon, "Remembering a 1966 'Sip-In' for Gay Rights," NPR, June 28, 2008, https://www.npr.org/2008/06/28/91993823/remembering-a-1966-sip-in-for-gay-rights.

10. "Designation Report: Julius' Bar Building," New York City Landmarks Preservation Commission. Dec. 6, 2022. https://www.nyclgbtsites.org/wp-content/uploads/2021/06/Julius.pdf.

11. Suzanne Cope, "Dewey's Sit-ins Sparked a Generation of LGBTQIA Social Change," *Philadelphia Inquirer*, June 16, 2022. https://www.inquirer.com/food/restaurants/philadelphiaa-dewey-sit-ins-legacy-20220616.html.

12. "Tavern Charges Police Brutality," *County Courier: The Voice of Los Angeles*, January 19, 1967, https://www.oneinstitute.org/wp-content/uploads/2019/02/one-archives-foundation-black-cat-riots.pdf.

13. Bill Shapiro and Vince Bielski, "Cracker Barrel," *Mother Jones*, March/April 1994, https://www.motherjones.com/politics/1994/03/cracker -barrel/.

14. "Cracker Barrel (@crackerbarrel). "We are excited to celebrate Pride Month with our employees and guests. Everyone is always welcome at our table (and our 🪑 rocker). Happy Pride!" June 8, 2023, https://www.instagram.com/p /CtPBuvgtAv-/?hl=en.

15. "Kim Chi on Childhood, Drag Delusion, and Cracker Barrel," *Good Children: The Podcast*, June 26, 2024, YouTube (video), https://youtu .be/8GDmaNmutD0?si=HOpoQ6G0VUJjcf0-.

16. Eric Marcus, host of *Making Gay History*, podcast, season 3, episode 5, "Deborah Johnson & Zandra Rolón Amato," November 16, 2017, https:// makinggayhistory.org/podcast/deborah-johnson-zandra-rolon-amato.

17. Myrna Oliver, "Lesbian Couple Lose Bid for Injunction," *Los Angeles Times*, July 14, 1983, https://www.newspapers.com/article/the-los-angeles -times/8179031/.

18. "A Binghamton woman who . . . " *Drag* 2, no. 8, https://archive.org /details/drag28unse/page/38/mode/2up.

Chapter 5. Myth America

1. Sam Levin, "Compton's Cafeteria Riot: A Historic Act of Trans Resistance, Three Years Before Stonewall," *Guardian*, June 21, 2019, https:// www.theguardian.com/lifeandstyle/2019/jun/21/stonewall-san-francisco-riot -tenderloin-neighborhood-trans-women.

2. Rick Paulas, "Before Stonewall: The Raucous Trans Riot That History Nearly Forgot," *Vice*, May 12, 2016, https://www.vice.com/en/article /before-stonewall-the-raucous-trans-riot-that-history-nearly-forgot/.

3. Gregorio Davila, dir., *Nancy From Eastside Clover*, Film Bliss Studios, 2014, short film.

4. Ryu Spaeth, "Cancel Culture Grows Up," *Intelligencer* (blog), September 23, 2023, https://nymag.com/intelligencer/article/cancel-culture -haruki-murakami-hasan-minhaj-jann-wenner.html.

5. Daniel Avery, "10 LGBT Uprisings Before Stonewall," *Newsweek*, June 23, 2019, https://www.newsweek.com/before-stonewall-riots-1445365.

Chapter 7. Bread and Butt

1. Jeremiah Moss, "The Gaiety Theater," *Jeremiah's Vanishing New York* (blog), October 11, 2007, http://vanishingnewyork.blogspot.com/2007/10 /gaiety-theater.html.

2. James Traub, *The Devil's Playground: A Century of Pleasure and Profit in Times Square* (New York: Penguin Random House, 2004).

3. Kathryn Belgiorno, "Quietly, a Bawdy Gay Beacon Goes Dark," *New York Times*, April 24, 2005, https://www.nytimes.com/2005/04/24/nyregion/thecity /quietly-a-bawdy-gay-beacon-goes-dark.html.

4. Belgiorno, "Quietly, a Bawdy Gay Beacon Goes Dark."

5. Robert Simonson, "Howard Johnson's, Landmark of Old Time New York, to Shut Down," *Playbill*, April 19, 2005, https://playbill.com/article /howard-johnsons-landmark-of-old-times-square-to-shut-down-com -125398.

6. Lee Robbins, "Brunch Munching," *Philadelphia Gay News*, December 11–24, 1981, https://jstor.org/stable/community.28042780.

7. Dennis Rubini, "Continental Baths Revisited," *Philadelphia Gay News*, September 1976, https://jstor.org/stable/community.28042742.

8. Jack Veasey, "Coming Clean at Philly's Gay Baths," *Philadelphia Gay News*, May 15–29, 1981, https://jstor.org/stable/community.28042773.

Chapter 8. It Was Never About the Food

1. Guy Beringer, "Brunch: A Plea," *Hunter's Weekly*, 1895, https://en.wiki source.org/wiki/Page%3ABrunch_a_plea_(Beringer).tif.

2. "And Yet, the Show Goes On." *Evening Independent* (Massillon, OH), June 5, 1936, https://www.newspapers.com/newspage/3751636/.

3. Steven McElroy, "Portal to Off Off Broadway's Early Days," *New York Times*, December 7, 2011, https://www.nytimes.com/2011/12/11/theater /donation-to-library-opens-new-portal-to-caffe-cino.html.

4. The Clown, advertisement, *Magpie* 1, no. 14, July 5, 1968, https://www .lavenderzines.com/magpie/volume-01-number-13?pgid=ldlci3ix-af3363_233 ddc516e104ac89b342488afb04909mv2.jpg.

5. Edward Siddons, "The Extraordinary Rise of Drag Brunch: A Dining Delight or a Betrayal of Queer History?" *Guardian*, March 17, 2019, https://www.theguardian.com/culture/2019/mar/17/the-extraordinary-rise -of-drag-brunch-a-dining-delight-or-a-betrayal-of-queer-history.

6. Dana B., "Grand Opening of the Newest TG Club/Restaurant in NYC!" *LadyLike: A Tasteful Magazine for Crossdressers With Class*, No. 28, 1996, https://archive.org/details/ladylike28unse/page/18/mode/2up?q=restaurant.

7. Rose Christensen, interview with the author, November 20, 2023.

8. Michael D. Craig, interview with the author, November 20, 2023.

9. Erik Piepenburg, "At Taco Bell, the Drag Brunch Goes Corporate," *New York Times*, May 27, 2022. https://www.nytimes.com/2022/05/27/dining /taco-bell-drag-brunch.html.

10. Louis Knuffke, "Catholics Protest Blasphemous 'Gospel' Drag Brunch at Washington, DC Restaurant," *LifeSiteNews*, September 1, 2023, https:// www.lifesitenews.com/news/catholics-protest-blasphemous-gospel-drag-brunch -at-washington-dc-restaurant/.

11. Troy Campbell, "Drag Show Restaurant Hamburger Mary's Sues Florida, Claiming Law Hurting Business," *ClickOrlando.com*, https://www.clickor lando.com/news/local/2023/05/22/hamburger-marys-sues-florida-claims-adult -performance-law-hurting-business/.

Chapter 10. Convenient Joy

1. Elaine T. Cicora, "Special Effect," *Cleveland Scene*. July 29, 1999. https://www.clevescene.com/food-drink/special-effect-1472530.

2. Cara De Silva, "Restaurants in the Gay '90s," *New York Newsday*, November 10, 1993.

3. Corinne Werder, "GO's New York 'Where to' Guide to Pride," *GOMAG*, August 17, 2007, https://gomag.com/article/gos_new_york_where_to_gui/.

4. Martin Padgett, "Your Fried Chicken Has Done Drag," *Southern Foodways*, https://www.southernfoodways.org/your-fried-chicken-has-done-drag/.

5. Edward Ferry and Shaun Young, "Eat, Drink & Be Mary," *Genre*, no. 71, June 1999.

Chapter 11. Because the Night

1. Michael Kasino, video by Joe E. Jeffries, "Pay It No Mind: After Movie Discussion," YouTube, September 23, 2016, https://www.youtube.com/watch?v=I6-Z19bZIeI.

2. Tray Butler, "God Save the Queen," *Creative Loafing*, October 9, 2003, https://creativeloafing.com/content-184726-cover-story-god-save-the-queen.

3. Butler, "God Save the Queen."

Chapter 12. "It Felt Safe"

1. Kevin Flynn, "Rudy Faces Hostile Gay Reception," *New York Newsday*, July 14, 1989.

2. Eric Marcus, host, *Making Gay History*, podcast, season 3, episode 5, "Coming of Age in the AIDS Crisis—Chapter 4: Complications of AIDS," August 12, 2021, https://makinggayhistory.org/podcast/coming-of-age-during-the-aids-crisis-chapter-4/.

3. UNAIDS, "How AIDS Changed Everything," July 24, 2015, https://www.unaids.org/sites/default/files/media_asset/MDG6Report_en.pdf.

4. Ronald Reagan, "Remarks at the American Foundation for AIDS Research Awards Dinner," Ronald Reagan Presidential Library & Museum. May 31, 1987, accessed September 2, 2024, https://www.presidency.ucsb.edu/documents/remarks-the-american-foundation-for-aids-research-awards-dinner.

5. Eugene L. Meyer and Eve Zibart, "AIDS Fear Closed Restaurant, Owners Say," *Washington Post*, October 10, 1987, accessed September 2, 2024, http://ezproxy.nypl.org/login?url=https://www.proquest.com/hnp washingtonpost/historical-newspapers/aids-fear-closed-restaurant-owners-say/docview/139269519/sem-2?accountid=35635.

6. Hanna Raskin, "Hospitality Industry's Response to AIDS Pandemic Offers Lessons for SC Restaurateurs Today," *Post and Courier* (Charleston, SC), July 8, 2020, updated September 14, 2020, https://www.postandcourier.com/health/covid19/hospitality-industrys-response-to-aids-pandemic-offers

-lessons-for-sc-restaurateurs-today/article_41c360b4-c156-11ea-8858-df71da
2fd184.html.

7. Raskin, "Hospitality Industry's Response."

8. Raskin, "Hospitality Industry's Response."

9. Gregory M. Herek and John P. Capitanio, "AIDS Stigma and Sexual Prejudice," University of California, Davis, preprint of a paper to appear in *American Behavioral Scientist*, 1999, 42, 1126–1143, https://lgbpsychology.org/html/abs99_sp_pre.pdf.

10. The ADA Project, "Special Collection: The Chapman Amendment," http://www.adalawproject.org/chapman-amendment.

11. Senator Helms, speaking on S. 2189, on July 11, 1990, 101st Cong., 2nd sess., Congressional Record 136, pt. 12, https://www.govinfo.gov/content/pkg/GPO-CRECB-1990-pt12/pdf/GPO-CRECB-1990-pt12-2-2.pdf.

Chapter 13. The Lifeline

1. David Amsden, "The 25th Hour of Florent Morellet," *New York*, May 23, 2008, https://nymag.com/restaurants/features/47227/.

2. Amsden, "The 25th Hour."

3. Amsden, "The 25th Hour."

4. Frank Bruni, "Genre-Bending Hangout Takes Its Final Bows," *New York Times*, May 21, 2008, https://www.nytimes.com/2008/05/21/dining/21florent.html.

5. "Behind the Bushes: The Queer History of the High Line," *High Line* (blog), June 24, 2021, https://www.thehighline.org/blog/2021/06/24/behind-the-bushes-the-gay-history-of-the-high-line/.

6. Jay Shockley, "Mineshaft," NYC LGBT Historic Sites Project, https://www.nyclgbtsites.org/site/mineshaft/.

7. Joyce Purnick, "City Closes Bar Frequented by Homosexuals, Citing Sexual Activity Linked to AIDS," *New York Times*, November 8, 1985, https://www.nytimes.com/1985/11/08/nyregion/city-closes-bar-frequented-by-homosexuals-citing-sexual-activity-linked-to-aids.html.

Chapter 14. The Trendsetter

1. Linda Burum and Charles Perry, "Cave Canem: Ancient History on a Plate," *Los Angeles Times*, February 7, 1988, https://www.latimes.com/archives/la-xpm-1988-02-07-ca-40931-story.html.

2. Amy Clyde, "Neither Guys Nor Dolls," *New Yorker*, April 3, 1994, https://www.newyorker.com/magazine/1994/04/11/neither-guys-nor-dolls.

3. Daniel Maurer, "Dirty Delta of Lucky Cheng's Serves Orgy Bowls to Britney Spears," *New York*, January 30, 2007, https://www.grubstreet.com/2007/01/dirty_delta_of_lucky_chengs_se.html.

4. Simon Rex Brown, "What a Drag: Lucky Cheng's Will Leave East Village for 52nd Street," *The Local: East Village* (blog), http://localeastvillage.com/2011/12/08/sayonara-lucky-chengs/.

5. Brown, "What a Drag."

6. David Kirby, "Maison de Sade Gets a Whipping," *New York Times*, March 7, 1999, https://www.nytimes.com/1999/03/07/nyregion/neighborhood-report -chelsea-maison-de-sade-gets-a-whipping.html.

7. Kirby, "Maison de Sade."

8. Hey Qween, "Ongina on the Legacy of the Legendary Drag Restaurant Lucky Cheng's," YouTube, July 12, 2017, https://www.youtube.com /watch?v=DUxfmCmpVIo.

Chapter 15. Now Serving

1. Steve Rothaus, "The Census Confirms It: Wilton Manors in No. 2 Nationally for Most Gay Couples per 1,000," *Miami Herald*, September 8, 2011, https://miamiherald.typepad.com/gaysouthflorida/2011/09/the -census-confirms-it-wilton-manors-is-one-of-the-united-states-gayest-places .html.

Bibliography

"75 Anniversary Celebration." Wilton Manors.gov. Accessed September 3, 2024. https://www.wiltonmanors.gov/799/75th-Anniversary-Celebration.

1450ATL. "Impulse Video Digest—Gallus Restaurant Spotlight." YouTube video, 5:04, October 9, 2014, originally aired July 1984. https://youtu.be/G7zBTWBxnqs?si=NaSvb_tJzjI-mnbt.

1450ATL. "The Silver Grill on Monroe Drive Atlanta—Impulse Video Digest." YouTube video, 4:38, May 16, 2015, originally aired August 27, 1984. https://youtu.be/NuAbmoBH6oE?si=nRKK2Is_oYLFYT43.

Abramson, Mark. Interview with the author, November 21, 2023.

ADA Project. "Special Collection: The Chapman Amendment." http://www.adalawproject.org/chapman-amendment.

Albo, Mike. "The Death and Life of America's Gay Restaurants." *Jarry*, no. 2, accessed on Medium, April 16, 2016. https://medium.com/jarry-mag/the-death-and-life-of-america-s-gay-restaurants-2ec9a24c68a3.

Allen, Mark. Interview with the author, August 21, 2023.

Allen, Ted. Interview with the author, October 20, 2023.

Allred, Gloria. June 9, 1983. Papa Choux press release.

Altman, Lawrence K. "Rare Cancer Seen in 41 Homosexuals." *New York Times*, July 3, 1981. https://www.nytimes.com/1981/07/03/us/rare-cancer-seen-in-41-homosexuals.html.

"America Responds to AIDS." National Library of Medicine, accessed September 2, 2024. https://www.nlm.nih.gov/exhibition/surviving-and-thriving/digitalgallery_theme_2.html.

Amsden, David. "The 25th Hour of Florent Morellet." *New York*, May 23, 2008. https://nymag.com/restaurants/features/47227.

Anderson, Brett. "With Chop Suey and Loyal Fans, a Montana Kitchen Keeps the Flame Burning." *New York Times*, August 3, 2021. http://www.nytimes.com/2021/08/03/dining/pekin-noodle-parlor-butte-montana.html.

"And Yet, the Show Goes On." *Evening Independent*, Massillon, OH, June 5, 1936. https://www.newspapers.com/newspage/3751636/.

Annie's Paramount Steakhouse Statement of Significance Summary, sec. 8, page 18, National Park Service / National Register of Historic Places Registration Form, United States Department of the Interior, Washington, D.C., October 27, 2020. https://planning.dc.gov/sites/default/files/dc/sites/op /publication/attachments/JRs%20and%20Annie%27s%20Paramount%20 Steakhouse%20Nomination_0.pdf.

Arino, Lisha. "City Waited 3 Decades to Rule Yaffa Cafe's Back Patio Illegal, Manager Says." *DNA Info*, October 6, 2014. https://www .dnainfo.com/new-york/20141006/east-village/city-waited-3-decades-rule -yaffa-cafes-back-patio-illegal-manager-says/.

"The Artistry Behind the Dolphin Spout: A Journey from Florence to the Automat." *Horn & Hardart* (blog), January 31, 2024. https://hornandhardart .com/blogs/blog/automat-dolphin-spout-history?srsltid=AfmBOooc 2k2SeLIbww_XIsHHO-ssCfh7BUakiEiayOC6jS4zcCuCmJYq.

Associated Press. "Automat Won't 'Boogey,'" *Philadelphia Gay News* 1, no. 5, February 1977. https://jstor.org/stable/community.28042747.

Associated Press. "Survey Finds Wide AIDS Ignorance." *New York Times*, January 30, 1988. https://www.nytimes.com/1988/01/30/us/survey-finds -wide-aids-ignorance.html.

Atlanta LGBTQ+ Historic Context Statement. New South Associates for Historic Atlanta and the City of Atlanta Office of Design, April 17, 2023. https://atlgbtq.atlantaga.gov/assets/files/Atlanta%20LGBTQHistoricContext Statement.pdf.

Azali, Saied. Interview with the author, January 31, 2023.

Bainbridge, Julia. "Friday Night at the Colonnade." *Atlanta*, October 26, 2017. https://www.atlantamagazine.com/dining-news/friday-night-at -the-colonnade/.

Baldridge, Charlene. "A Gender Bender." *Girl Talk* (newsletter), July 1999. https://www.digitaltransgenderarchive.net/downloads/2801pg534.

Barnes, Djuna. *Greenwich Village As It Is*. New York: Phoenix Bookshop, 1978. Originally published in *Pearson's* magazine, October 1916. https:// www.themorgan.org/printed-books/87521.

Barron, James. "Last Automat Closes, Its Era Long Gone." *New York Times*, April 11, 1991. https://www.nytimes.com/1991/04/11/nyregion/last-automat -closes-its-era-long-gone.html.

Beane, Douglas Carter (playwright). In discussion with the author, August 2022.

"Behind the Bushes: The Queer History of the High Line." *High Line* (blog), June 24, 2021. https://www.thehighline.org/blog/2021/06/24 /behind-the-bushes-the-gay-history-of-the-high-line.

Belgiorno, Kathryn. "Quietly, a Bawdy Gay Beacon Goes Dark." *New York Times*, April 24, 2005. https://www.nytimes.com/2005/04/24/nyregion/the city/quietly-a-bawdy-gay-beacon-goes-dark.html.

Beringer, Guy. "Brunch: A Plea." *Hunter's Weekly*, 1895. https://en.wikisource .org/wiki/Page%3ABrunch_a_plea_(Beringer).tif.

Berkman, Stephen. "Visiting Babylon Boulevard, New York's 19th-Century Bohemian Underworld." *Literary Hub* (blog), December 2, 2020. https://lithub.com/visiting-babylon-boulevard-new-yorks-19th-century-bohemian -underworld/.

Bérubé, Allan. *Coming Out Under Fire: The History of Gay Men and Women in World War II*. Chapel Hill: University of North Carolina Press, 1990.

Biederman, Marcia. "Journey to an Overlooked Past." *New York Times*, June 11, 2000. https://www.nytimes.com/2000/06/11/nyregion/journey-to -an-overlooked-past.html.

"A Binghamton woman who . . . " *Drag*, 2, no. 8. https://archive.org/details/drag 28unse/page/38/mode/2up?q=restaurant.

Birdsall, John. "The Forgotten Queer Legacy of Billy West and Zuni Cafe." *New York Times*, May 28, 2021. https://www.nytimes.com/2021/05/28 /dining/billy-west-zuni-cafe.html.

"The Black Cat." Los Angeles Conservancy, https://www.laconservancy.org /learn/historic-places/the-black-cat/.

Blalock, Stephanie M. *"GO TO PFAFF'S!": The History of a Restaurant and Lager Beer Saloon*. Lehigh, PA: Lehigh University Press, 2014. https://preserve.lehigh .edu/digital-special-collections/vault-pfaffs/go-pfaffs-history-restaurant -lager-beer-saloon-stephanie-m.

Bloodroot. "As many of you know, Bloodroot has recently come under attack. . . ." Facebook, December 31, 2017. https://www.facebook .com/BloodrootVegetarianRestaurant/posts/as-many-of-you-know-blood root-has-recently-come-under-attack-and-is-currently-be/152202001450 1063/.

Blount, Scott. Interview with the author, August 18, 2023.

Boyce, Martin. Interview with the author, August 1, 2022.

Boyd, Nan Alamilla. *Wide Open Town: A History of Queer San Francisco to 1965*. Berkeley: University of California Press, 2003.

Brantley, Ben. Review of *The Nance*, by Douglas Carter Beane. *New York Times*, April 16, 2013. https://www.nytimes.com/2013/04/16/theater /reviews/the-nance-starring-nathan-lane-at-lyceum-theater.html.

Bressler, Jill. "Hamburger Mary's: Hold the Mayo." *Campanile*, February 10, 1984. https://palyjournalismarchive.pausd.org/?a=d&d=CAM19840210 -01.1.6&e=—en-20—1—txt-txIN—.

"Brian Bradley." houstonlgbthistory.org. https://www.houstonlgbthistory.org /banner1991bb.html.

"Brian Douglas Bradley." Texas Obituary Project. https://www.texas obituaryproject.org/111095bradley.html.

Brown, Ricardo J. *The Evening Crowd at Kirmser's: A Gay Life in the 1940s*. Minneapolis: University of Minnesota Press, 2001.

Brown, Simon Rex. "What a Drag: Lucky Cheng's Will Leave East Village for 52nd Street." *The Local: East Village* (blog). http://localeastvillage .com/2011/12/08/sayonara-lucky-chengs/.

Bruni, Frank. "Genre-Bending Hangout Takes Its Final Bows." *New York Times*, May 21, 2008. https://www.nytimes.com/2008/05/21/dining/21 florent.html.

Buch, Clarissa. "Mayor Gary Resnick Discusses The Revival of Wilton Manors." *Fort Lauderdale Illustrated*, November 20, 2017. https://fort lauderdaleillustrated.com/fli-life/people/mayor-gary-resnick-discusses -the-revival-of-wilton-manors/.

"Buck Harris Interview, 20 April 2006," Cleveland Voices, accessed August 30, 2024. https://clevelandvoices.org/items/show/2620.

Buckley, Cara. "Closing Time at a Diner That Never Closed." *New York Times*, June 30, 2008. https://www.nytimes.com/2008/06/30/nyregion/30florent .html.

BU News Service. "Forty Years of Food and Friendship in Bloodroot." October 16, 2019. https://bunewsservice.com/forty-years-of-food-and -friendship-in-bloodroot/.

Burns, Kevin. Interview with the author, September 27, 2023.

Burum, Linda, and Charles Perry. "Cave Canem: Ancient History on a Plate." *Los Angeles Times*, February 7, 1988. https://www.latimes.com/archives /la-xpm-1988-02-07-ca-40931-story.html.

Butler, Tray. "God Save the Queen." *Creative Loafing*, October 9, 2003. https:// creativeloafing.com/content-184726-cover-story-god-save-the-queen.

Cabana Cafe and Cabaret at the Copa. Menu. Miami, Florida.

"Cafe Orlin signs off." *EV Grieve* (blog), October 16, 2017. https://evgrieve .com/2017/10/cafe-orlin-signs-off.htm.

Caffe Cino. NYC LGBT Historic Sites Project. Accessed on August 29, 2014. https://www.nyclgbtsites.org/site/caffe-cino/.

Campbell, Troy. "Drag Show Restaurant Hamburger Mary's Sues Florida, Claiming Law Hurting Business." *ClickOrlando.com*. https://www .clickorlando.com/news/local/2023/05/22/hamburger-marys-sues-florida -claims-adult-performance-law-hurting-business.

Carman, Tim. "Annie's Paramount Steakhouse, Long a Haven for D.C.'s Gay Community, Wins a James Beard Classics Award." *Washington Post*, January 31, 2019. https://www.washingtonpost.com/news/food/wp/2019/01/31 /annies-paramount-steakhouse-long-a-haven-for-d-c-s-gay-community -wins-a-james-beard-classics-award/.

Carr, Bonnie. "New Feminist Eatery Aims to 'Warm Belly and Mind.'" *Bridgeport Post*, March 27, 1977. https://www.newspapers.com /image/60219605/?terms=bloodroot&match=1.

"A Case of Sadism, Indifference." *The Chicago Tribune*, August 3, 1991, updated August 10, 2021. https://www.chicagotribune.com/1991/08/03 /a-case-of-sadism-indifference/.

Chauncey, George. *Gay New York: Gender, Urban Culture, and the Making of the Gay Male World 1890–1940*. New York: Basic Books/HarperCollins, 1994.

Christensen, Rose. Interview with the author, November 20, 2023.

Cicora, Elaine T. "Special Effect." *Cleveland Scene.* July 29, 1999. https://www
.clevescene.com/food-drink/special-effect-1472530.

Cinema Treasures. "Gaiety Burlesque." Accessed August 29, 2024. https://
cinematreasures.org/theaters/9809.

The Clown, advertisement. *Magpie* 1, no. 14, July 5, 1968. https://www
.lavenderzines.com/magpie/volume-01-number-13?pgid=ldlci3ix-af3363
_233ddc516e104ac89b342488afb04909mv2.jpg.

"Club Baths: New York City." *Welcome to My World* (blog), September 23,
2013. http://welclometomyworld0426.blogspot.com/2013/09/club-baths
-new-york-city.html?zx=2352bdee07d19376.

Clyde, Amy. "Neither Guys Nor Dolls." *New Yorker,* April 3, 1994. https://
www.newyorker.com/magazine/1994/04/11/neither-guys-nor-dolls.

Congressional Record, vol. 96, pt. 4, 81st Congress, 2nd Session, March
29–April 24, 1950, 4527–4528.

Cooper, Carly. "Lingering Shade Owners Take Over the 97-Year-Old Colonnade Restaurant." *Atlanta* magazine, September 10, 2024. https://www
.atlantamagazine.com/dining-news/lingering-shade-owners-take-over-the
-97-year-old-colonnade-restaurant/.

Cope, Suzanne. "Dewey's Sit-Ins Sparked a Generation of LGBTQIA Social
Change," *Philadelphia Inquirer,* June 16, 2022. https://www.inquirer.com
/food/restaurants/philadelphiaa-dewey-sit-ins-legacy-20220616.html.

Covarrubias, Miguel. "What Caused the Black Cat Tavern Riots?" *Out for
Safe Schools*, https://www.oneinstitute.org/wp-content/uploads/2019/02
/one-archives-foundation-black-cat-riots.pdf.

Cracker Barrel (@crackerbarrel). "We are excited to celebrate Pride Month with
our employees and guests. Everyone is always welcome at our table (and
our 🎸 rocker). Happy Pride!" June 8, 2023. https://www.instagram.com/p
/CtPBuvgtAv-/?hl=en.

Craig, Michael D. Interview with the author, November 20, 2023.

Crawford, Phillip. *The Mafia and the Gays.* Pub. by author, 2015.

Crowell, Merle. "Two Country Boys Who Serve 45,000,000 Meals a Year,"
American Magazine 92 no. 5, November 1921. https://www.mrlocalhistory
.org/oldmillinn-grain-house/.

Dana B. "Grand Opening of the Newest TG Club/Restaurant in NYC!" *Lady-
Like: A Tasteful Magazine for Crossdressers With Class*, No. 28, 1996.
https://archive.org/details/ladylike28unse/page/18/mode/2up?q=restaurant.

Davenport, Sharon. "LGBT Pride: Remembering The Brick Hut Cafe," KQED
Food. San Francisco, CA: KQED, June 23, 2011. https://www.kqed.org
/bayareabites/29308/lgbt-pride-remembering-the-brick-hut-cafe-part-1.

Davila, Gregorio, dir. *Nancy From Eastside Clover.* Film Bliss Studios, 2014.
Short film.

Dawson, Ashley Nicole. Interview with the author, August 25, 2023.

del Campo, Robert. Interview with the author, October 3, 2023.

"Designation Report: Julius' Bar Building." New York City Landmarks Preservation Commission. December 6, 2022. https://www.nyclgbtsites.org
/wp-content/uploads/2021/06/Julius.pdf.

Diamond Lil. *Diamond Lil Sings Silver Grill.* Glamour & Grease Records,
1984. Vinyl LP.

Dilallo, Kevin, and Krumholtz, Jack. *The Unofficial Gay Manual: Living the
Lifestyle (or at Least Appearing to).* New York: Doubleday, 1994.

"Dining Out for Life 2015: Celebrating 25 Years of Fellowship, Generosity, and
Good Food." ActionWellness, April 16, 2015. https://www.actionwellness
.org/archived/dining-out-for-life-2015-celebrating-25-years-of-fellowship
-generosity-and-good-food/.

Dominguez, Laura. "The Black Cat: Harbinger of LGBTQ Civil Rights,"
PBS SoCal. February 11, 2017. https://www.pbssocal.org/shows/lost-la
/the-black-cat-harbinger-of-lgbtq-civil-rights.

Dress, Tora. Interview with the author, January 22, 2023.

Dynasty, season 4, episode 5, "The Hearing: Part 2," directed by Irving J.
Moore, written by Edward DeBlasio, aired November 2, 1983, on ABC.

Enrico & Paglieri, postcard. Circa 1910. https://www.worthpoint.com
/worthopedia/1910-enrico-paglieri-restaurant-3821462199.

Evans, Jacquie, and Keith Evans. Interview with the author, Los Angeles, October 1, 2023.

"Eye Scoop." *Women's Wear Daily*, March 10, 1994. https://wwd.com/eye
/people/eye-scoop-1156334/.

F & C Holding Corp. v. State Liquor Authority, 222 F.3d 141, 145 (New York
Supreme Court, Appellate Division, 1966).

Fabricant, Florence. "Village Den, from Antoni Porowski of 'Queer Eye,'
Opens in West Village." *New York Times*, September 25, 2018. https://www
.nytimes.com/2018/09/25/dining/nyc-restaurant-openings.html.

Faderman, Lillian, and Stuart Timmons. *Gay L.A.: A History of Sexual Outlaws, Power Politics, and Lipstick Lesbians.* New York: Basic
Books, 2006. https://archive.org/details/gaylahistoryofse00lill/page/150
/mode/2up?q=arthur+J.

"Farewell, Florent: New York Loses a Mecca of Cool." NPR, June 9, 2008.
YouTube, accessed on September 2, 2024. https://www.youtube.com
/watch?v=-J1qO7AidqY.

Feniger, Susan. Interview with the author, December 23, 2023.

Ferentinos, Susan. "Dewey's Lunch Counter Sit-In." The Encyclope-
dia of Greater Philadelphia. https://www.scribbr.com/academic-writing
/writing-process/.

Ferry, Edward, and Shaun Young. "Eat, Drink & Be Mary," *Genre*, no. 71, June
1999.

Filloon, Whitney. "Lessons Learned from Tallywackers, Dallas' Male
Version of Hooters." *Eater*, March 24, 2016. https://www.eater.com
/2016/3/24/11300634/tallywackers-dallas-male-hooters.

Folsom, Ed, and Kenneth M. Price. *Re-Scripting Walt Whitman: An Introduction to His Life and Work*. Hoboken, NJ: Wiley-Blackwell, 2005.

Foster, James, and Rocky Joseph McCombs. Interview with the author, November 14, 2023.

Franklin, Jonathan. "An Orlando Drag Show Restaurant Files Lawsuit Against Florida and Gov. Ron DeSantis." NPR, May 25, 2023. https://www.npr.org/2023/05/25/1177727539/hamburger-marys-orlando-lawsuit-florida-desantis-drag-show.

Franklin, Jonathan. "Judge Blocks a Florida Law That Would Punish Venues Where Kids Can See Drag Shows." NPR, June 27, 2023. https://www.npr.org/2023/06/27/1184561373/hamburger-marys-orlando-anti-drag-law-blocked-florida.

Garcia, Ken. "Hamburger Mary's Will Be Missed/Folsom Street Hangout Is Sold." *SFGate*, March 6, 2001. https://www.sfgate.com/restaurants/article/hamburger-mary-s-will-be-missed-folsom-street-2945558.php.

Gates, Anita. "Looking at Bodies (and Peeking Into Souls)." *New York Times*, December 1, 2006. https://www.nytimes.com/2006/12/01/arts/television/01nake.html.

Gay Barchives. "Wilton Manors: Andy Martin Discusses Chardees, Andee's Creamery, Listen, Wilton Bier Garden & More." YouTube video, 26:08, posted September 7, 2023. https://www.youtube.com/watch?v=XB6YHNvtnmM.

Gay Morning America, season 2, show 1, aired October 17, 1984. http://gaycenter.prattsi.org/s/av/item/27.

Gay Morning America, season 2, show 2, aired October 26, 1984. http://gaycenter.prattsi.org/s/av/item/25.

Gay Morning America, season 2, show 3, aired October 30, 1984. http://gaycenter.prattsi.org/s/av/item/90.

Gay Morning America, season 2, show 6, aired November 20, 1984. http://gaycenter.prattsi.org/s/av/item/31.

"Gay News Lambda Awards." *Philadelphia Gay News* 6, no. 10 (March 5, 1982). https://jstor.org/stable/community.28042786.

Gersten, David. Interview with the author, July 15, 2024.

Gieseking, Jen Jack. *A Queer New York: Geographies of Lesbians, Dykes, and Queers*. New York University Press, 2020. https://mc.dlib.nyu.edu/files/nyupress/pdfs/9781479891672.pdf.

Gragnani, Vincent. "Lost Restaurants of NYC: Enrico & Paglieri." *I Happen to Like New York* (blog), February 3, 2014. https://ihappentolikenewyork.com/2014/02/03/lost-restaurants-of-nyc-enrico-paglieri/.

Green, Penelope. "Robert Patrick, Early and Prolific Playwright of Gay Life, Dies at 85. *New York Times*. May 2, 2023. https://www.nytimes.com/2023/05/02/theater/robert-patrick-dead.html.

Guerrero, Susana. "Retro Diner Orphan Andy's Gets Modern Makeover Fit for a Global Pandemic." *SF Gate*, June 24, 2020. https://www.sfgate.com/food/slideshow/Orphan-Andys-diner-plastic-barriers-SF-Castro-204221.php.

Hagedorn, David. Interview with the author, February 9, 2023.

Halo. Interview with the author, December 12, 2023.

Hamburg, Daniel. "Annie's Way Sign Officially Unveiled, Honoring Long-time DC LGBTQ Advocate." *DC News Now*, June 10, 2024. https://www.dcnewsnow.com/news/local-news/washington-dc/annies-way-sign-officially-unveiled-honoring-longtime-dc-lgbtq-advocate/.

"Hamburger Mary's." *Cuisinenet.* https://www.cuisinenet.com/restaurants/hamburger-marys/#google_vignette.

"The Handkerchief Code, According to 'Bob Damron's Address Book' in 1980," *Saint Foundation* (blog), April 25, 2019. https://www.thesaintfoundation.org/community/hanky-code-bob-damrons-address-book.

Hargitai, Quinn. "After Automats Died in New York, They Flourished in the Netherlands." *Atlas Obscura*, July 15, 2019. https://www.atlasobscura.com/articles/automat-history.

Harrison, Shane. "Pioneering Atlanta Drag Performer Diamond Lil Has Died." *Atlanta Journal-Constitution*, August 10, 2016. https://www.ajc.com/lifestyles/pioneering-atlanta-drag-performer-diamond-lil-has-died/fFIGPEvnJGV6ufuZtYNmoN/.

Hartke, Kristen. "For 47 Years, a Lesbian-Owned Restaurant Has Put Politics on the Menu." *Washington Post*, June 7, 2024. "https://www.washingtonpost.com/food/2024/06/07/bloodroot-collective-restaurant-lesbian-feminist/.

Harvey, Steve. "Papa Choux Serves Black Crepe at 'Wake for Romance.'" *Los Angeles Times*, May 25, 1984.

"Have You a Little Fairy in Your Home?" American Vaudeville Museum Archive. Accessed August 30, 2024. https://vaudeville.library.arizona.edu/items/have-you-a-little-fairy-in-your-home/.

Heide, Robert. "Magic Time at the Caffe Cino," *New York Native*, May 6–19, 1985, 29–30.

Helms, Senator Jesse, speaking on S. 2189, on July 11, 1990, 101st Cong., 2nd sess., Congressional Record 136, pt. 12. https://www.govinfo.gov/content/pkg/GPO-CRECB-1990-pt12/pdf/GPO-CRECB-1990-pt12-2-2.pdf.

Hemstreet, Charles. *Literary New York: Its Landmarks and Associations.* New York and London: G. P. Putnam and Sons, 1903. https://www.gutenberg.org/files/31814/31814-h/31814-h.htm.

Henry, Scott. "30 Years of the Good, the Bad and the Weird-as-Hell." *Creative Loafing*, June 5, 2002. https://creativeloafing.com/content-184564-cover-story-30-years-of-the-good-the-bad-and-the.

Herbkersman, Mara, and Emily Bielagus. Interview with the author, October 4, 2023.

Herek, Gregory M., and John P. Capitanio, "AIDS Stigma and Sexual Prejudice," University of California, Davis. This is a preprint of a paper to appear in *American Behavioral Scientist* 42, (1999): 1126–1143. https://lgbpsychology.org/html/abs99_sp_pre.pdf.

Hey Qween. "Ongina on the Legacy of the Legendary Drag Restaurant Lucky Cheng's." YouTube video, 3:34, posted July 12, 2017. https://www.youtube .com/watch?v=DUxfmCmpVIo.

Hippler, Mike. *So Little Time: Essays on Gay Life*. Berkeley: Celestial Arts, 1990.

"History of 2209 Wilton Drive." Eagle Bar, Wilton Manors, accessed September 3, 2024. https://eaglebarwm.com/wp-content/uploads/2021/09/History-of -2209-Wilton-Drive.pdf.

Hobo's. "The 'All My Children' Lunch Bunch," advertisement in *Cascade Voice*, June 3, 1983.

Holleran, Andrew. "The Wrinkle Room." *New York Times Magazine*, September 1, 1996. https://www.nytimes.com/1996/09/01/magazine/the-wrinkle -room.html.

"Hollywood Spa, One of LA's Oldest Gay Bathhouses, Will Close Soon." *WeHO Online*, February 10, 2014. https://wehoville.com/2014/02/10 /hollywood-spa-one-las-oldest-gay-bathhouses-will-close-soon/.

Horn & Hardart. Menu, October 1, 1958. 31x18 cm folded; 31x35.5 cm open. New York Public Library, New York. https://menus.nypl.org /menu_pages/52560/explore.

Horn of Plenty. *Queer Happened Here*. Instagram, August 7, 2023. https://www .instagram.com/queer_happened_here/p/Cvo0cMfOLxA/?img_index=2.

Hyman, Martin D. "'Where the Drinkers & Laughers Meet'—Pfaff's: Whitman's Literary Lair," *Seaport*, Spring 1992.

International House of Pancakes. "IHOP Supports LGT Pride," advertisement in *Cruise Weekly* 6, no. 25, 1981.

Jacobs, Andrew. "Tiffany's Refitted For Breakfast, And Other Meals." *New York Times*. September 24, 1995. https://www.nytimes.com/1995/09/24 /nyregion/neighborhood-report-greenwich-village-tiffany-s-refitted-for -breakfast-other.html.

Jason, Josephine. Interview with the author, January 22, 2023.

"John P. Dodd Is Dead; Lighting Designer, 50." *New York Times*, July 17, 1991. https://www.nytimes.com/1991/07/17/obituaries/john-p-dodd-is -dead-lighting-designer-50.html.

Johnson, Deborah, and Zandra Rolón. Interview with the author, November 21, 2023.

Johnson, Thomas A. "3 Deviates Invite Exclusion by Bars." *New York Times*, April 22, 1966. https://www.nytimes.com/1966/04/22/archives/3-deviates -invite-exclusion-by-bars-but-they-visit-four-before.html.

Johnson, Tom, Interview with the author, August 23, 2023.

Justice, Telly, and Camille Lindsley. Interview with the author, September 14, 2023.

Kacala, Alexander. "Florida City Elects Country's Second All-LGBTQ Local Government." *NBC News*, November 12, 2018. https://www.nbcnews .com/feature/nbc-out/florida-city-elects-country-s-second-all-lgbtq-local -government-n935156.

Karlin, Rick. Interview with the author, March 4, 2023.

Kasino, Michael, video by Joe E. Jeffries. "Pay It No Mind: After Movie Discussion." YouTube video, posted September 23, 2016. https://www.youtube .com/watch?v=I6-Z19bZIeI.

Kastor, Elizabeth, and Sandra G. Boodman. "The Flap at the AIDS Fundraiser." *Washington Post*, May 31, 1987. https://www.washington post.com/archive/lifestyle/1987/06/01/the-flap-at-the-aids-fundraiser /b673e8ee-b611-44fb-af78-a4c5880760eb/.

Katinas, Georgia. Interview with the author, Washington, D.C., January 2023.

Kauffman, Jonathan. "Hamburger Mary's Grandiose Return to SF Comes with Side of Controversy." *San Francisco Chronicle*, April 30, 2018. https://www .sfchronicle.com/restaurants/article/Hamburger-Mary-s-grandiose-return-to -SF-comes-12873176.php.

Kelly, Leslie. "A Report from the Grandest Restaurant Opening Ever." *Forbes*, January 31, 2024. https://www.forbes.com/sites /lesliekelly/2024/01/29/a-report-from-the-grandest-restaurant-opening-ever/.

Ketchum, Alex. *Ingredients for Revolution: A History of American Feminist Restaurants, Cafes, and Coffeehouses*. Montreal: Concordia University Press, 2022.

"Kim Chi on Childhood, Drag Delusion, and Cracker Barrel." *Good Children: The Podcast*, June 26, 2024. YouTube video. https://youtu .be/8GDmaNmutD0?si=HOpoQ6G0VUJjcf0-.

Kim, Colleen. "A Dining Experience to Remember: A Brief History of the Automat." *History Associates* (blog) https://www.historyassociates.com /automat.

Kirby, David. "Maison de Sade Gets a Whipping." *New York Times,* March 7, 1999. https://www.nytimes.com/1999/03/07/nyregion/neighborhood-report -chelsea-maison-de-sade-gets-a-whipping.html.

Knuffke, Louis. "Catholics Protest Blasphemous 'Gospel' Drag Brunch at Washington, DC restaurant," *LifeSiteNews*, September 1, 2023. https://www .lifesitenews.com/news/catholics-protest-blasphemous-gospel-drag-brunch -at-washington-dc-restaurant/.

Komisar, Lucy. "Three Homosexuals in Search of a Drink." *Village Voice*, May 5, 1966. https://www.thekomisarscoop.com/wp-content/uploads/2022/04 /Village-Voice-Three-Homoxexuals-in-Search-of-a-Drink-by-Lucy-Komisar -1.pdf.

Kravitz Hoeffner, Melissa. "Four Stages, One Drag Restaurant: The Evolution of Lucky Cheng's in NYC." *Thrillist*, August 17, 2016. https://www.thrillist .com/eat/new-york/lucky-chengs-nyc-drag-restaurant.

Kurutz, Steven. "Savoring a Last Cup at a Place All Their Own." *New York Times*, August 26, 2005. https://www.nytimes.com/2005/08/26/nyregion /savoring-a-last-cup-at-a-place-all-their-own.html.

Lait, Jack, and Lee Mortimer. *Washington Confidential*. New York: Crown Publishers, 1951.

Lambert, Bruce. "Gay Bar Shut in 'Loop.'" *New York Times*, September 4, 1994. https://www.nytimes.com/1994/09/04/nyregion/neighborhood-report-midtown-gay-bar-shut-in-loop.html?pagewanted=1.

Lavender Woman 2, no. 7 (November 1973). https://jstor.org/stable/community.28039114.

Lavender Woman 3, no. 5 (July 1974). https://jstor.org/stable/community.28039119.

Lavender Woman 4, no. 4 (August 1975). https://jstor.org/stable/community.28039125.

Lesbian Connection 3, no. 2 (June 1977). https://jstor.org/stable/community.28039174.

Levin, Sam. "Compton's Cafeteria Riot: A Historic Act of Trans Resistance, Three Years Before Stonewall." *Guardian*, June 21, 2019. https://www.theguardian.com/lifeandstyle/2019/jun/21/stonewall-san-francisco-riot-tenderloin-neighborhood-trans-women.

Lev-Tov, Devorah. "The Return of the Automat." *Food & Wine*, April 6, 2021. https://www.foodandwine.com/lifestyle/return-of-the-automat.

Li, Julie. Interview with the author, July 29, 2024.

Lieberman, Hallie. "The Devil Went Down to Georgia." *Atavist*, no. 149. March 2024. https://magazine.atavist.com/the-devil-went-down-to-georgia-handcuff-man-atlanta-crime-lgbt/.

Lookalikes. "Original La Cage aux Folles—Beverly Hills—www.icons.nu." Video, 1:52. July 19, 2006. https://www.youtube.com/watch?v=tyPk0_5gCgs.

Loudis, Jessica. "Florent Was the Most Progressive Diner in New York." *My Recipes*, February 13, 2018. https://www.myrecipes.com/extracrispy/florent-was-the-most-progressive-diner-in-new-york.

Mann, Walter L. "HoJoLand Times Square." HoJoLand.com, August 29, 2014. http://www.hojoland.com/timessquare.html.

Man's Country, Chicago. "An Indoor fantasy!" advertisement. Facebook, August 16, 2020. https://www.facebook.com/136472266406009/photos/a.549605131759385/3134866809899858/?type=3&source=57&_rdr.

Marcus, Eric, host. *Making Gay History*. Season 3, episode 5, "Deborah Johnson & Zandra Rolón Amato." November 16, 2017. Podcast, 19 min. https://makinggayhistory.org/podcast/deborah-johnson-zandra-rolon-amato.

Marcus, Eric, host. *Making Gay History*. Season 3, episode 5, "Coming of Age in the AIDS Crisis—Chapter 4: Complications of AIDS." August 12, 2021. Podcast, 41 min. https://makinggayhistory.org/podcast/coming-of-age-during-the-aids-crisis-chapter-4/.

Martha. Interview with the author, June 1–2, 2023.

Martin, Justin. *Rebel Souls: Walt Whitman and America's First Bohemians*. Boston: Da Capo, 2014.

Masello, David. "Time, Gentlemen." *New York Times*, September 26, 2004. https://www.nytimes.com/2004/09/26/nyregion/thecity/time-gentlemen.html.

Matthews, Jay. "LaRouche's Call to Quarantine AIDS Victims Trails in California." *Washington Post*, October 25, 1986. https://www.washingtonpost.com/archive/politics/1986/10/26/larouches-call-to-quarantine-aids-victims-trails-in-california/f79e0d33-02be-4fad-a643-08bf0d462f95/.

Mattson, Greggor. *Who Needs Gay Bars? Bar-Hopping Through America's Endangered LGBTQ+ Places*. Redwood City, CA: Redwood Press, 2023.

Maurer, Daniel. "Dirty Delta of Lucky Cheng's Serves Orgy Bowls to Britney Spears." *New York*, January 30, 2007. https://www.grubstreet.com/2007/01/dirty_delta_of_lucky_chengs_se.html.

Maxim, Nanette. "The Gourmet Q + A: Florent Morellet." *Gourmet*, June 9, 2008. http://www.gourmet.com.s3-website-us-east-1.amazonaws.com/restaurants/2008/06/florent_QA.html.

Maxine's. "For Your Dining Pleasure," advertisement in *New Gay Life*, April 1977.

McCarron, Meghan. "'Our Version of Hospitality Can't Exist Right Now': MeMe's Diner on Deciding to Permanently Close." *Eater New York*, November 16, 2020. https://ny.eater.com/2020/11/16/21570329/memes-diner-closed-interview-libby-willis-bill-clark.

McCart, Melissa. "Salt Bae Sprinkles His Way into the China Grill Location." *Eater New York*, February 27, 2017. https://ny.eater.com/2017/2/27/14750810/china-grill-closes-to-make-way-for-salt-bae.

McDaniel, Wayne. Interview with the author, August 9, 2023.

McDonough, Molly. "A Woman's Place." *Tufts Now* (blog), June 16, 2020. https://now.tufts.edu/2020/06/16/womans-place.

McElroy, Steven. "Portal to Off Off Broadway's Early Days." *New York Times*, December 7, 2011. https://www.nytimes.com/2011/12/11/theater/donation-to-library-opens-new-portal-to-caffe-cino.html.

McRae, James. Interview with the author, August 4, 2023.

"A Memoir About New York City's Famous Gay Hustler Bar ROUNDS." Data Lounge. Accessed on September 2, 2024. https://www.datalounge.com/thread/9210976-a-memoir-about-new-york-city-s-famous-gay-hustler-bar-rounds.

Meyer, Eugene L., and Eve Zibart. "AIDS Fear Closed Restaurant, Owners Say." *Washington Post*, October 10, 1987, accessed September 2, 2024. http://ezproxy.nypl.org/login?url=https://www.proquest.com/hnpwashingtonpost/historical-newspapers/aids-fear-closed-restaurant-owners-say/docview/139269519/sem-2?accountid=35635.

Miller, Tom. "Enrico & Paglieri's—No. 64 West 11th Street." *Daytonian in Manhattan* (blog), November 2, 2013. http://daytoninmanhattan.blogspot.com/2013/11/enrico-paglieris-no-64-west-11th-street.html#google_vignette.

Morellet, Florent. Interview with the author, November 28, 2023.

Moss, Jeremiah. "The Gaiety Theater." *Jeremiah's Vanishing New York* (blog), October 11, 2007. http://vanishingnewyork.blogspot.com/2007/10/gaiety-theater.html.

Moss, Jeremiah. "Tiffany Diner." *Jeremiah's Vanishing New York* (blog). January 25, 2012. http://vanishingnewyork.blogspot.com/2012/01/tiffany-diner.html.

Murderpedia. "Robert Lee Bennett, Jr." https://murderpedia.org/male.B/b/bennett-robert-lee.htm.

Museum of the City of New York. "Much like Schrafft's and Horn and Hardart's Automat, Childs Restaurant Was a Staple Eatery with Many Locations Across New York. . . ," Facebook, June 3, 2017. https://www.facebook.com/MuseumofCityNY/posts/much-like-schraffts-and-horn-and-hardarts-automat-childs-restaurant-was-a-staple/10154892557267690/?_rdr.

Nahmod, David-Elijah. "Orphan Andy's: The Story Behind the Popular Castro Eatery and Its Owners." *Hoodline San Francisco*, October 31, 2015. https://hoodline.com/2015/10/orphan-andy-s-the-story-behind-the-popular-castro-eatery-and-its-owners/.

The Nance, script by Douglas Carter Beane, Lyceum Theatre (Broadway), New York, March 21–August 11, 2013. https://www.dramatists.com/previews/4884.pdf.

NBC Universal Archives. "Anita Bryant's Pie to the Face." October 14, 1977. Video. https://www.youtube.com/watch?v=5tHGmSh7f-0.

New York City Gay Scene Guide, vol. 2, 1969. New York: Apollo Book Co. Digitized by the Metropolitan New York Library Council as part of the Culture In Transit project, funded by a grant from the John S. and James L. Knight Foundation. https://dcmny.org/do/0ef1b2e5-1e58-48ab-83b8-f737482549de#mode/2up.

Nugent, Richard Bruce. *Gay Rebel of the Harlem Renaissance: Selections from the Work of Richard Bruce Nugent*. Edited and with an introduction by Thomas H. Wirth. Durham and London: Duke University Press, 2002.

O'Connell, Elizabeth. "Truffles Pastry Shop Goes Dark." *Cleveland Plain Dealer*, August 13, 2007. https://www.cleveland.com/lifestyles/2007/08/truffles_pastry_shop_goes_dark.html.

O'Connor, Michael. Interview with the author, November 21, 2023.

Oliver, Myrna. "Two Women Refused Use of Booth Sue Restaurant." *Los Angeles Times*, June 10, 1983. https://www.newspapers.com/article/the-los-angeles-times/8179031/.

Oliver, Myrna. "Lesbian Couple Lose Bid for Injunction." *Los Angeles Times*, July 14, 1983.

"Orphan Andy's." *San Francisco Bay Times*, accessed September 2, 2024. https://sfbaytimes.com/orphan-andys/.

Ortega, Tony. "Three Homosexuals In Search of a Drink." *Village Voice*, December 2, 2009. https://www.villagevoice.com/three-homosexuals-in-search-of-a-drink.

Padgett, Martin. Interview with the author, August 5, 2022.

Parks, Brian. "Chopsticks Optional," *New York Times*, March 20, 1994. https://www.nytimes.com/1994/03/20/style/chopsticks-optional.html.

Paulas, Rick. "Before Stonewall: The Raucous Trans Riot That History Nearly Forgot." *Vice*, May 12, 2016. https://www.vice.com/en/article /before-stonewall-the-raucous-trans-riot-that-history-nearly-forgot/.

Pendergast, Arnold "Butch." Interview with the author, June 5, 2024.

Petronius. *New York Unexpurgated*. New York: Grove Press, 1966.

"Pfaff's." *NYC LGBT Historic Sites Project* (blog). https://www.nyclgbtsites .org/site/pfaffs/.

Piepenburg, Erik. "Still Here and Still Queer: The Gay Restaurant Endures." *New York Times*, May 28, 2021. https://www.nytimes.com/2021/05/28 /dining/gay-restaurants.html.

Piepenburg, Erik. "At Taco Bell, the Drag Brunch Goes Corporate." *New York Times*, May 27, 2022. https://www.nytimes.com/2022/05/27/dining /taco-bell-drag-brunch.html.

"The Poz Decade." *POZ*, May 2004. https://www.poz.com/article/poz -digital-editions-2004.

Pratt, Eric. "Mary: You in Danger, Gurl." *SF Weekly*, May 3, 2018. https:// www.sfweekly.com/dining/mary-you-in-danger-gurl/article_252e72cc-fc96 -5fdf-b15d-7d2d643e0d98.html.

Purnick, Joyce. "City Closes Bar Frequented by Homosexuals, Citing Sexual Activity Linked to AIDS." *New York Times*, November 8, 1985. https:// www.nytimes.com/1985/11/08/nyregion/city-closes-bar-frequented-by -homosexuals-citing-sexual-activity-linked-to-aids.html.

Rainbow, Greta. "Inside Out and Upside Down." Cooper Hewitt, August 28, 2017, accessed September 2, 2024. https://www.cooperhewitt.org /2017/08/18/inside-out-and-upside-down/.

Rao, Tejal. "Mixing Food and Feminism, Bloodroot Is 40 and Still Cooking." *New York Times*, March 14, 2017. https://www.nytimes.com/2017/03/14 /dining/bloodroot-feminist-restaurant.html.

Raposo, Jacqueline. "Meet the Women Who've Served Up 40 Years of Feminist Food." *Shondaland*, June 11, 2019. https://www.shondaland.com /change-makers/a27792899/bloodroot-restaurant-feminist-icons/.

Raskin, Hanna. "Hospitality Industry's Response to AIDS Pandemic Offers Lessons for SC Restaurateurs Today." *Post and Courier* (Charleston, SC), July 8, 2020, updated September 14, 2020. https://www.postandcourier.com/health /covid19/hospitality-industrys-response-to-aids-pandemic-offers-lessons -for-sc-restaurateurs-today/article_41c360b4-c156-11ea-8858-df7 1da2fd184.html.

Reagan, Ronald. "Remarks at the American Foundation for AIDS Research Awards Dinner." Ronald Reagan Presidential Library & Museum. May 31, 1987, accessed September 2, 2024. https://www.presidency.ucsb.edu/documents /remarks-the-american-foundation-for-aids-research-awards-dinner.

"Record Turn Out at Waterworks." *BWMT/Atlanta* newsletter 10, no. 2, February 1992.

"Restaurant Florent [1985–2008]." Modernism 101. https://modernism101 .com/products-page/graphic-design/mco-restaurant-florent-tibor-kalman-et -al-designed-archive-of-14-original-postcards-matchbooks-menus/.

Rhodes, Jesse. "The Birth of Brunch: Where Did This Meal Come from Anyway?" *Smithsonian*, May 6, 2011. https://www.smithsonianmag.com/arts-culture /the-birth-of-brunch-where-did-this-meal-come-from-anyway-164187758/.

Ricks, Dave. January 2, 2018 (4:09 a.m.) Comment on *Butterflies and Wheels* (blog), "Bloodroot has always welcomed and respected everyone." https:// www.butterfliesandwheels.org/2018/bloodroot-has-always-welcomed -and-respected-everyone/#comment-2710502.

"The Riot at Compton's Cafeteria: Coming Soon to a Theater Near You!" *Transgender Tapestry*, Spring 2004. https://archive.org/details /transgendertapes1052unse/page/46/mode/2up?q=restaurant.

Robbins, Lee. "Brunch Munching." *Philadelphia Gay News* 6, no. 4 (December 11–24, 1981). https://jstor.org/stable/community.28042780.

Rose, Veronica. "Landmarks Calendars Julius' Bar for Consideration as an Individual Landmark." *CityLand*. September 29, 2022. https://www .citylandnyc.org/landmarks-calendars-julius-bar-for-consideration-as-an -individual-landmark.

Rothaus, Steve. "The Census Confirms It: Wilton Manors in No. 2 Nationally for Most Gay Couples per 1,000." *Miami Herald*, September 8, 2011. https:// miamiherald.typepad.com/gaysouthflorida/2011/09/the-census-confirms-it -wilton-manors-is-one-of-the-united-states-gayest-places.html.

Rothaus, Steve. "Tony Dee Helped Make Wilton Manors Gay." *OUTSFL*, October 17, 2023. https://outsfl.com/history/tony-dee-helped-make-wilton -manors-gay.

Rubenstein, Hal. Review of Food Bar. *New York*. April 5, 1999. https://nymag .com/nymetro/food/reviews/restaurant/368/.

Rubini, Dennis. "Continental Baths Revisited." *Philadelphia Gay News*, no. 9, September 1976. https://jstor.org/stable/community.28042742.

Ryan, Hugh. Interview with the author, May 11, 2021.

Saladin v. Turner, 936 F. Supp. 1571 (N.D. Okla. 1996). Justia. May 23, 1996. https://law.justia.com/cases/federal/district-courts/FSupp/936 /1571/1487050/.

Santi, Federico. *A Night at the Gaiety: Male Burlesque in New York City.* CreateSpace Independent Publishing Platform, 2016.

Saunders, Patrick. "Atlanta Drag Icon Diamond Lil Dies at 80." *Georgia Voice*, August 9, 2016. https://thegavoice.com/news/georgia/atlanta -drag-icon-diamond-lil-dies/.

Scharkey, Kristin. "Who Serves the Best Date Shake in the Coachella Valley? Let Us Know." *Palm Springs Desert Sun*, August 20, 2019. https:// www.desertsun.com/story/life/2019/08/20/best-date-shake-coachella -valley-vote-here/3683107002/.

Schneck, Ken. *LGBTQ Cleveland*. Mount Pleasant, SC: Arcadia Publishing, 2018.

Schneier, Matthew. "Julius', the Gay-Elder Dive Bar of the Village, Gets Land-marked." *Curbed*, December 9, 2022. https://www.curbed.com/2022/12/julius-gay-elder-dive-bar-greenwich-village-landmarked.html.

Schudel, Matt. "Annie Kaylor Dies; Presided over Landmark D.C. Steakhouse." *Washington Post*, August 3, 2013. https://www.washingtonpost.com/local/obituaries/annie-kaylor-dies-at-85-presided-over-landmark-dc-steakhouse/2013/08/03/8e920c78-fc56-11e2-9bde-7ddaa186b751_story.html.

Schwalbe, Will. Interview with the author, October 12, 2023.

Schwartz, Stu. Interview with the author, September 7, 2023.

"Screaming Queens." Truly CA: KQED, July 21, 2016. YouTube video. https://www.youtube.com/watch?v=G-WASW9dRBU.

Seasoned. "An Interview with Selma Miriam and Noel Furie of Bloodroot." Aired September 11, 2020, on Connecticut Public Radio. YouTube video. https://youtu.be/qtxLyIqYhxQ?si=n_XEt40qq9n7n4dh.

Selvam, Ashok. "After 56 Years, the Melrose Diner Is Closed in Lakeview." Eater Chicago, August 2, 2017. https://chicago.eater.com/2017/8/2/16081488/melrose-diner-lakeview-boystown-closed.

"Seventeen Amusements." *Evening Independent*, Massillon, OH, October 2, 1936. https://www.newspapers.com/newspage/3848040/.

Shapiro, Bill, and Vince Bielski. "Cracker Barrel." *Mother Jones*, March/April 1994. https://www.motherjones.com/politics/1994/03/cracker-barrel/.

Sheraton, Mimi. Review of Horn of Plenty. *New York Times*. August 13, 1976. https://www.nytimes.com/1976/08/13/archives/restaurants.html.

Shockley, Jay. "Mineshaft." NYC LGBT Historic Sites Project. https://www.nyclgbtsites.org/site/mineshaft.

Sicha, Choire. "Michael Alig, Fixture of New York City Nightlife, Dies at 54." *New York Times*, December 26, 2020. https://www.nytimes.com/2020/12/26/style/michael-alig-dead.html.

Siddons, Edward. "The Extraordinary Rise of Drag Brunch: A Dining Delight or a Betrayal of Queer History?" *Guardian*, March 17, 2019. https://www.theguardian.com/culture/2019/mar/17/the-extraordinary-rise-of-drag-brunch-a-dining-delight-or-a-betrayal-of-queer-history.

Signorile, Michelangelo. Interview with the author, January 20, 2023.

Simon, Scott. "Remembering a 1966 'Sip-In' for Gay Rights." NPR, June 28, 2008. https://www.npr.org/2008/06/28/91993823/remembering-a-1966-sip-in-for-gay-rights.

Simonson, Robert. "Howard Johnson's, Landmark of Old Time New York, to Shut Down." *Playbill*, April 19, 2005. https://playbill.com/article/howard-johnsons-landmark-of-old-times-square-to-shut-down-com-125398.

Skiba, Bob. "So, What's the Oldest Gay Bar in Philadelphia?" *Philadelphia Gayborhood Guru* (blog), July 15, 2012. https://thegayborhoodguru.wordpress.com/tag/maxines/.

Skiba, Bob. "Before There Was Stonewall, There Was Dewey's," *Philadelphia Gay News*, May 24, 2017. https://epgn.com/2017/05/24/before-there-was-stonewall-there-was-dewey-s/.

Smith, Art. Interview with the author, July 29, 2022.

Sorene, Paul. "Walt Whitman Leading Light of America's First Gay Bar: The New York Bohemians Who Made Good at Pfaff's." *Flashbak*, August 26, 2015. https://flashbak.com/walt-whitman-leading-light-of-americas-first-gay-bar-the-new-york-bohemians-who-made-good-at-pfaffs-39034/.

Sosin, Kate. "Lesbian Feminist Staple Bloodroot Vegetarian Restaurant Is Accused of Transphobia." *INTO*, January 8, 2018, and updated on May 28, 2018. https://www.intomore.com/impact/lesbian-feminist-staple-bloodroot-vegetarian-restaurant-is-accused-of-transphobia/.

Spaeth, Ryu. "Cancel Culture Grows Up." *Intelligencer* (blog), September 23, 2023. https://nymag.com/intelligencer/article/cancel-culture-haruki-murakami-hasan-minhaj-jann-wenner.html.

"Special Section: Guide to Detroit, Bars." *Gay Liberator*, no. 38 (June 1, 1974). https://jstor.org/stable/community.28037208.

Staley, Peter. "Searching for ACT UP." *POZ*, October 25, 2021. https://www.poz.com/article/peter-staley-never-silent-searching-for-act-up.

Staley, Peter. *Never Silent: ACT UP and My Life in Activism*. Chicago: Chicago Review Press, 2021.

Staley, Peter. Interview with the author, February 3, 2022.

"Starting Tomorrow Night For One Full Week . . ." *Evening Independent*, Massillon, OH, February 18, 1936. https://www.newspapers.com/newspage/3751636/.

Stein, Marc. *City of Sisterly & Brotherly Loves: Lesbian and Gay Philadelphia, 1945-1972*. Philadelphia: Temple University Press, 2000.

Stephens, Todd. Interview with the author, March 10, 2023.

Stone, Wendell C. *Caffe Cino: The Birthplace of Off-Off-Broadway Theater*. Carbondale, IL: Southern Illinois University Press, 2005.

Strub, Sean. Interview with the author, January 6, 2023.

"Suddenly, Everyone's Discovering the Gay Market." *Philadelphia Gay News* 6, no. 6 (January 8, 1982). https://jstor.org/stable/community.28042782.

Suthon, Warrene. Obituary, *NOLA.com*, June 9, 2014. https://obits.nola.com/us/obituaries/nola/name/warrene-suthon-obituary?id=10475292.

Tanne, Janice Hopkins. "The Last Word on Avoiding AIDS." *New York*, October 7, 1985. https://books.google.com/books?id=ZckBAAAAMBAJ&lpg=PP1&pg=PP1#v=onepage&q&f=false.

"Tavern Charges Police Brutality." *County Courier: The Voice of Los Angeles*, January 19, 1967. https://www.oneinstitute.org/wp-content/uploads/2019/02/one-archives-foundation-black-cat-riots.pdf.

Tcholakian, Danielle. "Madewell Store Coming to Meatpacking District in 2016, Company Says." *DNAInfo*, August 3, 2015. https://www.dnainfo

.com/new-york/20150803/meatpacking-district/madewell-store-coming
-meatpacking-district-2016-company-says/.

"Telly Justice, Michelin Guide New York 2023 Young Chef Award Winner." *Michelin Guide*, November 7, 2023. https://guide.michelin.com/us
/en/article/michelin-guide-ceremony/telly-justice-hags-young-chef-award
-winner-michelin-star-guide-ceremony-new-york.

"Torch Club Tonight." *Evening Independent*, Massillon, OH, February 20, 1936. https://www.newspapers.com/image/3752479/?terms=%22Torch%20
Club%22&match=1.

Trattner, Douglas. "The Rustic Restaurant in Rocky River Is Closing After 75 Years." *Cleveland Scene*, September 8, 2011. https://www.clevescene
.com/food-drink/the-rustic-restaurant-in-rocky-river-is-closing-after-75
-years-40212418.

Traub, James. *The Devil's Playground: A Century of Pleasure and Profit in Times Square*. New York: Penguin Random House, 2004.

UNAIDS. "How AIDS Changed Everything." July 24, 2015. https://www
.unaids.org/sites/default/files/media_asset/MDG6Report_en.pdf.

Veasey, Jack. "Coming Clean at Philly's Gay Baths." *Philadelphia Gay News* 5, no. 15 (May 15–29, 1981). https://jstor.org/stable/community.28042773.

Villegas, Pepe. Interview with the author, November 1, 2023.

Voigt, Henry. "Pfaff's." *The American Menu* (blog). September 23, 2017. https://www.theamericanmenu.com/2017/09/pfaffs.html.

Walsh, Kenneth M. "The Heyday of Chelsea's Eighth Avenue." *Kenneth in the 212* (blog). Accessed September 2, 2024. http://www.kennethinthe212
.com/2015/06/the-heyday-of-chelseas-8th-avenue.html.

Watts, Gabbie. "Remembering Diamond Lil, Atlanta Drag Pioneer." *WABE*, August 12, 2015. https://www.wabe.org/remembering-diamond
-lil-atlanta-drag-pioneer/.

Wayne's Meat Rack at the Stud, Los Angeles, menu. https://digital
library.usc.edu/asset-management/2A3BF1O3LB0XM?FR_=1&W=1119
&H=629.

Waxmann, Laura. "SF Mission's La Rondalla Closed." *Mission Local*, July 27, 2016. https://missionlocal.org/2016/07/fate-of-sf-missions-la
-rondalla-unclear/.

Werder, Corinne. "GO's New York 'Where to' Guide to Pride." *GOMAG*, August 17, 2007. https://gomag.com/article/gos_new_york_where_to_gui/.

White, Edmund. "The Gay Bar." *New York*, December 13, 2002. https://
nymag.com/nymetro/news/classicnewyork/n_8167.

Whitley, Edward. *The Saturday Press*. The Vault at Pfaff's: An Archive of Art and Literature by the Bohemians of Antebellum New York. https://pfaffs
.web.lehigh.edu/node/54193.

Whitman, Walt. "Calamus 29." In *Leaves of Grass*. Boston: Thayer and Eldridge, 1860. https://whitmanarchive.org/item/ppp.01500_01605, https://
whitmanarchive.org/item/ppp.01500#gallery-9.

Wicker, Randy. Interview with the author, August 5, 2022.

Wingfield, Valerie. "Before the Big Mac: Horn & Hardart Automats." NYPL Blog, New York Public Library. https://www.nypl.org/blog/2010/12/08/horn -hardart-automats.

Woods, Diana R., David Davis, and Bonita J. Westover. "'America Responds to AIDS': Its Content, Development Process, and Outcome." Centers for Disease Control and Prevention. November–December 1991. https://stacks.cdc.gov /view/cdc/63655.

"Young Homos Picket Compton's Restaurant," *Cruise News & World Report* 11, no. 8, August 1966. https://commiepinkofag.org/post/126199580495 /young-homos-picket-comptons-restaurant-cruise-news.

"You Won't Get AIDS in a Restaurant" (poster), Louise M. Darling Biomedical Library. History and Special Collections for the Sciences, UCLA Library Digital Collections, accessed September 2, 2024. https://digital.library.ucla .edu/catalog/ark:/21198/zz0002m3bv.

Index

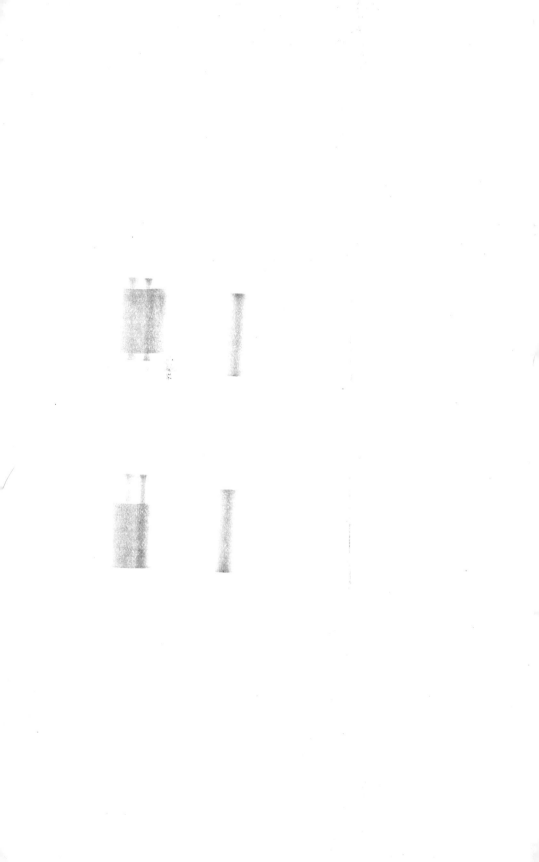